# Clans and Religion in Ancient Japan

*Clans and Religion in Ancient Japan* presents the latest research on the origin of Japanese religion and the clans in charge of religious services in ancient Japan. This book is written from a new analytical perspective, and it utilizes not only well-known historical manuscripts but also mythology, archaeological antiquities, pictorial materials, and genealogies.

The book aims to differentiate between the religious systems of Japan and those of other Asian countries, as well as between eastern and western cultures. Although different and unique, the book aims to show how Japan plays a part in the global environment and captures attention by answering questions from a historical perspective such as "What is Japan?" and "How should Japan relate to the world?"

**Masanobu Suzuki** is Senior Analyst for Textbooks at the Elementary and Secondary Education Bureau at the Ministry of Education, Culture, Sports, Science and Technology, Japan. He was formerly Associate Professor at Waseda University, Japan and has taught ancient Japanese history in many universities since 2008. He received his Ph.D. in Literature at Waseda University in 2012.

**Routledge–WIAS Interdisciplinary Studies**
Edited by Hideaki Miyajima and Shinko Taniguchi
*Waseda University, Japan*

1 **Corporate Crime in China**
   History and contemporary debates
   *Zhenjie Zhou*

2 **Why Policy Representation Matters**
   The consequences of ideological proximity between citizens and their governments
   *Willy Jou, Luigi Curini and Vincenzo Memoli*

3 **Electoral Survey Methodology**
   Insight from Japan on using computer assisted personal interviews
   *Edited by Masaru Kohno and Yoshitaka Nishizawa*

4 **Corpus Methodologies Explained**
   An empirical approach to translation studies
   *Edited by Meng Ji, Lidun Hareide, Defeng Li and Michael Oakes*

5 **Clans and Religion in Ancient Japan**
   The mythology of Mt. Miwa
   *Masanobu Suzuki*

# Clans and Religion in Ancient Japan
The mythology of Mt. Miwa

Masanobu Suzuki

First published 2016
by Routledge

2 Park Square, Milton Park, Abingdon, Oxfordshire OX14 4RN
711 Third Avenue, New York, NY 10017

*Routledge is an imprint of the Taylor & Francis Group,
an informa business*

Copyright © 2016 Masanobu Suzuki

The right of Masanobu Suzuki to be identified as author of this
work has been asserted by him in accordance with sections 77 and
78 of the Copyright, Designs and Patents Act 1988.

All rights reserved. No part of this book may be reprinted or reproduced
or utilised in any form or by any electronic, mechanical, or other means,
now known or hereafter invented, including photocopying and recording,
or in any information storage or retrieval system, without permission in
writing from the publishers.

Notice:
Product or corporate names may be trademarks or registered trademarks,
and are used only for identification and explanation without intent to infringe.

*British Library Cataloguing in Publication Data*
A catalogue record for this book is available from the British Library

*Library of Congress Cataloging-in-Publication Data*
Names: Suzuki, Masanobu, 1977– author.
Title: Clans and religion in ancient Japan : the mythology of
　Mt. Miwa / Masanobu Suzuki.
Description: First [edition]. | New York : Routledge, 2016. |
　Series: Routledge-WIAS interdisciplinary studies ; 5 | Includes
　bibliographical references and index.
Identifiers: LCCN 2015046994 | ISBN 9781138922877
　(hardback) | ISBN 9781315617909 (ebook)
Subjects: LCSH: Clans—Japan—History—To 1500. | Miwa
　Mountain (Japan)—Religious life and customs. | āOmiwa Jinja
　(Sakurai-shi, Japan)—History—To 1500.
Classification: LCC DS855.3 .S883 2016 | DDC 299.5/6—dc23
LC record available at http://lccn.loc.gov/2015046994

ISBN: 978-1-138-92287-7 (hbk)
ISBN: 978-1-138-31789-5 (pbk)

Typeset in Galliard
by Apex CoVantage, LLC

# Contents

*Preface*   vii
*Acknowledgments*   viii

Introduction   1

1   History of study and points of controversy   4

    1.1   *Introduction* 4
    1.2   *The Uji and Kabane of the Ōmiwa clan* 4
    1.3   *Previous research by the Ōmiwa-jinja Shrine* 5
    1.4   *History of research and layout of this book* 6
    1.5   *Conclusion* 8

2   The rise and decline of the Ōmiwa clan   10

    2.1   *Introduction* 10
    2.2   *Fictional members of the Ōmiwa clan* 10
    2.3   *The Ōmiwa clan in the late fifth century* 15
    2.4   *The Ōmiwa clan in the sixth century* 19
    2.5   *The Ōmiwa clan from the early to mid-seventh century* 23
    2.6   *The Ōmiwa clan from the late seventh century to the beginning of the eighth century* 26
    2.7   *Conclusion* 31

3   The constitution of the Ōmiwa clan   36

    3.1   *Introduction* 36
    3.2   *The cognate clans that lived in Yamato Province* 36
    3.3   *The cognate clans that lived in Yamashiro and Settsu Provinces* 40
    3.4   *The cognate clans that lived in Izumo and Buzen Provinces* 41
    3.5   *Conclusion* 43

vi  Contents

4  **The dispersal of the Ōmiwa clan**  47

   *4.1  Introduction 47*
   *4.2  Circumstances of dispersal throughout Japan 47*
   *4.3  Advancement to western Japan and to foreign countries 53*
   *4.4  Advancement to eastern Japan 56*
   *4.5  Local ruling systems of the Yamato Kingdom 59*
   *4.6  Conclusion 62*

5  **Characterizations of the Ōmiwa god**  66

   *5.1  Introduction 66*
   *5.2  Reexamining the Kunimi ceremony 67*
   *5.3  Reexamining the worship of the sun god 71*
   *5.4  Characterizations of the Ōmiwa god 75*
   *5.5  Conclusion 82*

6  **The transition of religious services at Mt. Miwa**  86

   *6.1  Introduction 86*
   *6.2  The change of dynasties theory 86*
   *6.3  Archaeological ruins and relics 89*
   *6.4  The notation of "Mt. Miwa" and "Mt. Mimoro" 96*
   *6.5  The Ōmiwa clan and religious services at Mt. Miwa 104*
   *6.6  Conclusion 106*

7  **The legend of religious services at Mt. Miwa**  112

   *7.1  Introduction 112*
   *7.2  The production of Sue ware and the Miwabe clan 114*
   *7.3  Clans that lived in Suemura Village 119*
   *7.4  The Miwa clan of Suemura Village and the Ōmiwa clan 122*
   *7.5  The nodal point of the genealogical relationships 127*
   *7.6  Conclusion 132*

8  **Conclusion and future prospects**  139

   *8.1  Introduction 139*
   *8.2  Summary and conclusion of each chapter 139*
   *8.3  Future prospects 141*

   *Bibliography*  145
   *Index*  159

# Preface

Mt. Miwa (三輪山) is in present-day Nara Prefecture (奈良県), western Japan. Since ancient times, locals have believed that a god resides in the mountain and they worship the mountain devoutly. The Ōmiwa-jinja Shrine (大神神社) at the foot of the mountain lacks a Honden (本殿), or main hall. Therefore, people worship the mountain from the Haiden (拝殿), or worship hall. They worship the mountain as though it were a god. This is the oldest form of religious ceremony in Japan. Therefore, the Ōmiwa-jinja Shrine has great historical significance.

The ancient Ōmiwa clan (大神氏), one of the most powerful, served the Yamato Kingdom (大和王権) and oversaw this religious service in ancient times. After the eighth century, they became Shintō priests (神主) at the Ōmiwa-jinja Shrine, and their lineage continues today. Therefore, knowledge of how the imperial family and the Ōmiwa clan conducted religious services at Mt. Miwa is indispensable for understanding the nature of politics in the Yamato Kingdom. Furthermore, it is essential for understanding the formation of the Japanese nation in the ancient past.

Previous research has described two periods of religious service at Mt. Miwa. From the fourth century to the fifth century, the imperial family worshipped the sun god. After the mid-sixth century, the Ōmiwa clan worshipped the god of curses. Between these periods, religious services were discontinued. To verify this earlier theory, I comprehensively investigated the myths and legends recorded in ancient history books, archaeological ruins and relics discovered around Mt. Miwa, and pictorial and genealogical materials handed down to the Ōmiwa-jinja Shrine.

Consequently, I determined that the god in Mt. Miwa is attributed many characteristics. Furthermore, the religious service conducted by the Ōmiwa clan was held without interruption from the end of the fifth century to the late sixth century. In ancient times, it was quite common for the imperial family to order local powerful clans to worship locally enshrined gods. This method of worship was systematized after the late seventh century. It eventually formed the foundation of the religious service system of the ancient Japanese nation after the eighth century.

In this book, I explain this theme, clans, and religion in ancient Japan in more detail.

# Acknowledgments

The ideas presented in each chapter originally appeared in the following book and article. In writing this book, I extensively rearranged and reconstituted their contents and then translated them into English.

- Masanobu Suzuki, *Study of Ōmiwa Clan (Ōmiwa-uji no Kenkyū)*, Yūzankaku, Tōkyō, Japan, 2014.
- Masanobu Suzuki, "Methodology for Analyzing the Genealogy of Ancient Japanese Clans," *WIAS Research Bulletin no. 7*, 2015.

    I am deeply grateful to Professor Tokio Shinkawa and Professor Akio Kawajiri at Waseda University for providing me with abundant advice and instruction from my school days until today. I give special thanks to Professor Hideaki Miyajima, Professor Tadashi Ebisawa, and Professor Shinko Taniguchi at Waseda University for giving me the opportunity to write a research book in English. I also owe a heavy debt to the Waseda Institute for Advanced Study (WIAS) at Waseda University for offering me such a fulfilling research environment.
    This work was supported by JSPS KAKENHI Grant Number 15K16834.

# Introduction

Shintō is the unique and traditional Japanese religion. In recent years, interest in and enthusiasm for Shintō shrines among Japanese people and foreign tourists has increased. For example, the Ise-jingu Grand Shrine's lavish ceremony for the reconstruction of its main building was broadcast on a large scale in Japan, as well as internationally. The Izumo-taisha Shrine, the Fushimiinari-jinja Shrine, the Kumano-taisha Shrine, and other famous shrines are extremely popular tourist destinations. In fact, many people have visited such shrines while traveling in Japan.

As a result, interest in the Ōmiwa-jinja Shrine is increasing among historians, researchers, and the general public. Situated at the foot of Mt. Miwa in western Japan, the Ōmiwa-jinja Shrine is one of the oldest Shintō shrines in the country. From this shrine, people worship the mountain as though it were a god; this represents the oldest form of religious service in Japan. To understand Shintō's origin, it is valuable to focus on Mt. Miwa, the Ōmiwa-jinja Shrine, and the Ōmiwa clan, which is in charge of religious services there.

Many classic works in Japanese literature have been translated into English and are widely read abroad. However, no comprehensive text in English offers foreign scholars the latest research on religious services and clans in ancient Japan. This book may shed light on differences between the religious systems of Japan and those of other Asian countries and even differences between Eastern and Western cultures. In addition, it may help scholars answer questions such as "What is Japan?" and "How should Japan relate to the world?" from a historical perspective.

Each chapter of this book refers to current arguments and the latest research, using an interdisciplinary approach to advance the study of ancient Japanese history. It is hoped that this book will also have an impact on the fields of archaeology, the science of religion, mythology, literature, folklore, and cultural anthropology.

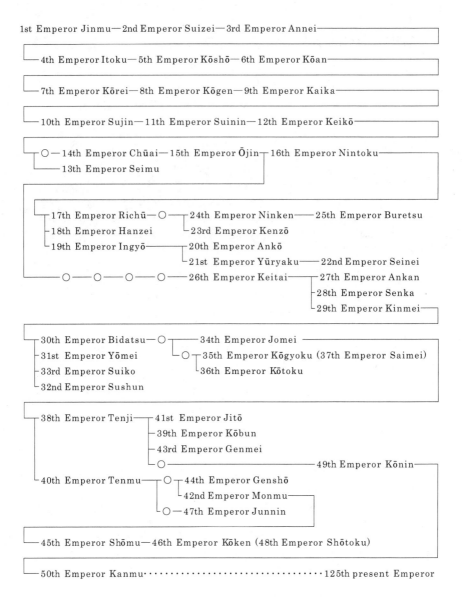

*Figure 1* Genealogy of the Japanese **imperial family** in ancient times
*This figure is based on the genealogy presented by the Imperial Household Agency.

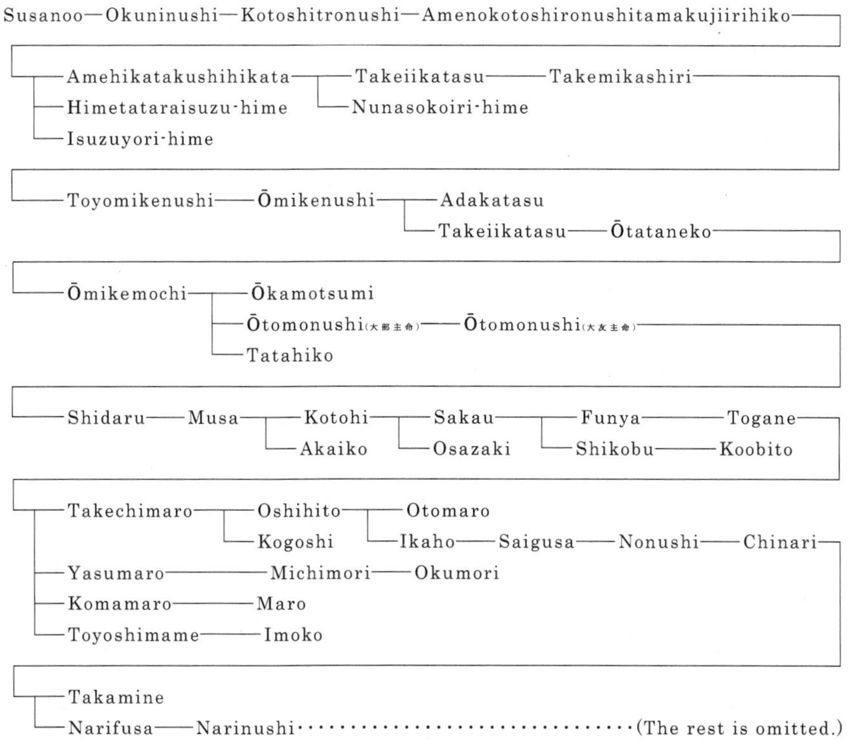

```
Susanoo─Okuninushi─Kotoshitronushi─Amenokotoshironushitamakujiirihiko─┐
┌─────────────────────────────────────────────────────────────────────┘
├─Amehikatakushihikata──┬─Takeiikatasu──────Takemikashiri──────────────┐
├─Himetataraisuzu-hime  └─Nunasokoiri-hime                             │
└─Isuzuyori-hime                                                       │
┌─────────────────────────────────────────────────────────────────────┘
└─Toyomikenushi──────Ōmikenushi──┬─Adakatasu                           ┐
                                 └─Takeiikatasu──────Ōtataneko         │
┌─────────────────────────────────────────────────────────────────────┘
└─Ōmikemochi──┬─Ōkamotsumi                                             ┐
              ├─Ōtomonushi(大郡主命)──────Ōtomonushi(大友主命)            │
              └─Tatahiko                                                │
┌─────────────────────────────────────────────────────────────────────┘
└─Shidaru──Musa──┬─Kotohi──┬─Sakau────┬─Funya──────Togane              ┐
                 └─Akaiko  └─Osazaki  └─Shikobu────Koobito              │
┌─────────────────────────────────────────────────────────────────────┘
├─Takechimaro──┬─Oshihito──┬─Otomaro                                   ┐
│              └─Kogoshi   └─Ikaho──Saigusa──Nonushi──Chinari─┐        │
├─Yasumaro──────────Michimori──Okumori                                 │
├─Komamaro──────────Maro                                               │
└─Toyoshimame───────Imoko                                              │
┌─────────────────────────────────────────────────────────────────────┘
├─Takamine
└─Narifusa──Narinushi·························(The rest is omitted.)
```

*Figure 2* Genealogy of the Ōmiwa clan in ancient times
\*This figure is based on *Ōmiwa-no-Ason-Honkeichōryaku*.

# 1 History of study and points of controversy

## 1.1 Introduction

Mt. Miwa (三輪山) is in the southeastern part of the Nara Basin, in present-day Sakurai City, Nara Prefecture (奈良県桜井市). Since ancient times, people have devoutly worshipped this mountain, believing it to be the home of a god. The Ōmiwa-jinja Shrine[1] (大神神社) was established at the foot of this mountain. This shrine does not have a Honden[2] (本殿). Instead, the people worship the mountain as a Goshintai[3] (御神体) directly from the Haiden[4] (拝殿) through the Mitsutorii[5] (三ツ鳥居). Many archaeological relics used for religious services have been discovered at this site. This form of religious service is the oldest in Japan. The shrine is thus of great historical significance.

The Ōmiwa clan[6] (大神氏) took charge of these religious services in ancient times. This clan was one of the most powerful clans serving the Yamato Kingdom (大和王権) and was believed to have descended from the Ōmiwa god[7] (大三輪神); it produced many well-known historical figures. After the eighth century AD, members of the clan became Shintō priests (神主) at the Ōmiwa-jinja Shrine, and their lineage continues there to this day.

Understanding how the Ōmiwa clan and the imperial family conducted religious services at Mt. Miwa is crucial to understanding the formation of the Yamato Kingdom and the ancient nation of Japan.

In this book, I discuss in detail ancient Japanese clans and mythology related to them, with a specific focus on the Ōmiwa clan and religious services at Mt. Miwa from the fifth century to the eighth century.

## 1.2 The Uji and Kabane of the Ōmiwa clan

The name of the central lineage (本宗) of the Ōmiwa clan changed over time. Ancient clan names included the Uji (氏) and the Kabane (姓). The Ōmiwa clan was also known as Miwa[8]-no-Kimi (三輪君氏・神君氏), Ōmiwa-no-Kimi[9] (大三輪君氏・大神君氏), and Ōmiwa-no-Ason[10] (大三輪朝臣氏・大神朝臣氏). "Miwa" (三輪・神) and "Ōmiwa" (大三輪・大神) are the Uji; this is an ancient family name showing the clan's stronghold or occupation. "Kimi" (君) and "Ason" (朝臣) are the Kabane (姓); this is a hereditary title, roughly indicating the hierarchy of clans serving the Yamato Kingdom.

Contemporary histories record the changing Uji and Kabane of the clan. In *Kojiki*[11] (古事記), this clan's Uji was written as "Miwa" (神), while in *Nihonshoki*[12] (日本書紀), it was written as "Miwa" (三輪) and "Ōmiwa" (大三輪). "Miwa" was used relatively early; "Ōmiwa" was used later. In *Shokunihongi*[13] (続日本紀), it was mostly written as "Ōmiwa" (大神). It was also written as "Ōmiwa" (大神) on Mokkan[14] (木簡). Thus, the clan's Uji changed from "Miwa" (神) and "Miwa" (三輪) to "Ōmiwa" (大三輪) and "Ōmiwa" (大神).

Similarly, the clan's Kabane was first written as "Kimi"[15] (君) but later changed, as seen in the following articles.

### Article 1: 『日本書紀』天武十三年（六八四）十一月戊申条
(Boshin,[16] November, the thirteenth year of Emperor Tenmu[17] (天武天皇) [684], *Nihonshoki*)

大三輪君・大春日臣・阿倍臣・巨勢臣・膳臣・紀臣・波多臣・物部連・平群臣・雀部臣・中臣連・大宅臣・栗田臣・石川臣・桜井臣・采女臣・田中臣・小墾田臣・穂積臣・山背臣・鴨君・小野臣・川辺臣・櫟井臣・柿本臣・軽部臣・若桜部臣・岸田臣・高向臣・宍人臣・来目臣・犬上君・上毛野君・角臣・星川臣・多臣・胸方君・車持君・綾君・下道臣・伊賀臣・阿閇臣・林臣・波弥臣・下毛野君・佐味君・道守臣・大野君・坂本臣・池田君・玉手臣・笠臣、凡五十二氏、賜姓曰朝臣。

In this article, the Ōmiwa clan appears at the head of a list of fifty-two clans granted the Kabane "Ason" (朝臣). At this time, the Ōmiwa clan's Kabane changed from "Kimi" to "Ason."

In this book, I refer to periods in which different Uji and Kabane were used. Therefore, to avoid confusion, I use the Uji "Ōmiwa" (大神), as seen in the name of the Ōmiwa-jinja Shrine (大神神社), and omit the Kabane, except where it is useful to mention it.

## 1.3 Previous research by the Ōmiwa-jinja Shrine

In the following section, I present previous research concerning the Ōmiwa clan and religious services at Mt. Miwa. These subjects have been the focus of many previous studies. I first discuss the technical books edited by persons connected to the Ōmiwa-jinja Shrine.

Misumi Saitō (斎藤美澄), the editor of *Yamatoshiryō*[18] (大和志料) (Nara Prefecture 1914–1915), served as the chief priest of the Ōmiwa-jinja Shrine from 1893 to 1894. During his time in office, Saitō collected historical documents that had been handed down in the Ōmiwa-jinja Shrine and used them to edit *Miwasōsho*[19] (三輪叢書). When the book was completed, it was copied by hand. It was published by the shrine office after Saitō's death (Shrine Office of the Ōmiwa-jinja Shrine 1928).

Many basic historical documents, such as *Ōmiwashinsansha-Chinzanoshidai*[20] (大三輪神三社鎮座次第), *Miwadaimyōjinengi*[21] (三輪大明神縁起),

*Ōmiwabunshinruisyashō*[22] (大神分身類社抄), *Ōyamatojinjachūshinjō-narabini-Isagawajinjaki*[23] (大倭神社註進状並率川神社記), and *Miwatakamiya-Kakeizu*[24] (三輪髙宮家系図), were included in *Miwasōsho*. This book is the starting point for research on the Ōmiwa clan and religious services held at Mt. Miwa after the Meiji period (明治時代).

The next significant work on this subject was *Ōmiwa-jinja-shiryō* (大神神社史料) (Publication Committee on Editing the Sourcebook of the Ōmiwa-jinja Shrine 1968–1991), a series of eleven volumes published in honor of the 100th anniversary of the Meiji Restoration (明治維新). Historical documents were included in Volumes 1 and 2, treatises in Volume 3, and historical Shintō documents in Volumes 5, 6, and 10. Other documents were published in Volumes 4, 7, and 8, and a list of related Shintō shrines was included in Volume 9. A chronological table and index were provided in a supplementary volume. The series contains many important historical documents, including treatises dating from the end of the Edo period (江戸時代) to the pre-war Showa period (昭和時代). Some of these treatises are no longer available, making the series an indispensable resource.

When this series was being compiled, Wakei Nakayama (中山和敬), the chief priest of the Ōmiwa-jinja Shrine, wrote *Ōmiwa-jinja* (Nakayama 1971). Subsequently, the Ōmiwa-jinja Shrine edited *Ōmiwa-jinja Shi* (大神神社史), a complete history of the shrine (Publication Committee on Editing the Sourcebook of the Ōmiwa-jinja Shrine 1975). This collection of eighteen treatises features contributions by many distinguished researchers, including Kiyoyuki Higuchi (樋口清之), Mikio Sasaki (佐々木幹雄), Isao Nishiyama (西山徳), and Takehiko Abe (阿部武彦). An essential resource for researchers, this book represents many years of effort by the Ōmiwa-jinja Shrine.[25]

## 1.4 History of research and layout of this book

Individual scholars have long studied the Ōmiwa-jinja Shrine from different perspectives, including the study of historical documents, archaeology, literature, and mythology. This research can be roughly divided into two categories.

The first category is a study of the Ōmiwa clan's prosperity and decline. Junichi Shida (志田諄一) analyzes the legends of the Ōmiwa clan and the achievements of all its members appearing in *Nihonshoki*. He then focuses on the god worshipped by the Ōmiwa clan. According to Shida, this god was originally associated with the imperial family. By enshrining this god at the foot of Mt. Miwa, where the clan was based, the Ōmiwa clan gained a high political and religious position in the Yamato Kingdom (Shida 1971). Shida thus examines the Ōmiwa clan's prosperity from the perspective of their worship practices.

Takehiko Abe analyzes the achievements of individual clan members and looks at how the Ōmiwa clan was distributed throughout the Japanese islands. According to him, the Ōmiwa clan developed a close relationship with the imperial family and played an important role in sending troops to eastern and western Japan, as well as to foreign countries. They thus became a powerful clan in the late seventh century; however, the clan subsequently declined, and many of its members devoted themselves to the Ōmiwa-jinja Shrine as Shintō priests (Abe 1975).

Abe has studied the history of the Ōmiwa clan before and after the era of Emperor Tenmu. However, few scholars have analyzed the clan's long-term fortunes from a general standpoint. Furthermore, Shida and Abe have missed some important points. Therefore, in Chapters 2, 3, and 4, I reexamine and explain in detail the Ōmiwa clan's prosperity and decline.

The second category of research is the study of the Ōmiwa clan's official duties in the Yamato Kingdom. This is the main area of research. Many scholars have been interested not only in the fortunes of the Ōmiwa clan, but also in (a) the legends related to the religious services the Ōmiwa clan conducted at Mt. Miwa, (b) the relationship between the Ōmiwa clan and the imperial family, and (c) the formation of the ancient nation of Japan. The best-known scholars in this category are Kōjirō Naoki (直木孝次郎), Atsumu Wada (和田萃), and Tetsuo Hishida (菱田哲郎).

Naoki bases his argument on the change of dynasties theory[26] (王朝交替説). He analyzes the legend of the curse of the Ōmiwa god in the era of Emperor Sujin[27] (崇神天皇). In the fifth century, the Kawachi dynasty (河内政権) arose in Kawachi Province[28] (河内国) and invaded Yamato Province[29] (大和国), destroying the early Yamato dynasty (初期大和政権) that had ruled over Yamato Province and conducted religious services at Mt. Miwa since the fourth century. The Kawachi dynasty claimed both of these rights. As a result, the imperial family became displeased with the Ōmiwa god (Naoki 1964, Naoki 1977).

Wada proposes two periods of religious service at Mt. Miwa. From the fourth century to the mid-fifth century, the imperial family worshipped the sun god. However, religious services at Mt. Miwa were discontinued after the late fifth century, leading the people to regard the Ōmiwa god as a god of curses.[30] When religious services were resumed by the Ōmiwa clan in the mid-sixth century, the Ōmiwa god thus was worshipped as a god of curses (Wada 1979, Wada 1985). According to Wada, the antagonism between the imperial family and the Ōmiwa god was caused by the interruption of religious services at Mt. Miwa. Wada's research departs from the change of dynasties theory and combines the study of historical documents and archaeology.

In recent years, Hishida has studied this subject from an archaeological perspective. In *Nihonshoki*, Ōtataneko (大田田根子), the ancestor of the Ōmiwa clan, lived in Sue Village, Chinu Region[31] (茅渟県陶邑). Hishida observes that many examples of Sue ware[32] (須恵器) made in this village were discovered at the foot of Mt. Miwa. He also notes that the Ōmiwa clan took charge of the production of Sue ware from the late sixth century to the early seventh century (Hishida 2005, Hishida 2007). Previously, scholars had only emphasized the relationship between the Ōmiwa clan and the religious services at Mt. Miwa. Hishida's work offers a chance to reexamine previous research from the perspective of handicraft manufacturing.

From the 1960s to the 1970s, many researchers, including Naoki, based their work on the change of dynasties theory; however, recent research has challenged this theory. Similarly, whether religious services at Mt. Miwa from the late fifth century to the mid-sixth century were ever interrupted, as stated by Wada, has also been questioned; whether the relationship between the Ōmiwa clan and the production of Sue ware was as universal as assumed by Hishida too has been questioned. In light of these questions, I reexamine and discuss the Ōmiwa god's characteristics in Chapter 5 and the transition of and mythology around religious services at Mt. Miwa in Chapters 6 and 7.

I summarize my arguments and conclude the book in Chapter 8. I also mention the Ōmiwa clan's fate in the eighth century, when they became priests at the Ōmiwa-jinja Shrine, where they remain to this day. I thus examine the Ōmiwa clan and the Ōmiwa-jinja Shrine over the course of several generations.

## 1.5  Conclusion

In this book, I attempt to portray the Ōmiwa clan and religious services at Mt. Miwa accurately and in their correct context. Many books written in, or translated into, English offer an overview of Shintō in ancient Japan; however, this book's objectives are markedly different. There is an urgent need for Japanese scholars of ancient Japanese history to share their research with the international academic community. Therefore, I have described my subject matter as systematically and concisely as possible, and I provide a simple commentary for technical terms, unique to the study of ancient Japanese history.

## Notes

1 The Ōmiwa-jinja Shrine (大神神社) is located in Miwa, Sakurai City, Nara Prefecture (奈良県桜井市三輪). In pre-modern times, this place was called Ōmiwa Village, Shikinokami County, Yamato Province (大和国城上郡大神郷).
2 A Honden (本殿) is a main hall. Most Shintō shrines in Japan have a Honden.
3 A Goshintai (御神体) is an object of worship believed to contain the spirit of a god.
4 A Haiden (拝殿) is a worship hall.
5 A Torii (鳥居) is a Shintō shrine gate. A Mitsutorii (三ツ鳥居) is a special gate that combines three common Toriis.
6 To be precise, "clan" in English is different from "Uji" in Japanese, in that "Uji" does not merely refer to non-political groups related by blood. These groups were politically organized to serve the Yamato Kingdom, and they included a primary group of blood relatives but also unrelated people. Since this is a complicated point, in this book, I have provisionally translated "Uji" as "clan."
7 The Ōmiwa god (大三輪神) was the god living in Mt. Miwa. This god is called Ōmononushi-no-Kami (大物主神) in ancient history books.
8 Miwa (三輪・神) is the name of a place, also referring to the foot of Mt. Miwa. It survives in Miwa, Sakurai City, Nara Prefecture (奈良県桜井市三輪).
9 Ō (大) means "great."
10 Ason (朝臣) refers to the second grade of vassals, according to the eight hereditary titles (八色の姓) established in 684.

11 *Kojiki* (古事記) is a record of ancient matters in Japan. It was edited in 712.
12 *Nihonshoki* (日本書紀) is a chronicle of ancient Japan. It was edited in 720.
13 *Shokunihongi* (続日本紀) is the history book that recorded the period after *Nihonshoki*. It was edited in 797.
14 A Mokkan (木簡) is a narrow strip of wood on which official messages were written; it was mainly used in ancient times.
15 Kimi (君) is an ancient word meaning "local leader."
16 This is a Kanshi (干支), a combination of signs used in the sexagenary cycle. There are sixty possible combinations showing the year, month, day, time, point of the compass, and so on. They were used in history books and similar texts in Japan and other East Asian countries.
17 Tenmu (天武天皇) was the fortieth emperor, according to *Kōtōfu* (皇統譜), the modern genealogy of the imperial family. However, in pre-modern times there were various ways of counting the generation of the emperor. For example, the beginning of *Kōtōfu* includes fictitious emperors. In this book, I provide the number of the emperor as given in *Kōtōfu*.
18 *Yamatoshiryō* (大和志料) is a sourcebook of Yamato Province.
19 *Miwasōsho* (三輪叢書) is a sourcebook of the Ōmiwa-jinja Shrine.
20 *Ōmiwashinsansha-Chinzanoshidai* (大三輪神三社鎮座次第) is a historical chronicle of the Ōmiwa-jinja Shrine.
21 *Miwadaimyōjinengi* (三輪大明神縁起) records the origins and history of the Ōmiwa-jinja Shrine.
22 *Ōmiwabunshinruisyashō* (大神分身類社抄) contains records of the Sessha (摂社, auxiliary shrine) and Massha (末社, affiliated sub-shrines) of the Ōmiwa-jinja Shrine.
23 *Ōyamatojinjachūshinjō-narabini-Isagawajinjaki* (大倭神社註進状並率川神社記) is a historical chronicle of the Ōyamato-jinja Shrine (大倭神社) and the Isagawa-jinja Shrine (率川神社).
24 *Miwatakamiya-Kakeizu* (三輪髙宮家系図) records the family tree of the Ōmiwa clan and its descendants, the Takamiya family (髙宮家).
25 The Ōmiwa-jinja Shrine publishes a magazine called *Ōmiwa* (大美和) twice a year. The shrine also holds a seminar every month. The contents of these seminars have been published (Ueno et al. 2003, Aboshi et al. 2003, Ueda et al. 2003, Ishino et al. 2008, Ogasawara et al. 2008, Kasai et al. 2008, Ōmiwa-jinja Shrine 2013).
26 The change of dynasties theory (王朝交替説) was proposed by Yū Mizuno (水野祐). According to this theory, the imperial family in ancient Japan changed several times (Mizuno 1952).
27 Sujin (崇神天皇) was the tenth emperor.
28 In the eastern part of present-day Ōsaka Prefecture (大阪府).
29 In present-day Nara Prefecture (奈良県).
30 In ancient times, people believed that the Ōmiwa god brought curses upon people.
31 Sue Village (陶邑) was in present-day Sakai, Ōsakasayama, Izumi, and Kishiwada City, Ōsaka Prefecture (大阪府堺市, 大阪狭山市, 和泉市, 岸和田市).
32 Sue ware (須恵器) is an unglazed earthenware produced from the latter half of the Kofun period (古墳時代) through the Heian period (平安時代).

# 2 The rise and decline of the Ōmiwa clan

## 2.1 Introduction

Numerous researchers have studied the Ōmiwa clan (大神氏), religious services at Mt. Miwa (三輪山)[1], and the Ōmiwa-jinja Shrine (大神神社) from various perspectives, such as historical documents study, archaeology, literature, and mythology. However, their study has not considered trends in the Ōmiwa clan as a whole; rather, they have examined individual clan members and investigated what kind of role they played. Therefore, in this chapter, I first investigate the fictional members of this clan. Then, I look at members of the clan in the fifth and sixth centuries, the early to mid-seventh century, and the late seventh century to the early eighth century. Thus, I divide the clan's history into four phases: the rising period, the prosperous period, the decline period, and the revival period.

## 2.2 Fictional members of the Ōmiwa clan

The oldest Japanese history books are *Kojiki*[2] (古事記) and *Nihonshoki*[3] (日本書紀). Ōtataneko (大田田根子) first appears in these history books as a member of the Ōmiwa clan. In this chapter, I present a summary of his myth.

> **Article 1:** 『古事記』崇神段
> (The part of Emperor Sujin[4] in *Kojiki*)
>
> 此天皇御世、疫病多起、人民死為㆑尽。爾天皇愁歎而、坐㆓神牀㆒之夜、大物主大神、顕㆑於㆓御夢㆒曰、是者我之御心。故、以㆓意富多多泥古㆒而、令㆑祭㆓我御前㆒者、神気不㆑起、国安平。是以駅使班㆑于㆓四方㆒、求㆗謂㆓意富多多泥古㆒人㆖之時、於㆓河内之美努村㆒、見㆑得其人㆑貢進。爾天皇問㆑賜之汝者誰子㆒也、答曰、僕者大物主大神、娶㆓陶津耳命之女、活玉依毘売㆒、生子、名櫛御方命之子、飯肩巣見命之子、建甕槌命之子、僕意富多多泥古白。於㆑是天皇大歓以詔之、天下平、人民栄。即以㆓意富多多泥古命㆒、為㆓神主㆒而、於㆓御諸山㆒拝㆑祭意富美和之大神前㆒、又仰㆓伊迦賀色許男命㆒、作㆓天之八十毘羅訶㆒。〈此参字以㆑音也。〉定㆑奉天神地祇之社、又於㆓宇陀墨坂神㆒、祭㆓赤色楯矛㆒、又於㆓大坂神㆒、祭㆓墨色楯矛㆒、又於㆓坂之御尾神及河

瀬神_、悉無_遺忘_、以奉_幣帛_也。因_此而疫気悉息、国家安平也。(略)
〈此意富多多泥古命者、神君・鴨君之祖。〉

### Article 2:『日本書紀』崇神七年二月辛卯条
(Shinbō, February, the seventh year of Emperor Sujin, *Nihonshoki*)

詔曰、昔我皇祖、大啓_鴻基_。其後、聖業逾高、王風転盛。不_意、今当_
朕世_、数有_災害_。恐朝無_善政_、取_咎於神祇_耶。蓋下命神亀、以極中
致_災之所由_上也。於是、天皇乃幸_于神浅茅原_、而会_八十万神_、以卜
問之。是時、神明憑_倭迹々日百襲姫命_曰、天皇、何憂_国之不_治也。
若能敬_祭我_者、必当自平矣。天皇問曰、教_如此_者誰神也。答曰、我
是倭国域内所居神、名為_大物主神_。時得_神語_、随_教祭祀。然猶於_
事無_験。天皇乃沐浴斎戒、潔_浄殿内_、而祈之曰、朕礼_神尚未_尽耶。何
不_享之甚也。冀亦夢裏教之、以畢_神恩_。是夜夢、有_一貴人_、対_立
殿戸_、自称_大物主神_曰、天皇、勿_復為_愁。国之不_治、是吾意也。
若以_吾児大田々根子_、令_祭吾_者、則立平矣。亦有_海外之国_、自当
帰伏。

### Article 3:『日本書紀』崇神七年八月己酉条
(Kiyū, August, the seventh year of Emperor Sujin, *Nihonshoki*)

倭迹速神浅茅原目妙姫・穂積臣遠祖大水口宿禰・伊勢麻績君、参人共同_
夢、而奏言、昨夜夢之、有_一貴人_、誨曰、以_大田々根子命_、為下祭_大
物主大神_之主_上、亦以_市磯長尾市_、為下祭_倭大国魂神_主_上、必天下太
平矣。天皇得_夢辞_、益歓_於心_。布告_天下_、求_大田々根子_、即於_
茅渟県陶邑_得_大田々根子_而貢之。天皇、即親臨_于神浅茅原_、会_諸
王卿及八十諸部_、而問_大田々根子_曰、汝其誰子。対曰、父曰_大物主大
神_。母曰_活玉依媛_。陶津耳之女。亦云、奇日方天日方武茅渟祇之女也。
天皇曰、朕当栄楽。乃卜下使_物部連祖伊香色雄_、為中神班物者_上、吉之。
又卜_便祭_他神_、不_吉。

### Article 4:『日本書紀』崇神七年十一月己卯条
(Kibō, November, the seventh year of Emperor Sujin, *Nihonshoki*)

命_伊香色雄_、而以_物部八十平瓮_、作_祭神之物_。即以_大田々根子_、
為下祭_大物主大神_之主_上。又以_長尾市_、為下祭_倭大国魂神_之主_上。然
後、卜_祭_他神_、吉焉。便別祭_八十万群神_。仍定_天社・国社、及神地・
神戸_。於是、疫病始息、国内漸謐。五穀既成、百姓饒之。

### Article 5:『日本書紀』崇神八年四月乙卯条
(Itsubō, April, the eighth year of Emperor Sujin, *Nihonshoki*)

以_高橋邑人活日_、為_大神之掌酒_。〈掌酒、此云_佐介弭苔_。〉

### Article 6: 『日本書紀』崇神八年十二月乙卯条
### (Itsubō, December, the eighth year of Emperor Sujin, *Nihonshoki*)

天皇、以_大田々根子_、令レ祭_大神_。是日活日自挙神酒。献天皇。(略)所謂大田々根子、今三輪君等之始祖也。

Ōtataneko appears in the articles of Emperor Sujin (崇神天皇) in *Kojiki*:[5] during a deadly epidemic, Ōmononushi-no-Kami (大物主神), the god living in Mt. Miwa, appeared to the emperor in a dream. The god said that the epidemic would end if the emperor commanded Ōtataneko to worship the god. Therefore, the emperor looked for Ōtataneko, found him in Mino Village, Kawachi Province (河内之美努村), and commanded him to worship the god at Mt. Miwa. Thus, the epidemic ended.

Ōtataneko appears in the articles of Emperor Sujin in *Nihonshoki*[6] as well. The summary of the story is similar to that in *Kojiki*. An epidemic was killing Emperor Sujin's subjects. The imperial princess Yamatototohimomoso-hime[7] (倭迹迹日百襲姫命) said that the epidemic was a curse from the god Ōmononushi. The emperor conducted a religious service according to her instructions. However, he was unsuccessful. Then, the god appeared in the emperor's dream and said that the emperor must command Ōtataneko to worship the god. The same night, Yamatotohayakamuasajiharamakuwashi-hime (倭迹速神浅茅原目妙姫), Ominakuchi-no-Sukune (大水口宿禰), and Ise-no-Omi-no-Kimi (伊勢麻績君) had the same dream. Therefore, the emperor looked for Ōtataneko, found him in Sue Village[8] (茅渟県陶邑), and commanded him to worship the god at Mt. Miwa. As a result, the epidemic ended. Furthermore, the next year, the emperor appointed Takahashimura-no-Ikuhi (高橋邑活日) as manager of rice wine[9] (神酒). The emperor again commanded Ōtataneko to worship the god at Mt. Miwa and commanded Ikuhi to present rice wine to the god.

These stories explain the origin of the religious service conducted at Mt. Miwa. Ōtataneko, who took charge of religious services at the mountain, is the most famous ancestor of the Ōmiwa clan. The Ōmiwa clan insisted on its legitimacy to serve the Yamato Kingdom (大和王権) on the basis of this myth. In other words, it insisted that it had the right to serve the emperor as the clan that took charge of religious services at the mountain, because its ancestor took charge in the same way.

This myth is recorded in *Kojiki*. *Kojiki* was based on *Kyūji* (旧辞), which was written in the sixth century. Tarō Sakamoto (坂本太郎) acknowledges this point and suggests that the myth had already been mentioned in *Kyūji* (Sakamoto 1946). Many researchers argue about the character of *Kyūji* even today.[10] However, Sakamoto's opinion is partially correct because the name of the Ōmiwa clan is noted as 三輪 (Miwa) and 神 (Miwa) in the above articles. These are old notations of the clan name. After the late seventh century, these notations changed to 大三輪 (Ōmiwa) and 大神 (Ōmiwa). 大 (Ō) means "great." Thus, many researchers think that the original form of this myth was established before the late seventh century.

After Ōtataneko, Ōtomonushi (大友主) appears in *Nihonshoki*.

### Article 7:『日本書紀』垂仁三年三月条
(March, the third year of Emperor Suinin,[11] *Nihonshoki*)

新羅王子天日槍来帰焉。(略)〈一云、初天日槍、乗艇泊于播磨国、在於完粟邑。時天皇遣三輪君祖大友主、与倭直祖長尾市於播磨、而問天日槍曰、汝也誰人、且何国人也。天日槍対曰、僕新羅国主之子也。然聞日本国有聖皇、則以己国授弟知古而化帰之。(略)〉

### Article 8:『日本書紀』仲哀九年二月丁未条
(Teibi,[12] February, the ninth year of Emperor Chūai,[13] *Nihonshoki*)

天皇忽有痛身、而明日崩。時年五十二。即知、不用神言而早崩。(略)於是、皇后及大臣武内宿禰、匿天皇之喪、不令知天下。則皇后詔大臣及中臣烏賊津連・大三輪大友主君・物部膽咋連・大伴武以連曰、今天下未知天皇之崩。若百姓知之、有懈怠者乎。則命四大夫、領百寮、令守宮中。(略)

In Article 7, Ame-no-Hiboko (天日槍), the prince of Silla (新羅), visited Japan. He temporarily lived in Harima Province[14] (播磨国). Ōtomonushi was dispatched with Nagaochi (長尾市), the ancestor of the Ōyamato clan (大倭氏), to question Hiboko. In Article 8, when Emperor Chūai (仲哀天皇) died, Empress Jingū[15] (神功皇后) and Takeshiuchi-no-Sukune (武内宿禰) commanded the four ministers (四大夫) to guard the place where the funeral ceremony was held. The four ministers were Ōmiwa-no-Ōtomonushi, Nakatomi-no-Ikatsu (中臣烏賊津), Mononobe-no-Ikui (物部膽咋), and Ōtomo-no-Takemochi (大伴武以).

In Article 8, Ōtomonushi was one of the four ministers. Previous research on political organizations before the seventh century suggests that the Ōmiwa clan belonged to the Maetsukimi class (大夫層), which means the ruling class, and its members could be appointed as ministers (Saeki 1975, Katō 1986, Kuramoto 1991). Ōmiwa-no-Sakau (逆) was said to be a favorite retainer of Emperor Bidatsu[16] (敏達天皇). This also demonstrates that the Ōmiwa clan was ranked highly in the Yamato Kingdom.

The composition of the four ministers is very important. In this article, the four ministers were from the Ōmiwa, Nakatomi, Mononobe, and Ōtomo clans. However, the descendants of these four clans all participated in the funeral ceremony of Emperor Tenmu[17] (天武天皇). Isonokami-no-Maro[18] (石上麻呂) made a funeral address (誄) as a representative of the Hōkan[19] (法官), Ōmiwa-no-Takechimaro (大神高市麻呂) did so as a representative of the Rikan[20] (理官), Ōtomo-no-Yasumaro (大伴安麻呂) did so as a representative of the Ōkura[21] (大蔵), and Fujiwara-no-Ōshima[22] (藤原大嶋) did so as a representative of the Heiseikan[23] (兵政官). In addition, in this article, "Ōmiwa" is noted as 大三輪. This is a new notation used after the late seventh century.

This shows that the composition of the four ministers in Article 8 reflects the constitution of the ruling class in the late seventh century. Of course, this article is not all fiction, but the constitution of the four ministers was modified when *Nihonshoki* was edited.

In contrast, in Article 13, the Ōmiwa clan is noted as 三輪. In addition, Nagaochi, accompanying Ōtomonushi, was the ancestor of the Ōyamato clan. Ōyamato is noted as 倭 (Yamato). Both 三輪 and 倭 are notations used before the late seventh century. Therefore, it is thought that Article 13 was written based on legends established before the late seventh century.

Furthermore, in Article 13, Ōtomonushi is described as the ancestor of the Ōmiwa clan. In contrast, in Articles 1 and 6, Ōtataneko is described as the ancestor of the Ōmiwa clan and also other clans.[24] The Kamo clan (賀茂氏) is included among those other clans.

### Article 9: 『日本書紀』神代上第八段一書第六
### (The first book of the eighth part of Jindaiki,[25] *Nihonshoki*)

此大三輪之神也。此神之子、即甘茂君等大三輪君等。

In this article, the ancestor of the Ōmiwa clan and that of the Kamo clan are one and the same. In addition, in *Shinsenshōjiroku*[26] (新撰姓氏録), the ancestors of the Ōmiwa, Kamo, Miwahito (神人氏), and Mitoshi-no-Hahuri (三歳祝氏) clans are identical. Therefore, Ōtomonushi was the ancestor only of the Ōmiwa clan. In contrast, Ōtataneko was a common ancestor of the Ōmiwa clan and many other clans.[27]

I believe that Ōtomonushi was the ancestor of the Ōmiwa clan at first. When the Ōmiwa clan and other clans allied politically, they tied their genealogies together. At that time, the Ōmiwa clan and other clans created a fictional character called Ōtataneko. They insisted that they were all descendants of Ōtataneko. Therefore, the genealogy is not necessarily a historical fact, but it is true that the ancient clans really believed their genealogies. Ancient clans' genealogies closely and strongly reflected political alliances.

After Ōtomonushi, Iwatoko (石床) appears only in *Miwa-Takamiya-Kakeizu*[28] (三輪高宮家系図). There is no description of his achievements. However, the name Iwatoko is reminiscent of the huge stones called Iwakura[29] (磐座) which were used for religious services conducted at Mt. Miwa.

The Hegurinimasu-Iwatoko-jinja Shrine (平群坐石床神社), for example, was located in Heguri County, Yamato Province[30] (大和国平群郡). The name of the shrine includes "Iwatoko" as well. This shrine is still in existence. The objects of worship of this shrine are the huge stones on the premises. It is thought that "Iwatoko" refers to these huge stones as well as to Iwakura from ancient times.

In addition, the Ōmiwa clan had many cognate clans; for example the Ōmiwa-no-Hikita (大神引田氏), Ōmiwa-no-Kisaibe (大神私部氏), and Ōmiwa-no-Hata (大神波多氏) clans. According to Takehiko Abe (阿部武彦), these clans were the closest relatives to the head linage of the Ōmiwa clan (Abe 1975). According to *Takamiya-Kakeizu*, the ancestor of these clans was Iwatoko. Iwatoko's children were Musa (身狭) and Ioshima (五百島). Ioshima's children were

Urushi (宇留志) and Inoko (猪子). Urushi's children were Mura (牟良) and Kakoshi (加古志). Musa's descendants were the head linage of the Ōmiwa clan. In contrast, Mura was the ancestor of the Ōmiwa-no-Hikita clan, Kakoshi was the ancestor of the Ōmiwa-no-Kisaibe clan, and Inoko was the ancestor of the Ōmiwa-no-Hata clan. In other words, the head linage of the Ōmiwa clan and the cognate clans diverged from Iwatoko.

Therefore, Iwatoko was thought to be a fictional character created by the Ōmiwa clan and the cognate clans when they formed a political alliance and tied their genealogies together. The name Iwatoko is based on Iwakura, the symbol of the religious service conducted at Mt. Miwa. This genealogy seems to have been formed in the early eighth century. From this time to the early ninth century, the movement to reorganize many ancient clans was very active. For example, the government commanded clans to submit *Honkeichō*[31] (本系帳) and, based on these, edited *Shinsenshōjiroku* in 815. Under these circumstances, the constitution of the Ōmiwa clan was thought to be reorganized and its genealogy revised, which is why Iwatoko appears in the genealogy.

## 2.3 The Ōmiwa clan in the late fifth century

After Iwatoko, Musa (身狹) appears in this article.

### Article 10: 『日本書紀』雄略即位前紀
### (The record before the enthronement of Emperor Yūryaku,[32] *Nihonshoki*)

御馬皇子、以﹦会善﹦三輪君身狹﹦故、思﹦欲遣﹦慮而往。不意、道逢﹦邀軍﹦、於﹦三輪磐井側﹦逆戰。不ﾚ久被ﾚ捉。臨ﾚ刑指ﾚ井。而詛曰、此水者百姓唯得ﾚ飲焉。王者独不ﾚ能ﾚ飲矣。

In this article, Ōhatsuse-no-miko[33] (大泊瀬皇子) and Mima-no-miko (御馬皇子) fought over succession to the imperial throne. Musa and Mima were friends, so Mima called for Musa's help. However, Mima met with Ōhatsuse's armies on the way to meet with Musa. They fought at a place called Miwa-no-Iwai (三輪磐井), and finally Mima gave way to Ōhatsuse. When Mima was about to be executed, he cursed Ōhatsuse so that he would be prevented from drinking the water of a nearby well.

Before this article, Ōhatsuse murdered princes of the same generation in sequence over succession to the imperial throne, including Yatsurishirohiko-no-miko (八釣白彦皇子), Sakaikurohiko-no-miko (坂合黒彦皇子), and Ichinobeoshiwa-no-miko (市辺押磐皇子). Mima expected that he would be murdered, so he called for Musa's help. Considering this article, I present the following two points.

First, Musa is different from his ancestors. Ōtataneko and Ōtomonushi are both described as "the ancestor" of the Ōmiwa clan in *Kojiki* and *Nihonshoki*.

In contrast, Musa and his descendants are not described as "the ancestor" of the Ōmiwa clan. It is thought that Musa was the first true person in the Ōmiwa clan.

Second, the specific person and the place appear in this article as "Musa" and "Miwa-no-Iwai." Tarō Sakamoto pays attention to these points and assumes that this article was based on the *Boki*[34] (墓記) of the Ōmiwa clan (Sakamoto 1946). However, if this article was based on the *Boki*, it is not obvious why the battle between Mima and Ōhatsuse is central and Musa plays only a supporting role.

This article focuses on restrictions on the emperor's eating and drinking habits. I compare this article with other examples. In the era of Emperor Buretsu[35] (武烈天皇), the emperor and Ōtomo-no-Kanamura (大伴金村) subdued Heguri-no-Matori (平群真鳥).[36] Surrounded by Kanamura's soldiers and realizing that he could not escape, Matori cursed the salt produced in Japan (it is unknown why he did so). But he forgot to curse the salt produced only in Tsunuga[37] (角鹿). That is why it is said that in ancient times, the emperor would only eat salt produced in Tsunuga. In this article, Matori was killed. Furthermore, the result of the curse is described clearly.

In contrast, Article 10 does not describe the result of Mima's cursing the water. In addition, it is not clear whether he was executed, although the text is clear that other princes were murdered by Ōhatsuse.

Therefore, it is thought that Article 10 had a second half describing the result of the curse and Mima's activities. When *Nihonshoki* was edited, so the thinking goes, the editor left that part out. Therefore, the Ōmiwa clan participated in a fight for succession to the imperial throne, though *Nihonshoki* does not say so. This shows that the Ōmiwa clan had formed and begun to gain power in the Yamato Kingdom in the late fifth century.

By this time, many legends had materialized about the Ōmiwa clan and Mt. Miwa. I pay special attention to the following three articles.

### Article 11: 『日本書紀』雄略七年七月丙子条
(Heishi, July, the seventh year of Emperor Yūryaku, *Nihonshoki*)

天皇詔_少子部連蜾蠃_曰、朕欲レ見三諸岳神之形_。〈或云、此山之神為_大物主神_也。或云、菟田墨坂神也。〉汝膂力過_人。自行捉来。蜾蠃答曰、試往捉之。乃登_三諸岳_、捉_取大蛇_、奉レ示_天皇_。天皇不_齋戒_。其雷虺虺、目精赫赫。天皇畏、蔽レ目不レ見、却_入殿中_。使レ放_於岳_。仍改賜レ名為レ雷。

### Article 12: 『日本書紀』雄略十四年三月条
(March, the seventeenth year of Emperor Yūryaku, *Nihonshoki*)

命_臣連_迎_呉使_。即安_置呉人於檜隈野_。因名_呉原_。以_衣縫兄媛_、奉_大三輪神_。以_弟媛_為_漢衣縫部_也。漢織・呉織衣縫、是飛鳥衣縫部・伊勢衣縫之先也。

## Article 13: 『古事記』雄略段
(The part of Emperor Yūryaku in *Kojiki*)

亦一時、天皇遊行。到᠑於_美和河_之時、河辺有᠑洗᠑衣童女_。其容姿甚麗。天皇問_其童女_、汝者誰子、答白、己名謂_引田部赤猪子_。爾令᠑詔者、汝不᠑嫁᠑夫。今将᠑喚而、還᠑坐於᠑宮。故其赤猪子、仰_待天皇之命_、既経_八十歳_。於᠑是赤猪子以為、望᠑命之間、已経_多年_、姿体痩萎、更無᠑所᠑恃。然非᠑顯_待情_、不᠑忍於᠑悒而、令᠑持_百取之机代物_、参出貢献。然天皇、既忘_先所᠑命之事_。問_其赤猪子_曰、汝者誰老女。何由以参来。爾赤猪子答白、其年其月、被_天皇之命_、仰_待大命_、至于_今日_経_八十歳_。今容姿既耆、更無᠑所᠑恃。然顕᠑白己志᠑以参出耳。於᠑是天皇、大驚、吾既忘᠑先事。然汝守᠑志待᠑命。徒過᠑盛年_、是甚愛悲。心裏欲᠑婚、憚᠑其極老_、不᠑得᠑成婚而、賜᠑御歌_。其歌曰、
    美母呂能。伊都加斯賀母登。賀斯賀母登。由由斯伎加母。加志波良袁登売。
又歌曰、
    比気多能。和加久流須婆良。和加久閇爾。韋泥弖麻斯母能。淤伊爾祁流加母。
爾赤猪子之泣涙、悉濕_其所᠑服之丹摺袖_。答_其大御歌_而歌曰、
    美母呂爾。都久夜多麻加岐。都岐阿麻斯。多爾加母余良牟。加微能美夜比登。
又歌曰、
    久佐迦延能。伊理延能波知須。波那婆知須。微能佐加理毘登。登母志岐呂加母。
爾多禄給_其老᠑女以返遣也。故、此四歌、志都歌也。

Article 11 is a legend about Chiisakobe-no-Sugaru (少子部螺贏). In this article, Emperor Yūryaku wanted to take a look at the god of Mt. Miwa and commanded Sugaru to capture the god. Sugaru climbed Mt. Miwa, captured a huge snake, and gave it to the emperor. However, the emperor did not perform his ablutions. Therefore, the snake summoned thunder, made its eyes shine strangely, and threatened the emperor. The emperor hid for fear of the snake and commanded Sugaru to set it free at Mt. Miwa. The emperor then gave Sugaru the name Ikazuchi (雷), which means "thunder."

From this article, I understand that ancient people believed in the Ōmiwa god and that the god took the form of a huge snake. In this article, the god threatened the emperor. Although Emperor Sujin worshipped the god, his worship was totally ineffective.[38] This shows that the Ōmiwa god was seen as a god of curses.

Previous research interpreted the last sentence of this article in two different ways. One is that Sugaru changed his name to Chiisakobe-no-Ikazuchi. The other is that Mt. Miwa changed its name to Ikazuchi-no-Oka (雷丘). *Shinsenshōjiroku* insists on the former, while *Nihonryōiki*[39] (日本霊異記) insists on the latter. There were already two interpretations in the ninth century, during the Heian period (平安時代).

However, previous research has overlooked one important point. Before Article 11, there is the following description in *Nihonshoki*.

### Article 14: 『日本書紀』雄略六年三月丁亥条
### (Teigai, July, the seventh year of Emperor Yūryaku, *Nihonshoki*)

天皇欲_下_使_二_后妃親桑_一_、以勧_中_蚕事_上_。爰命_二_蜾蠃_一_〈蜾蠃、人名也。此云_二_須我屡_一_。〉聚_二_国内蚕_一_。於是、蜾蠃、誤聚_二_嬰児_一_、奉_献天皇_一_。天皇大咲。賜_二_嬰児於蜾蠃_一_曰、汝宜自養。蜾蠃即養_二_嬰児於宮墻下_一_。仍賜レ姓為_二_少子部連_一_。

Sugaru appears in this article as well. Here, Emperor Yūryaku commanded Sugaru to collect silkworms (蚕) to allow Empress Kusaka-no-Hatabi-no-Himemiko (草香幡梭姫皇后) to do sericulture. Sugaru gathered infants by mistake.[40] The emperor commanded Sugaru to raise the infants, giving him the name Chiisakobe (少子部).

Comparing Articles 11 and 14 shows that the former describes Sugaru's personal name and the latter describes the name of his clan. The final sentences of those two articles are related. In other words, Article 11 explains the origin of the name Ikazuchi, whereas Article 14 explains the origin of the name Chiisakobe. Therefore, it seems that Sugaru, not Mt. Miwa, was given the name Ikazuchi. Because the people of later ages forgot about the relationship between the two articles, they created a new interpretation, the basis of the legend in *Nihonryōiki*.

Next, in Article 12, Emperor Yūryaku commanded Kinunui-no-Ehime (衣縫兄媛) to worship the Ōmiwa god. This legend shows that people worshipped the Ōmiwa god in the era of Emperor Yūryaku, in the late fifth century. *Kojiki* and *Nihonshoki* note that religious services had been conducted at Mt. Miwa for a long time. However, archaeological excavations have found many relics in the ruins at the foot of Mt. Miwa. The relics were used from the late fifth century to the sixth century (Sasaki 1975, Terasawa 1988, Koike 1997). In addition, as I mentioned earlier, Musa is regarded as the first person in the Ōmiwa clan geneaology who actually existed. He played an active role in the late fifth century. Putting all these things together suggests that religious services were conducted at Mt. Miwa beginning in the late fifth century.

Article 13 is a story about Hikitabe-no-Akaiko (引田部赤猪子). In this article, Emperor Yūryaku walked along the Miwagawa River (美和川) and found a woman doing her laundry at the river. When he asked for her name, she introduced herself as Akaiko. The emperor wanted to make her his wife and commanded her to remain single. She waited for him to contact her for eighty years, but she did not hear from him. She went to see him, but he did not remember her. She described their encounter, much to his surprise. He gave her classic Japanese poems, and she gave him poems in return. Then he showered her with presents.

The Miwagawa River, where Akaiko met the emperor, flows past the foot of Mt. Miwa. Akaiko is thought to have been related to the Ōmiwa-no-Hikita clan, because "Hikita" is common to her name and the name of the clan.

It is important that the emperor compared Akaiko to a maiden in the poems. The emperor and Akaiko exchanged four poems. In the first poem, the emperor compared Akaiko to a holy oak that grows on Mt. Miwa. In the third poem, Akaiko compared herself to a court lady who had served the Ōmiwa god for many years. These expressions show that people at the time worshipped the tree that grew on Mt. Miwa, and they show that a medium served the Ōmiwa god in the late fifth century. Considering these points, religious services at Mt. Miwa seem to have been first conducted in the late fifth century, just as Articles 11 and 12 suggest.

## 2.4  The Ōmiwa clan in the sixth century

After Musa, Kotohi (特牛) appears in *Ōmiwa-no-Ason-Honkeichōryaku* (大神朝臣本系牒略) and *Takamiya-Kakeizu*. He does not appear in *Kojiki* or *Nihonshoki*.

> **Article 15:** 『大神朝臣本系牒略』特牛尻付（抜粋）
> (The part of Kotohi in *Ōmiwa-no-Ason-Honkeichōryaku*)
>
> 欽明天皇元年四月辛卯、令₋大神祭₋。之四月祭始乎。〈字類抄。〉
>
> **Article 16:** 『三輪❐宮家系図』特牛尻付（抜粋）
> (The part of Kotohi in *Miwa-Takamiya-Kakeizu*)
>
> 金刺宮御宇元年四年辛卯、令ₗ祭₌大神₋。是四月祭之始也。

In these articles, Kotohi began the April festival (四月祭) held in the first year of Emperor Kinmei[41] (欽明天皇). The April festival is the Ōmiwa-sai Festival (大神祭), the main festival later held at the Ōmiwa-jinja Shrine. In other words, this article is about the origin of the Ōmiwa-sai Festival.

Citing as evidence the article from *Takamiya-Kakeizu*, Atsumu Wada (和田萃) insists that the imperial family conducted religious services at Mt. Miwa from the fourth century to the fifth century before they bestowed the right to conduct religious services on the Ōmiwa clan in the mid-sixth century (Wada 1979, Wada 1985).

However, Wada does not refer to *Honkeichōryaku*. *Takamiya-Kakeizu* was edited based on *Honkeichōryaku* in the nineteenth century. Therefore, wherever the contents of both books overlap, *Honkeichōryaku* should be considered the original. The article from *Honkeichōryaku* should thus be reexamined.

Article 15 ends with the words *Jiruishō* (字類抄), indicating that either the editor quoted this article from *Jiruishō* or this article was written based on *Jiruishō*.

*Jiruishō* refers to either *Iroha-Jiruishō*[42] (色葉字類抄・伊呂波字類抄) or *Sezoku-Jiruishō*[43] (世俗字類抄). Their contents are quite different from manuscript copy to manuscript copy. I have not been able to find an article related to Kotohi. However, Wada's belief that the Ōmiwa clan conducted the religious service after the sixth century must be reexamined, because this article is not an original from *Honkeichōryaku*. I believe that the religious service at Mt. Miwa began earlier and that the system of conducting these religious services developed gradually from the Kinmei era and turned into the Ōmiwa-sai Festival later.

After Kotohi, Sakau (逆) appears in the following articles.

### Article 17: 『日本書紀』敏達十四年（五八五）六月条
(June, the forty-seventh year of Emperor Bidatsu [585],[44] *Nihonshoki*)

馬子宿禰奏曰、臣之疾病、至今未愈。不蒙参宝之力、難可救治。於是、詔馬子宿禰曰、汝可独行仏法。宜断余人。乃以三尼、還付馬子宿禰。馬子宿禰、受而歓悦。嘆未曾有、頂礼三尼。新営精舎、迎入供養。〈或本云、物部弓削守屋大連・大三輪逆君・中臣磐余連、倶謀滅仏法、欲焼寺塔、并棄仏像。馬子宿禰、靜而不従。〉

### Article 18: 『日本書紀』敏達十四年八月己亥条
(Kigai, August, the forty-seventh year of Emperor Bidatsu, *Nihonshoki*)

天皇病彌留、崩于大殿。是時、起殯宮於広瀬。(略)三輪君逆、使隼人相距於殯庭。穴穂部皇子、欲取天下。発憤称曰、何故事死王之庭、弗事生王之所也。

### Article 19: 『日本書紀』用明元年（五八六）五月条
(May, the first year of Emperor Yōmei[45] [586], *Nihonshoki*)

穴穂部皇子、欲奸炊屋姫皇后、而自強入於殯宮。寵臣三輪君逆、乃喚兵衛、重璅宮門、拒而勿入。穴穂部皇子問曰、何人在此。兵衛答曰、三輪君逆在焉。七呼開門。遂不聴入。於是、穴穂部皇子、謂大臣与大連曰、逆頻無礼矣。於殯庭誄曰、不荒朝庭、浄如鏡面、臣治平奉仕。即是無礼。方今天皇子弟多在。両大臣侍。詎得恣情、専言奉仕。又余観殯内、拒不聴入。自呼開門、七廻不応。願欲斬之。両大臣曰、随命。於是、穴穂部皇子、陰謀王天下之事、而口詐在於殺逆君、遂与物部守屋大連、率兵囲繞磐余池辺。逆君知之、隠於三諸之岳。是日夜半、潜自山出、隠於後宮。〈謂炊屋姫皇后之別業。是名海石榴市宮也。〉逆之同姓白堤与横山、言逆君在処。穴穂部皇子、即遣守屋大連〈或本云、穴穂部皇子与泊瀬部皇子、相計而遣守屋大連。〉曰、汝応往討逆君并其二子。大連率兵去。蘇我馬子宿禰、外聞斯計、詣皇子所、即逢門底。

〈謂_皇子家門_也。〉将_之_大連所_。時諫曰、王者不_近_刑人_。不_可_自往_。皇子不_聴而行。馬子宿禰、即便随去_到於磐余_、〈行至_於池辺_。〉而切諫之。皇子乃従_諫止。仍於_此処_、踞_坐胡床_、待_大連_焉。大連良久而至。率_衆報命曰、斬_逆等_訖。〈或本云、穴穂部皇子、自行射殺。〉於是、馬子宿禰、惻然頽歎曰、天下之乱不_久矣。大連聞而答曰、汝小臣所_不_識也。〈此三輪君逆者、訳語田天皇之所二寵愛一。悉委二内外之事一焉。由_是炊屋姫皇后与_蘇我馬子宿禰_、倶発恨_於穴穂部皇子_。〉

In Article 17, Emperor Bidatsu permitted Soga-no-Umako (蘇我馬子) to convert to Buddhism (仏教). Umako built a temple and allowed three priestesses to live there. However, Sakau, Mononobe-no-Moriya (物部守屋), and Nakatomi-no-Iware (中臣磐余) strongly opposed Buddhism. They burnt the temple built by Umako and threw away a Buddha statue that Umako worshipped.

This article is thought to be one of a series of articles about the dispute on the following of Buddhism (崇仏・排仏論争). Previous research suggests that the Soga clan (蘇我氏) – who believed in Buddhism – were at odds with the Mononobe clan (物部氏) and the Nakatomi clan (中臣氏) – who opposed Buddhism – and the Ōmiwa clan joined the latter (Tsukaguchi 2003). However, recent research questions this dispute on the following of Buddhism (Katō 1983, Hōjō 2005). It is thought that this article was written based *Nihonshoki*'s editor's interpretation of history. In other words, the Mononobe, Nakatomi, and Ōmiwa clans were thought to have believed in Shintō (神道), *and* they were grouped together by *Nihonshoki*'s editor (Shinokawa 2009).

In addition, Ōmiwa is noted as 大三輪. This notation shows that this article was written after the late seventh century. In contrast, in Articles 18 and 19, Ōmiwa is noted as 三輪. This notation shows that these articles were written before the late seventh century. At minimum, it is thought that Articles 18 and 19 were written at a different time than Article 17. As noted below, in Articles 18 and 19, the Ōmiwa clan opposed the Mononobe clan, and Mononobe-no-Moriya conquered Sakau. Furthermore, Umako bore a grudge against Prince Anahobe (穴穂部皇子), who murdered Sakau. This shows that the Ōmiwa clan was politically close to the Soga clan. Therefore, it is thought that the Ōmiwa clan acted in concert with not only the Mononobe clan and the Nakatomi clan but also the Soga clan, depending on the time and situation.

Next, I examine Articles 18 and 19. In Article 18, when Emperor Bidatsu died, Sakau guarded the place of the funeral ceremony with his subordinates. Anahobe, who sought the throne, was angry with Sakau and asked why he served "the dead emperor" and not "the living emperor." According to Anahobe, "the dead emperor" referred to Emperor Bidatsu, and "the living emperor" referred to Anahobe himself.

Article 19 describes the same scene in more detail. Sakau was the favorite retainer of Emperor Bidatsu, and the emperor left all politics to him. When the emperor died, Sakau took charge of guarding the place where the funeral ceremony was held. Anahobe tried to break into the place. Sakau guarded the gate together with a subordinate and prevented Anahobe from passing through. Anahobe demanded seven times that Sakau open the gate, but Sakau did not comply. Therefore, Anahobe appealed to Moriya and Umako to address Sakau's rudeness. Anahobe commanded Moriya to kill Sakau. Moriya approached Sakau with an armed force. Sakau knew that Moriya was coming, and he hid at Mt. Miwa before hiding in the palace of Empress Kashikiya-hime[46] (炊屋姫皇后). However, Shiratsutsumi (白堤) and Yokoyama (横山), who were relatives of Sakau, betrayed him and disclosed his location to Anahobe and Moriya. Moriya again mobilized his forces and killed Sakau. Umako and the empress predicted that this would disturb the political landscape and bore a grudge against Anahobe.

In Article 19, Sakau is described as "the favorite retainer of Emperor Bidatsu." In addition, the article says that "politics will be in turmoil" because Sakau was killed. This shows that Sakau had a big influence on politics at that time.

Previous research assumed that Sakau gained power because he built a close relationship with the Naitei[47] (内廷). One of the Naitei organizations was Kisaibe (私部), which was established for the empress.[48] The Ōmiwa-no-Kisaibe clan, a cognate clan of the Ōmiwa, took charge of the management of Kisaibe. Therefore, Takehiko Abe argues that the Ōmiwa clan came to have close relations with the Naitei by managing Kisaibe (Abe 1975). Kaoru Nakayama (中山薫) is of the same opinion (Nakayama 2002).

When Sakau knew that Moriya's forces were coming, he hid in the empress's palace. The empress protected Sakau because she trusted him, as he had helped establish Kisaibe. In Article 19, Emperor Bidatsu left "inside politics and outside politics" (内外之事) to Sakau. Typically, "inside politics and outside politics" are understood to mean "domestic politics and international politics" or "center officials and local officials." However, "inside politics and outside politics" also refers to "the Naitei and the Gaitei"[49] (外廷). It shows that the Ōmiwa clan had a relationship with the Naitei, too. Collectively, it is thought that Sakau helped establish and manage Kisaibe and that he built direct relationships with the emperor and empress and thus gained power in the era of Emperor Bidatsu. This was the golden age of the Ōmiwa clan.

In addition, Shiratsutsumi and Yokoyama, relatives of Sakau, appear in Article 19. They were members of the Ōmiwa clan. Therefore, the lineage of the Ōmiwa clan diverged along multiple paths in the mid-sixth century. Yokoyama's achievements are unknown, because he does not appear in other historical materials. Shiratsutsumi built the Isagawa-jinja Shrine (率川神社), which was the auxiliary shrine of the Ōmiwa-jinja Shrine. The Ōmiwa-jinja Shrine was in Shikinokami County, Yamato Province (大和国式上郡), and the Isagawa-jinja Shrine was far away in Sōnokami County, Yamato Province[50] (大和国添上郡). This shows that Shiratsutsumi and his lineage temporarily gained influence in the Ōmiwa clan after Sakau's death, but his lineage performed badly, so he moved his stronghold elsewhere.

## 2.5 The Ōmiwa clan from the early to mid-seventh century

From the early to mid-seventh century, many members of the Ōmiwa clan played significant roles. These clan members include Osazaki (小鷦鷯), Fumiya (文屋), and Togane (利金). First, Osazaki appears in the following article.

### Article 20:『日本書紀』舒明八年（六三六）三月条
(March, the eighth year of Emperor Jomei [636], *Nihonshoki*)

悉劾下奸采女者上、皆罪之。是時、三輪君小鷦鷯、苦其推鞫、刺頸而死。

In this article, Osazaki committed suicide because he was suspected of illicit intercourse with Uneme[51] (采女), the emperor's maid of honor. Most likely, he had been falsely accused and insisted on his innocence by suicide.

From Sakau's death to Osazaki's appearance – a time span of approximately fifty years – no member of the Ōmiwa clan appears in a historical manuscript. The Ōmiwa clan's power declined remarkably after Sakau's death. In Article 19, Anahobe commanded Moriya to kill Sakau and his two children, and Moriya reported to Anahobe that he had killed them. The reason why the Ōmiwa clan declined was that Sakau's successor was killed too.

After Osazaki, Fumiya appears in the following article.

### Article 21:『日本書紀』皇極二年（六四三）十一月丙子条
(Heishi, November, the second year of Emperor Kōgyoku[52] [643], *Nihonshoki*)

蘇我臣入鹿、遣小勢徳太臣・大仁土師娑婆連、掩山背大兄王等於斑鳩。（略）山背大兄、仍取馬骨、投置内寢。遂率其妃并子弟等、得間逃出、隠膽駒山。三輪文屋君・舎人田目連及其女・菟田諸石・伊勢阿部堅経従焉。（略）由是、山背大兄王等、四五日間、淹留於山、不得喫飯。三輪文屋君、進而勧曰、請、移向於深草屯倉、從茲乘馬、詣東国、以乳部為本、興師還戦。其勝必矣。（略）於是、山背大兄王等、自山還、入斑鳩寺。軍將等即以兵圍寺。於是、山背大兄王、使三輪文屋君謂軍將等曰、吾起兵伐入鹿者、其勝定之。然由一身之故、不欲残害百姓。是以、吾之一身、賜於入鹿、終与子弟妃妾一時自経倶死也。

In this article, the military of Soga-no-Iruka (蘇我入鹿) stormed Yamashiro-no-Ōe-no-miko (山背大兄王). Fumiya escaped from the palace with Yamashiro and hid at Mt. Ikoma (生駒山). Fumiya suggested that Yamashiro run away to eastern Japan, gather soldiers there, return to Yamato Province with an army, and fight Iruka. However, Yamashiro rejected this suggestion and returned to the palace. When Yamashiro again was surrounded by Iruka's soldiers, he entrusted Fumiya with a message to the enemy: "If I fight against you, I will win. But I do not want to injure the people. So I will give my life to Iruka." Then, Yamashiro committed suicide. Fumiya's fate is unknown, but he likely committed suicide as well, after relaying the message.

In this article, Fumiya was the first on the list of Yamashiro's retainers. He played an important role in sharing Yamashiro's message with the enemy. Nevertheless, he does not appear in the history book *Jyogushōtokutaishiden-Hoketsuki*[53] (上宮聖徳太子伝補闕記), which describes Yamashiro's family in detail. That is why Tarō Sakamoto insists that this article was written based on the legend of the Ōmiwa clan and Fumiya did not actually play an important role (Sakamoto 1946). I can support this opinion.

In *Nihonshoki*, when the argument about the succession to the imperial throne happened, Sakaibe-no-Marise (境合部摩理勢), Kose-no-Ōmaro (許勢大摩呂), Saeki-no-Azumahito (佐伯東人), and Kii-no-Shiote (紀塩手) supported Yamashiro. However, Fumiya is not listed among the people who supported Yamashiro. He appears only in Article 21. Therefore, I do not fully understand Fumiya's political position. At least his achievement was included in the legend of the Ōmiwa clan.

After Fumiya, Togane appears in the following article.

### Article 22: 『続日本紀』慶雲三年（七〇六）二月庚辰条
(Kōshin, February, the third year of Keiun [706], *Nihonshoki*)

左京大夫従四位上大神朝臣高市麻呂卒。以_壬申年功_、詔贈_従三位_。大花上利金之子也。

In this article, Togane was the father of Takechimaro (高市麻呂). Takechimaro will be mentioned later. Togane was ranked Taikajō[54] (大花上). His concrete achievement was not recorded. However, this was a very high crown rank. The Ōmiwa clan regained power in the mid-seventh century, after a long decline.

Until now, I only mentioned the head linage of the Ōmiwa clan, but members of the branch family played active roles in this period too. They include Shikobu (色夫), Ōkuchi (大口), Mikaho (甕穂), and Nemaro (根麻呂). This also shows that the Ōmiwa clan regained power.

Shikobu appears in the following articles.

### Article 23: 『日本書紀』大化元年（六四五）八月癸卯条
(Kibō, August, the first year of Taika [645], *Nihonshoki*)

遣_使於大寺_、喚_聚僧尼_、而詔曰（略）朕更復思┬崇_正教_、光中啓大猷上。故以_沙門狛大法師・福亮・惠雲・常安・霊雲・惠至・寺主僧旻・道登・惠隣・惠妙_、而為_十師_。別以_惠妙法師_、為_百済寺々主_。此十師等、宜能教導_衆僧_、修_行釈教_、要使レ如レ法。凡自_天皇_至_于伴造_、所レ造之寺、不レ能レ営者、朕皆助作。令拝_寺司等_与寺主_。巡_行諸寺_、験_僧尼・奴婢・田畝之実_、而尽顕奏。即以_来目臣〈闕名。〉・三輪色夫君・額田部連甥_、為_法頭_。

### Article 24: 『日本書紀』大化五年（六四九）五月癸卯条
(Kibō, May, the fifth year of Taika [649], *Nihonshoki*)

遣_小華下三輪君色夫・大山上掃部連角麻呂等於新羅_。

In Article 23, Shikobu was appointed Hōzu (法頭). The Hōzu was in charge of investigating the number of monks and nuns living at the temples and the number of slaves and fields that temples possessed (Inoue 1971, Shinkawa 1994). This shows that the Ōmiwa clan was positively concerned with Buddhism as well as religious service, which was later called Shintō.

In Article 24, Shikobu was dispatched to Silla. Shortly afterwards, refugees and their attendants visited Japan from Silla. Shikobu was in charge of receiving the refugees as a diplomatic delegation.

Ōkuchi appears in the following article.

### Article 25: 『日本書紀』大化二年（六四六）三月辛巳条
(Shinshi, March, the second year of Taika [646], *Nihonshoki*)

今問_朝集使及諸国造等_、国司至_任、奉_所_誨不。於是、朝集使等、具陳_其状_。（略）其紀麻利耆拕臣所_犯者、使_人於朝倉君・井上君、二人之所_、而為牽_来其馬_視之。復使_朝倉君_作刀。復得_朝倉君之弓・布_。復以_国造所_送兵代之物_、不_明還_主_、妄伝_国造_。復於_所任之国_、被_他偸_刀。復於_倭国_、被_他偸_刀。是其紀臣・其介三輪君大口・河辺臣百依等過也。

In this article, Ōkuchi was dispatched as a local governor of the eastern country (東国国司), and he committed crimes. According to a remark by the messenger, Ōkuchi embezzled a bow, cloth, and other weapons of local clan members and gave them to the Kokuzō[55] (国造). Furthermore, a robber stole Ōkuchi's sword in the eastern country and Yamato Province. However, Ōkuchi was granted amnesty, so he was ultimately not charged with any crime.

Mikaho appears in the following article.

### Article 26: 『日本書紀』白雉元年（六五〇）二月甲申条
(Kōshin, February, the first year of Hakuchi [650], *Nihonshoki*)

朝庭隊仗、如_元会儀_。（略）使_三国公麻呂・猪名公高見・三輪君甕穂・紀臣乎麻呂岐太四人_、代執_雉輿_、而進_殿前_。

This is an article about an imperial court ceremony. Just before this ceremony, Kusakabe-no-Shikobu (草壁醜経) found a white pheasant and presented it to the emperor. It was regarded as a good omen (祥瑞). Then, he transported the white pheasant to the main hall of the imperial palace together with Mikuni-no-Maro (三国麻呂), Ina-no-Takami (猪名高見), and Kii-no-Omarokida (紀臣乎麻呂岐太).

At last, Nemaro appears in *Nihonshoki*.

### Article 27:『日本書紀』天智二年（六六三）三月条
(March, the second year of Emperor Tenji[56] [663], *Nihonshoki*)

遣_前将軍上毛野君稚子・間人連大盖、中将軍巨勢神前臣訳語・三輪君根麻呂、後将軍阿倍引田臣比邏夫・大宅臣鎌柄_、率_二万七千人_、打_新羅_。

In this article, Nemaro was appointed a lieutenant general with Kose-no-Kamusaki-no-Osa (巨勢神崎訳語) and dispatched to the Korean Peninsula with 27,000 soldiers in the year 663.

Till then, the Ōmiwa clan's main role had been to manage the religious services at Mt. Miwa. However, Shikobu, Ōkuchi, Mikaho, and Nemaro engaged in various duties other than religious services. This shows that the significance of the religious service faded at this time, so the Ōmiwa clan had to demand other areas of activity. Through their activities in new fields, the Ōmiwa clan regained power. Togane's crown rank, mentioned above, demonstrates this clearly.

## 2.6 The Ōmiwa clan from the late seventh century to the beginning of the eighth century

I mentioned Takechimaro earlier. He was a son of Togane. Takechimaro was very famous for playing an active role in the Jinshin War (壬申の乱). He appears in the following articles.

### Article 28:『日本書紀』天武元年（六七二）六月己丑条
(Kichū, June, the first year of Emperor Tenmu [672], *Nihonshoki*)

因乃命_吹負_拝_将軍_。是時、三輪君高市麻呂・鴨君蝦夷等、及群豪傑者、如╱響悉會_将軍麾下_。乃規╱襲_近江_。撰_衆中之英俊_、為_別将及軍監_。

### Article 29:『日本書紀』天武元年七月是日条
(July, the first year of Emperor Tenmu, *Nihonshoki*)

三輪君高市麻呂・置始連菟、当_上道_、戦_于箸陵_。大破_近江軍_、而乗╱勝、兼断_鯨軍之後_。鯨軍悉解走、多殺_士卒_。鯨乗_白馬_以逃之。馬墮_泥田_、不╱能╱進行_。則将軍吹負、謂_甲斐勇者_曰、其乗_白馬_者、廬井鯨也。急追以射。於是、甲斐勇者馳追之。比╱及╱鯨、々々急鞭╱馬。々々能抜以出╱泥。即馳之得╱脱。将軍亦更還_本処_而軍之。自╱此以後、近江軍遂不╱至。

In Article 28, Emperor Tenmu appointed Ōtomo-no-Fukei (大伴吹負) as general. Many brave men, such as Takechimaro and Kamo-no-Emishi (鴨蝦夷), gathered and became retainers of the general. They then developed a strategy.

In Article 29, the army of Takechimaro and Okisome-no-Usagi (置始菟) fought against the army of Ioi-no-Kujira (廬井鯨) at the site of the Hashihaka-kofun Tumulus (箸墓古墳), in Yamato Province.[57] Takechimaro and Usagi won a great victory over Kujira. Afterwards, the enemy army did not attack Yamato Province.

Two points are noteworthy here. The first is that Ōmiwa-no-Takechimaro acted alongside Kamo-no-Emishi. According to *Kojiki*, *Nihonshoki*, and *Shinsenshōjiroku*, the Ōmiwa clan and the Kamo clan shared a common ancestor. In technical terms, they share a "fictitious blood relationship" (擬制的同祖関係). The reason why the Ōmiwa clan and the Kamo clan acted together was that such a relationship played an important role during wartime. Previous research originally assumed such a relationship to be established by a real blood relationship, territorial relationship, official duty, or mutual daily interchange (Mizoguchi M. 1982). However, I emphasize that military operations also played an important role in establishing such a relationship.

Another point is that Takechimaro fought against the enemy at the site of the Hashihaka-kofun Tumulus, in Yamato Province. The Ōmiwa clan's stronghold was in Ōmiwa Village, Shikinokami County, Yamato Province[58] (大和国城上郡大神郷). This place was very close to the Hashihaka-kofun Tumulus. Takechimaro must have had a good sense of location. Therefore, General Fukei placed Takechimaro at this place in order to gain advantage over the enemy during the war. In fact, he beat the enemy. The general's expectation was proven right.

### Article 30: 『日本書紀』朱鳥元年（六八六）九月乙丑条
(Icchū, September, the first year of Shuchō [686], *Nihonshoki*)

直大参布勢朝臣御主人、誄＿太政官事＿。次直広参石上朝臣麻呂、誄＿法官事＿。次直大肆大三輪朝臣高市麻呂、誄＿理官事＿。次直広参大伴宿禰安麻呂、誄＿大蔵事＿。次直大肆藤原朝臣大嶋、誄＿兵政官事＿。

I mentioned this article earlier. In this article, Takechimaro made a funeral address as a representative of the Rikan at Emperor Tenmu's funeral. The Rikan was the predecessor of the Jibushō (Naitō 1958, Kumagai 1979). When the government established Uji-no-Kami (氏上), which was the commander of a clan, for the first time, it was recorded in an account book.[59] Kimio Kumagai (熊谷公男) says that the account book was a genealogy of clans, and it was kept by the Rikan (Kumagai 1979). After that, the government commanded clans that had not yet chosen an Uji-no-Kami to decide immediately and to share their choice with the Jibushō.[60] This article shows that the Jibushō took charge of the Uji-no-Kami of clans. The legal codes called Ritsuryō (律令) describe that the Jibushō take down the names, successors, and genealogies of a clan.[61] When Sazakibe-no-Mahito (雀部真人) hoped to correct his genealogy, the government approved his demand after confirming it with the Jibushō.[62] This article shows that the Jibushō kept the genealogy of clans. Considering these facts, the Rikan and Jibushō were the government offices that controlled clans and genealogies.

In connection with this point, I take a closer look at the following article.

### Article 31: 『日本書紀』持統五年八月辛亥条
(Shingai, October, the fifth year of Emperor Jitō[63] [691], *Nihonshoki*)

詔_十八氏_、〈大三輪・雀部・石上・藤原・石川・巨勢・膳部・春日・上毛野・大伴・紀伊・平群・羽田・阿倍・佐伯・釆女・穂積・阿曇。〉上二進其祖等墓記_。

In this article, eighteen clans submitted *Boki* to the government. The Ōmiwa clan was placed at the head of these eighteen clans. Previous research assumed *Boki* to be a genealogy or legend that described how the ancestors of a clan served the Yamato Kingdom from generation to generation (Sakamoto 1970, Noguchi 1992, Katō 2004, Nakamura 2009). I support this opinion. Therefore, the Rikan took charge of *Boki*. In addition, the representative of the Rikan was Takechimaro. Considering these points, it seems logical that when the government commanded clans to submit their *Boki*, Takechimaro took the lead in editing and submitting the Ōmiwa clan's *Boki*, because he was a representative of the Rikan. As a result, the Ōmiwa clan was placed at the head of the eighteen clans. Until now, researchers could not explain why the Ōmiwa clan was placed first, ahead of other powerful clans such as the Isonokami, Fujiwara, Ishikawa, Ōtomo, and Abe clans. However, I can explain the reason very clearly.

In addition to his activity in the Jinshin War, Takechimaro was made famous by an episode during the imperial visit (行幸) to Ise Province[64] (伊勢国).

### Article 32: 『日本書紀』持統六年（六九二）二月丁未条
(Teibi, February, the sixth year of Emperor Jitō [692], *Nihonshoki*)

詔諸官曰、当以_三月三日_、将_幸_伊勢_。宜下知_此意_備中諸衣物_上。

### Article 33: 『日本書紀』持統六年二月乙卯条
(Itsubō, February, the sixth year of Emperor Jitō, *Nihonshoki*)

是日、中納言直大弐三輪朝臣高市麻呂、上_表敢直言、諌下争天皇、欲_幸_伊勢_、妨中於農時_上。

### Article 34: 『日本書紀』持統六年三月戊辰条
(Boshin, March, the sixth year of Emperor Jitō, *Nihonshoki*)

於是、中納言三輪朝臣高市麻呂、脱_其冠位_、擎_上於朝_、重諌曰、農作之節、車駕未_可_以動_。

### Article 35: 『日本書紀』持統六年三月辛未条
(Shinbi, March, the sixth year of Emperor Jitō, *Nihonshoki*)

天皇不_従_諌。遂幸_伊勢_。

In these articles, Takechimaro was appointed Chūnagon[65] (中納言) and Jikidaini[66] (直大弐). He was the fifth most important man in the government, after Takechi-no-Miko (高市皇子), Tajihi-no-Shima (丹比嶋), Abe-no-Miushi (阿倍御主人), and Ōtomo-no-Miyuki (大伴御行). At this time, the Ōmiwa clan was at the height of its power, just as during Sakau's generation.

However, this success did not last long. According to these articles, Emperor Jitō decided to visit Ise Province in February 692. Takechimaro objected to this decision because it was a busy season for farmers, and an imperial visit would disturb farming. Despite his opposition, the preparations for the visit continued. On the day of departure, Takechimaro again objected to the imperial visit, risking his crown rank. Emperor Jitō ignored his advice and departed to Ise Province three days behind schedule.

After this, though it is not described in these articles, Takechimaro likely resigned from office. This assumption is based on the following Chinese poems.

### Article 36: 『懐風藻』九五・九六
### (Chinese poems Nos. 95 and 96, *Kaifūsō*[67])

従三位兵部卿兼左右京大夫藤原朝臣萬里五首。
五言。過二神納言墟一。一首。
(九五) 一旦辞栄去。千年奉諫余。松竹含春彩。容暉寂旧墟。
　　　 清夜琴樽罷。傾門車馬疎。普天皆帝国。吾帰遂焉如。
(九六) 君道誰云易。臣義本自難。奉規終不用。帰去遂辞官。
　　　 放曠遊荘竹。沈吟佩楚蘭。天闇若一啓。将得水魚歓。

These poems were written by Fujiwara-no-Maro (藤原麻呂) when he was walking along Takechimaro's residence. These poems say that Takechimaro resigned his political position and left. It is clear that he resigned.

Then, in the decade from 692 to 702, Takechimaro did not appear in the record at all. In the meantime, according to Hidesato Tosa (土佐秀里), Takechimaro was a Sani[68] (散位) (Tosa 1999). In contrast, Sakamoto pays attention to Ōmiwa-no-Taifu (大神大夫), who appears in *Manyōshū*[69] (万葉集) 9–1772 (Sakamoto 1970). Ōmiwa-no-Taifu was relegated to a post in Chikushi Province[70] (筑紫国) in this poem. Furthermore, Ōmiwa-no-Taifu appears in *Manyōshū* 9–1770 and 9–1771, too. In these poems, he held a banquet on the bank of the Miwagawa River before he went to Nagato Province[71] (長門国). According to Sakamoto, Ōmiwa-no-Taifu and Takechimaro were the same person. Sakamoto's opinion is reasonable because the Miwagawa River flows through the Ōmiwa clan's stronghold. Therefore, Takechimaro, who was also called Ōmiwa-no-Taifu in *Manyōshū*, was relegated to a post in Chikushi Province after his resignation because he met with Emperor Jitō's anger.

It is unknown for how many years Takechimaro was in Chikushi Province. Afterwards, he appears in the record again.

**Article 37:**『続日本紀』大宝二年正月乙酉条
(Itsuyū, January, the second year of Taihō [702], *Nihonshoki*)

従四位上大神朝臣高市麻呂為<sub>_</sub>長門守<sub>_</sub>。

**Article 38:**『続日本紀』大宝三年（七〇三）六月乙丑条
(Icchū, June, the third year of Taihō [703], *Nihonshoki*)

以<sub>_</sub>従四位上大神朝臣高市麻呂<sub>_</sub>為<sub>_</sub>左京大夫<sub>_</sub>。

Takechimaro was appointed Nagato-no-Kami[72] (長門守) in 702 and Sakyō-Taifu[73] (左京大夫) in 703. Eleven years after his relegation, he made his comeback on the national political stage at last. Then, as mentioned earlier, he died in 706.

In Article 37, Takechimaro was Jushiijō (従四位上). He was not deprived of his crown rank after he resigned. However, he was Jikidaini when he resigned. Jikidaini is equivalent to the later Jushiijō. If he had been promoted, as could have been expected, he should have held a higher rank than Jushiijō. In addition, Nagato-no-Kami was the position to which a person who ranked equivalent to Shōrokuige (正六位下) should be appointed.[74] Sakyo-Taifu was the position to which a person who ranked equivalent to Shōgoijō (正五位上) should be appointed.[75] A Jushiijō should be appointed to a more important government position according to the law, but he was appointed to a lower position.

Furthermore, Takechimaro was awarded Jusanmi (従三位) after his death. This was the highest rank within the Ōmiwa clan. However, compared with the other people who also gave a funeral address at Emperor Tenmu's funeral ceremony, Takechimaro held a lower political position. For example, Isonokami-no-Maro (石上麻呂) was Shōnii (正二位) and Sadaijin (左大臣), Fuse-no-Miushi (布勢御主人) was Junii (従二位) and Udaijin (右大臣), and Ōtomo-no-Yasumaro (大伴安麻呂) was Shōsami (正三位) and Dainagon (大納言). This shows that because he objected to a decision of Emperor Jitō, Takechimaro could not succeed in life as planned. If he had not taken objection, he might have reached a much higher political position.

So, why did Takechimaro take objection to the imperial visit at the risk of his crown rank? In *Nihonshoki*, it was because the imperial visit would disturb farming. Some researchers insist on a different reason. They say that the planned purpose of the imperial visit to Ise Province was to establish the Ise-jingū Grand Shrine[76] (伊勢神宮), which would have amounted to ignoring the Ōmiwa god who had long protected the emperor, so Takechimaro could not approve of the imperial visit. For example, Toshihiko Moriya (守屋俊彦) claims that it was Takechimaro's "egoism" that prompted him to oppose the Ise-jingū Grand Shrine, as he was the head of the Ōmiwa clan, which had long controlled the religious services at Mt. Miwa (Moriya 1968). Isao Nishiyama (西山徳) states that Takechimaro did so because of his pride as the head of the Ōmiwa clan based at the foot of Mt. Miwa (Nishiyama 1975). Enchō Tamura (田村圓澄) proposes that the establishment of the Ise-jingū Grand Shrine represents the decline of the religious service at Mt. Miwa, so Takechimaro worried that the Ōmiwa clan would decline in the face of this situation (Tamura 1996). Thus, most scholars agree that Takechimaro objected to the imperial visit because of the opposition between the Mt. Miwa god and the god at the Ise-jingū Grand Shrine.

However, I think that such opposition did not exist, because the conventional religious service at Mt. Miwa was not conducted at that time. As I mention in Chapter 6, many archaeological relics were excavated from the ruins at the foot of Mt. Miwa. Many originate from the fifth century to the sixth century, but few are from the seventh century. The exhumation of relics from the same period was concentrated at only one spot at the foot of Mt. Miwa (Sasaki 1975, Terasawa 1988, Koike 1997). Later, this spot became the tabooed land of the Ōmiwa-jinja Shrine. Therefore, the significance of the religious service at Mt. Miwa changed dramatically for the Yamato Kingdom in the late seventh century, when Takechimaro objected to the imperial visit.

In addition, it was prescribed that the Chinka-sai Festival (鎮花祭) be held at the Ōmiwa-jinja Shrine.[77] This festival was derived from the religious service at Mt. Miwa. In the late seventh century, the Yamato Kingdom systematically conducted many religious services at various places, and the religious service at Mt. Miwa was merely one of many. However, Amaterasu-Ōmikami (天照大神), regarded as the ancestor of the imperial family, was worshipped at the Ise-jingū Grand Shrine, so it was the most important sacred place for the Yamato Kingdom at that time. Considering this, Mt. Miwa must be discussed separately from the Ise-jingū Grand Shrine.[78]

Furthermore, Takechimaro was praised as a great person with loyalty and tenderness by the people of the following ages in *Nihonryōiki*. If he resigned because of his "egoism," he had only himself to blame, and it is not obvious why he would be praised in such a way. Therefore, his description in *Nihonshoki* suggests that he did not resign because of his own "egoism" but because he tried to protect farmers at the cost of his high crown rank. That is why people praised him and his courageous action was remembered by future generations.

## 2.7 Conclusion

In this chapter, I investigated the fictional members of the Ōmiwa clan. I then looked at the actual members of the clan in the fifth and sixth centuries, the early to mid-seventh century, and the late seventh century to the early eighth century. I then analyzed their achievements in detail one by one and examined the trends of the Ōmiwa clan. Thus, I divided the Ōmiwa clan's history into four phases: the rising period, the prosperous period, the decline period, and the revival period.

The rising period was during the era of Emperor Yūryaku, in the late fifth century. During this period, Musa played an important role. Ōtataneko, Ōtomonushi, and Iwatoko appear in historical documents before Musa. However, these three people were fictional characters, created to explain the origin of the religious services at Mt. Miwa, support the Ōmiwa clan's right to serve the Yamato Kingdom, and tie together the genealogies of the Ōmiwa clan and its cognate clans. Musa was the first person in the Ōmiwa clan who actually existed. He participated in a fight for succession to the imperial throne. In the late fifth century, the Ōmiwa clan had begun to gain power in the Yamato Kingdom.

The prosperous period was during the era of Emperors Kinmei and Bidatsu, in the sixth century. During this period, Kotohi and Sakau played important roles. In Kotohi's generation, the system of conducting religious services at Mt. Miwa was gradually set up, and it later developed into the Ōmiwa-sai Festival. Sakau was one of Emperor Bidatsu's favorite retainers, and the emperor left all politics to him. He built direct relationships with the emperor and the empress, so he gained significant power. This was the golden age of the Ōmiwa clan.

The decline period spanned from the era of Emperor Yōmei to the era of Emperor Kōgyoku (i.e. from the early to mid-seventh century). Osazaki and Fumiya appear in historical documents from and about this period. However, Osazaki committed suicide because he was suspected of illicit intercourse with Uneme. Fumiya also probably committed suicide, according to Yamashiro. After Sakau's death, therefore, the power of the Ōmiwa clan declined remarkably for a long period.

The revival period began in the era of Emperor Kōtoku[79] (孝徳天皇) and included the era of Emperors Tenmu and Jitō, in the late seventh century. During this period, Togane and Takechimaro played important roles. Togane was ranked Taikajo, which was a high crown rank. The Ōmiwa clan regained power during his generation. Takechimaro was famous for fighting successfully in the Jinshin War. He gave a funeral address as a representative of the Rikan at Emperor Tenmu's funeral. Then, Takechimaro was appointed Chunagon and Jikidaini. He held the fifth-highest position in the government of that time. The Ōmiwa clan again reached a golden age of power and prosperity during his generation. However, Takechimaro risked his crown rank when he objected to Emperor Jitō's decision to visit Ise Province, incurring the emperor's anger. As a result, he was relegated to a post in Chikushi Province. Eleven years later, he returned to the national political stage, but he soon died. After his death, he was awarded Jusanmi, the highest rank within the Ōmiwa clan.

As I explained earlier, the Ōmiwa clan rose in the late fifth century, gained power in the sixth century, declined from the early to mid-seventh century, and revived in the late seventh century. Until now, very few studies have discussed the path of the Ōmiwa clan as a whole. In addition, I reexamined archaeological excavations. Many relics were excavated from the ruins at the foot of Mt. Miwa. Many of them date from the fifth century to the sixth century, but there is a sudden decrease in relics dating from the seventh century. This archaeological tendency corresponds with the rise and decline of the Ōmiwa clan. This shows that the Ōmiwa clan consistently was in charge of the religious services at Mt. Miwa at least from the late fifth century to the sixth century. I will address this point again in Chapter 6.

# Notes

1. Mt. Miwa is in present-day Sakurai City, Nara Prefecture (奈良県桜井市).
2. *Kojiki* (古事記) is a record of ancient matters in Japan. It was edited in 712.
3. *Nihonshoki* (日本書紀) is the chronicle of ancient Japan. It was edited in 720.
4. Sujin (崇神天皇) was the tenth emperor.
5. The part of Emperor Sujin in *Kojiki*.
6. Shinbō, February, the seventh year of Emperor Sujin, *Nihonshoki*. Kiyū, August, the seventh year of Emperor Sujin, *Nihonshoki*. Kibō, November, the seventh year of Emperor Sujin, *Nihonshoki*. Itsuō, December, the eighth year of Emperor Sujin, *Nihonshoki*.
7. Princess Yamatototohimomoso-hime (倭迹迹日百襲姫命) was a daughter of Emperor Kōrei (孝霊天皇), the seventh emperor. She was later the grand-aunt of Emperor Sujin.
8. The names Mino Village (美努村) and Sue Village (陶邑) refer to the same place. Today, this place is in Sakai, Ōsakasayama, Izumi, and Kishiwada City, Ōsaka Prefecture (大阪府堺市, 大阪狭山市, 和泉市, 岸和田市).
9. Today, the Ōmiwa god is worshipped as the god of rice wine production.
10. According to Sōkichi Tsuda, *Teiki* contained imperial genealogy, while *Kyūji* recorded old myths and legends (Tsuda 1946, Tsuda 1950). However, recent research suggests that the decision to cleanly distinguish between the contents of the two books should be reexamined (Nitō 2011).
11. Suinin (垂仁天皇) was the eleventh emperor.
12. This is a Kanshi (干支), a combination of signs used in the sexagenarian cycle. There are sixty possible combinations showing the year, month, day, time, point of the compass, and so on. They were used in history books and similar texts in Japan and other East Asian countries.
13. Chūai (仲哀天皇) was the fourteenth emperor.
14. In present-day Hyōgo Prefecture (兵庫県).
15. Jingū (神功皇后) was the wife of Emperor Chūai (仲哀天皇).
16. Bidatsu (敏達天皇) was the thirtieth emperor.
17. Tenmu (天武天皇) was the fortieth emperor.
18. In later times, the Mononobe clan (物部氏) changed its name to the Isonokami clan (石上氏).
19. The Hōkan (法官) was the predecessor of the Shikibushō (式部省). It was a government office controlling ceremonies and other affairs.
20. The Rikan (理官) was the predecessor of the Jibushō (治部省). It was a government office controlling clans, genealogies, and other matters. It will be discussed in detail later.
21. The Ōkura (大蔵) was the predecessor of the Ōkurashō (大蔵省). It was a government office controlling finances.
22. In later times, part of the Nakatomi clan (中臣氏) changed its name to the Fujiwara clan (藤原氏).
23. The Heiseikan (兵政官) was the predecessor of the Hyōbushō (兵部省). It was a government office controlling military affairs.
24. Kibō, December, the eighth year of Emperor Sujin, *Nihonshoki*.
25. Jindaiki (神代紀) is part of the myth in *Nihonshoki*.
26. *Shinsenshōjiroku* (新撰姓氏録) was a register of clan names and noble titles. It was edited in 815.
27. According to Akira Takemoto (竹本晃), ancient clans tied their genealogies together through the creation of a common ancestor (Takemoto 2006). In my previous book, I took up the Kii clan (紀氏) and demonstrated the same tendency (Suzuki M. 2012).

28 *Miwa-Takamiya-Kakeizu* (三輪髙宮家系図) records the family tree of the Ōmiwa clan and their descendants, the Takamiya family (髙宮家).
29 Iwakura (磐座) means the huge stones in which a god dwelled. Ancient people conducted religious services around Iwakura.
30 In present-day Heguri-cho, Ikoma County, Nara Prefecture (奈良県生駒市平群町).
31 *Honkeichō* (本系帳) was the genealogy of a clan. Many clans submitted a genealogy. Only some surviving fragments are in existence.
32 Yūryaku (雄略天皇) was the twenty-first emperor.
33 Ōhatsuse-no-miko (大泊瀬皇子) later succeeded to the throne. He was Emperor Yūryaku.
34 *Boki* (墓記) was the genealogy of a clan. It will be explained in detail later.
35 Buretsu (武烈天皇) was the twenty-fifth emperor.
36 The record before the enthronement of Emperor Buretsu, *Nihonshoki*.
37 In present-day Turuga City, Fukui Prefecture (福井県敦賀市).
38 Shinbō, February, the seventh year of Emperor Sujin, *Nihonshoki*.
39 *Nihonryōiki* (日本靈異記) is a collection of Buddhist stories. It was edited in the ninth century, in the Heian period (平安時代).
40 The pronunciation of "silkworms" (蚕) and "infants" (児) is the same: "ko."
41 Kinmei (欽明天皇) was the twenty-ninth emperor.
42 *Iroha-Jiruishō* (色葉字類抄・伊呂波字類抄) is an ancient Japanese dictionary from the end of the Heian period.
43 *Sezoku-Jiruishō* (世俗字類抄) is another ancient Japanese dictionary. It was edited before *Iroha-Jiruishō*.
44 Where available, I provided the exact year AD.
45 Yōmei (用明天皇) was the thirty-first emperor.
46 Empress Kashikiya-hime (炊屋姫皇后) succeeded the imperial throne later and became Empress Suiko (推古天皇), the thirty-third emperor.
47 Naitei (内廷) refers to the private organization of the imperial family.
48 Kōshin, February, the sixth year of Emperor Bidatsu [577], *Nihonshoki*.
49 Gaitei (外廷) refers to the public place where the emperor performs political actions.
50 In present-day Nara City, Nara Prefecture (奈良県奈良市).
51 Uneme (采女) was a beautiful maid of honor who served the emperor and prepared meals for him. Maids of honor were presented to the emperor by local ruling clans of various provinces.
52 Kōgyoku (皇極天皇) was the thirty-fifth emperor.
53 *Jyogushōtokutaishiden-Hoketsuki* (上宮聖徳太子伝補闕記) was a biography of Prince Shōtoku (聖徳太子), Yamashiro's father. It was edited in the early Heian period.
54 Taikajō (大花上) was the seventh grade for vassals of the crown rank grades, established in 649.
55 In the Kokuzō system (国造制), the government appointed the local powerful clan as chief officer, or Kokuzō (国造), of a local region, and granted them local rule. In return, the Kokuzō was required to supply goods, workers, and military power to the government. The Kokuzō was strictly called Kuni-no-Miyatsuko in Japanese. However, in recent research, it is commonly called Kokuzō, after the sound of the Chinese character.
56 Tenji (天智天皇) was the thirty-eighth emperor.
57 In present-day Hashinaka, Sakurai City, Nara Prefecture (奈良県桜井市箸中).
58 In present-day Miwa, Sakurai City, Nara Prefecture (奈良県桜井市三輪).
59 Kichū, September, the second year of Taihō [702], *Shokunihongi* (続日本紀). *Shokunihongi* is the history book that records the period after *Nihonshoki*. It was edited in 797.

60 Kōshin, September, the tenth year of Emperor Tenmu, *Nihonshoki*.
61 The part of Jibushō-jō in *Shikiin-Ryō* (職員令).
62 Kibō, February, the third year of Tenpyōshōhō [751], *Shokunihongi*.
63 Jitō (持統天皇) was the forty-first emperor.
64 In present-day Mie Prefecture (三重県).
65 Chūnagon (中納言) was the middle councilor of state in the government of ancient Japan.
66 Jikidaini (直大弐) was the eleventh grade for vassals of the crown rank grades, established in 685.
67 *Kaifūsō* (懐風藻) is the oldest collection of Chinese poems produced in Japan. It was edited in 751.
68 Sani (散位) was a court rank with no government post.
69 *Manyōshū* (万葉集) is the oldest anthology of classic Japanese poems. It was edited in the mid-eighth century.
70 In present-day Fukuoka Prefecture (福岡県).
71 In present-day Yamaguchi Prefecture (山口県).
72 Nagato-no-Kami (長門守) was the governor of Nagato Province (長門国).
73 Sakyō-Taifu (左京大夫) was the master of the eastern capital offices.
74 The part of Shōrokuijō in *Kani-Ryō* (官位令).
75 The part of Shōgoijō in *Kani-Ryō*.
76 The Ise-jingū Grand Shrine is in Ise City, Mie Prefecture (三重県伊勢市).
77 The part of Kishun-jo in *Jingi-Ryō* (神祇令).
78 According to Masao Sugano (菅野雅雄), Takechimaro objected to the imperial visit in his role as a member of government, not as a member of the Ōmiwa clan (Sugano 2008).
79 Kōtoku (孝徳天皇) was the thirty-sixth emperor.

# 3 The constitution of the Ōmiwa clan

## 3.1 Introduction

In Chapter 2, I elucidated the Ōmiwa clan's broad trend of prosperity and decline. Drawing on this, in this chapter, I analyze the constitution of this clan. Specifically, I address the relationship of the head lineage of the Ōmiwa clan with the cognate clans and the achievements and distribution of the cognate clans.[1]

In technical terms, in ancient Japanese history, cognate clans are referred to as Fukusei (複姓) clans. The cognate clans of the Ōmiwa clan include the Ōmiwa-no-Hikita clan (大神引田氏), the Ōmiwa-no-Kisaibe clan (大神私部氏), the Ōmiwa-no-Hata clan (大神波多氏), the Ōmiwa-no-Makamuta clan (大神真神田氏), the Miwa-no-Kurukuma clan (三輪栗隈氏), the Miwa-no-Miyabe clan (神宮部氏), the Ōmiwa-no-Ōyosami clan (大神大網氏), the Ōmiwa-no-Hakishi clan (大神掃石氏), and the Ōmiwa-no-Shimototа clan (大神楷田氏). Fukusei means "plural names." For example, the Ōmiwa-no-Hikita clan had two names, Ōmiwa and Hikita; and the Miwa-no-Kurukuma clan had two names, Miwa and Kurukuma. "Ōmiwa" and "Miwa" mean that they were relatives of the Ōmiwa clan. "Hikita" and "Kurukuma" were the clans' original names, referring to their stronghold or occupation.

## 3.2 The cognate clans that lived in Yamato Province

First, I examine the Ōmiwa-no-Hikita, Ōmiwa-no-Kisaibe, and Ōmiwa-no-Hata clans.

The Ōmiwa-no-Hikita clan's stronghold was Hikita Village, Shikinokami County, Yamato Province (大和国城上郡辟田郷).[2] The Hikita-jinja Shrine (曳田神社) is listed in *Engishiki-Jinmyōchō*[3] (延喜式神名帳). A member of this clan appears in the following article.

> **Article 1:** 『日本書紀』天武十三年（六八四）五月戊寅条
> (Boin, May, the thirteenth year of Emperor Tenmu[4] [684], *Nihonshoki*)
>
> 三輪引田君難波麻呂為二大使ｽ、桑原連人足為二小使ｽ、遣二高麗ｽ。

In this article, Miwa-no-Hikita-no-Naniwamaro (三輪引田君難波麻呂) was dispatched to Kokuryo (高句麗) as an ambassador. Furthermore, in Yamashiro Province[5] (山城国), Ōmiwa-no-Hikita-no-Okina (大神曳田老人) was in charge of rice field allotment.[6]

Kisaibe (私部) was established for the empress in the era of Emperor Bidatsu[7] (Kishi 1957). The Ōmiwa-no-Kisaibe clan took charge of the management of Kisaibe, which were installed across the country (Abe 1975). I described in Chapter 2 how the Ōmiwa clan gained power because Sakau (逆) helped establish and manage Kisaibe and built direct relationships with the emperor and the empress.

The Ōmiwa-no-Hata clan's stronghold was Hata Village, Takaichi County, Yamato Province (大和国高市郡波多郷).[8] The Hata-jinja Shrine (波多神社) is listed in *Engishiki-Jinmyōchō*.

These three clans appear in the following article.

### Article 2: 『続日本紀』神護景雲二年（七六八）二月壬午条
(Jingo, February, the second year of Jingokeiun [768], *Shokunihongi*)

大和国人従七位下大神引田公足人・大神私部公猪養・大神波多公石持等廿人、賜_姓大神朝臣_。

In this article, twenty people, including Ōmiwa-no-Hikita-no-Taruhito (大神引田公足人), Ōmiwa-no-Kisaibe-no-Ikai (大神私部公猪養), and Ōmiwa-no-Hata-no-Iwamochi (大神波多公石持), were granted the clan name Ōmiwa-no-Ason (大神朝臣). This clan name referred to the head lineage of the Ōmiwa clan. This shows that these three clans had relatively close relationships with the head linage of the Ōmiwa clan. Furthermore, the strongholds of the Ōmiwa-no-Hikita clan and the Ōmiwa-no-Hata clan were close to Yamato Province[9] (大和国). The relationship between these two clans was organized along territorial lines. It is thought that the Ōmiwa-no-Kisaibe clan's stronghold was very close to those of these two clans.

Next, we consider the Ōmiwa-no-Makamuta clan. Makamuta is the name of a place that was derived from Makamuhara (真神原). In 588, Hōkō-ji Temple (法興寺), also known as Asuka-dera Temple (飛鳥寺), was established, and that place was named Makamuhara.[10] Therefore, the Ōmiwa-no-Makamuta clan's stronghold was the Makamuhara region, Takaichi County, Yamato Province (大和国高市郡真神原).[11]

This clan's most famous member was Koobito (子首). He appears in the following article.

### Article 3: 『日本書紀』天武元年（六七二）六月甲申条
(Kōshin, June, the first year of Emperor Tenmu [672], *Nihonshoki*)

越_大山_、至_伊勢鈴鹿_。爰国司守三宅連石床・介三輪君子首、及湯沐令田中臣足麻呂・高田首新家等、参_遇于鈴鹿郡_。則且発_五百軍_、塞_鈴鹿山道_。

### Article 4:『日本書紀』天武元年七月辛卯条
(Shinbō, July, the first year of Emperor Tenmu, *Nihonshoki*)

天皇遣_紀臣阿閇麻呂・多臣品治・三輪君子首・置始連菟_、率_数萬衆_、自_伊勢大山_、越之向╷倭。

### Article 5:『日本書紀』天武五年（六七六）八月是月条
(August, the fifth year of Emperor Tenmu [676], *Nihonshoki*)

大三輪真上田子人君卒。天皇聞之大哀。以_壬申年之功_、贈_内小紫位_。仍諡曰_大三輪神真上田迎君_。

### Article 6:『続日本紀』大宝元年（七〇一）七月壬辰条
(Jinshin, July, the fifth year of Taihō [701], *Shokunihongi*)

勅、親王已下、准_其官位_賜_食封_。又壬申年功臣、隨_功第_亦賜_食封_。並各有╷差。又勅、先朝論╷功行╷封時、賜_村国小依百廿戸、當麻公国見・郡犬養連大侶・榎井連小君・書直知徳・書首尼麻呂・黄文造大伴・大伴連馬来田・大伴連御行・阿倍普勢臣御主人・神麻加牟陀君児首一十人各一百戸、若桜部臣五百瀬(略)四人各八十戸_。凡十五人、賞雖_各異_、而同居_中第_。宜_依╷令四分之一伝╷子。(略)

In Articles 3 and 4, Koobito was vice-head of the local officers in Ise Province[12] (伊勢国). When the Jinshin War (壬申の乱) broke out in 672, he met Prince Ōama[13] (大海人皇子) at the Suzuka-no-seki checking station (鈴鹿関). Then, he left Ise Province to invade Yamato Province.

Article 5 is Koobito's obituary. In this article, Emperor Tenmu mourned Koobito's death, and he posthumously awarded the title of Naishōshii (内小紫位) to Koobito, giving him the name Ōmiwa-no-Makamuta-no-Mukae-no-Kimi (大三輪神真上田迎君). Mukae means "the reception." This posthumous name was derived from the fact that Koobito had met Prince Ōama at the Suzuka-no-seki checking station, as mentioned earlier. Many people received rewards for participating in the Jinshin War. However, only Koobito was given a posthumous name. This shows that the emperor held Koobito's actions in high regard.

Furthermore, the clan name is noted merely as "Miwa" in Articles 3 and 4. In contrast, the clan name is noted as "Ōmiwa-no-Makamuta" in Article 5. In the beginning, Koobito's lineage was part of the head lineage of the Ōmiwa clan. After the Jinshin War, his lineage was independent and was called the Ōmiwa-no-Makamuta clan, as a cognate clan of the Ōmiwa clan (Katō 1973).

In Article 6, in the era of Emperor Tenmu, Koobito was granted Jikifu[14] (食封) for his activity in the Jinshin War. Then, Koobito was permitted to pass on one-quarter of the Jikifu to his children. This measure was carried out based on the Taihō Ritsuryō[15] (Satō 1976).

As an aside, for approximately 200 years, none of Koobito's descendants appeared in historical documents. Masao (全雄) and Yoshiomi (良臣) appear in the following articles from the early Heian period (平安時代), in the late ninth century.

### Article 7: 『日本三代実録』貞観四年（八六二）三月己巳条
(Kishi, March, the fourth year of Jōgan [862], *Nihonsandaijitsuroku*[16])

右京人左大史正六位上真神田朝臣全雄賜二姓大神朝臣一。大三輪大田田根子命之後也。

### Article 8: 『日本三代実録』仁和三年（八八七）三月乙亥条
(Kigai, March, the third year of Ninna [887], *Nihonsandaijitsuroku*)

授₋豊後介外従五位下大神朝臣良臣従五位下₋。先レ是、良臣向官披訴。清御原天皇壬申年入₋伊勢₋之時、良臣高祖父三輪君子首、為₋伊勢介₋従レ軍有レ功、卒後贈₋内小紫位₋。古之小紫位准₋従三位₋。然則、子首子孫、不レ可レ叙₋外位₋。於レ是、下₋外記₋而考₋実之₋。外記申明云、贈従三位大神朝臣高市麻呂・従四位上安麻呂・正五位上狛麻呂兄弟三人之後、皆叙₋内位₋。大神引田朝臣・大神楷田朝臣・大神掃石朝臣・大神真神田朝臣等、遠祖雖レ同、派別各異、不レ見レ応レ叙₋内位₋之由₋。加之、神亀五年以降、有レ格、諸氏先叙₋外位₋、後預₋内叙₋。良臣姓大神真神田朝臣也。子首之後、至₋于全雄₋、无下預₋五位₋者上。今請叙₋内₋品、事乖₋格旨₋。勅、毀₋良臣及故兄全雄外位告身₋、特賜₋内階₋。

In Article 7, Ōmiwa-no-Makamuta-no-Masao was granted the clan name Ōmiwa-no-Ason. After that, he was promoted to Shōrokuijō (正六位上), Gejugoige (外従五位下),[17] and Jugoige (従五位下).

In contrast, as noted in previous articles,[18] Yoshiomi was granted Gei[19] (外位). In Article 8, he contested it. He insisted on receiving Naii (内位) because his ancestor Koobito was granted Naishōshii. As a result, his argument was accepted, and he was granted Naii.

The Ōmiwa-no-Hikita, Ōmiwa-no-Shimotota, Ōmiwa-no-Hakishi, and Ōmiwa-no-Makamuta clans had a common ancestor in Ōtataneko (大田々根子), as Article 7 states that the Ōmiwa-no-Makamuta clan was descended from Ōtataneko. However, the ancestors of the Ōmiwa-no-Hikita, Ōmiwa-no-Shimotota, and Ōmiwa-no-Hakishi clans are not described in *Kojiki*[20] (古事記) or *Nihonshoki*[21] (日本書紀). Furthermore, according to Articles 13–16, the Ōmiwa-no-Shimotota clan was originally merely called the Shimotota clan, and later the name was changed to Ōmiwa-no-Shimotota. This shows that the Ōmiwa-no-Shimotota clan joined the cognate clans of the Ōmiwa clan later. Then, finally, the Ōmiwa-no-Hikita, Ōmiwa-no-Shimotota, Ōmiwa-no-Hakishi, and Ōmiwa-no-Makamuta clans came to insist that they were descendants of Ōtataneko. Therefore, "the fictitious blood relationship" (擬制的同祖関係) between these four clans was established after the Ōmiwa-no-Shimotota clan joined the cognate clans of the Ōmiwa clan. I discuss this period in the conclusion.

## 3.3 The cognate clans that lived in Yamashiro and Settsu Provinces

Next, I examine the Miwa-no-Kurukuma, Miwa-no-Miyabe, and Ōmiwa-no-Ōyosami clans. They lived in Yamashiro Province and Settsu Province[22] (摂津国).

The Miwa-no-Kurukuma clan's stronghold was Kurukuma Village, Kuze County, Yamashiro Province (山城国久世郡栗隈郷).[23] The place name appears in *Nihonshoki*, as in Kurukuma District[24] (栗隈県), Kurukuma Long Waterway[25] (栗隈大溝), and Kurukuma Field[26] (栗隈野). A member of this clan appears in the following article.

### Article 9: 『日本書紀』大化元年七月丙子条
(Heishi, July, the first year of Taika [645], *Nihonshoki*)

又詔_於百済使_日、明神御宇日本天皇詔旨、始我遠皇祖之世、以_百済国_、為_内官家_、譬如_三絞之綱_。中間以_任那国_、属_賜百済_。後遣_三輪栗隈君東人_、観_察任那国堺_。是故、百済王隨_勅、悉示_其堺_。而調有_闕。由_是、却_還其調_。任那所出物者、天皇之所_明覧_。夫自_今以後、可_具題_国与_所_出調_。汝佐平等、不易面来。早須明報。今重遣_三輪君東人_・馬飼造_〈闕_名。〉

In this article, Miwa-no-Kurukuma-no-Azumahito (三輪栗隈君東人) was dispatched to confirm the border between Baekje (百済) and Mimana (任那). Azumahito is described as belonging to both the "Miwa-no-Kurukuma" clan and the "Miwa" clan. "Miwa" was the old notation of "Ōmiwa." This shows that there was no distinction between the "Miwa-no-Kurukuma" clan and the "Miwa" clan. In the beginning, this clan was called either the Miwa-no-Kurukuma clan or the Miwa clan, and the former name became fixed over time.

The Miwa-no-Miyabe clan appears in the following article.

### Article 10: 『新撰姓氏録』山城国神別 神宮部造条
(Part of the Miwa-no-Miyabe clan, Shinbetsu,[27] Yamashiro Province, *Shinsenshōjiroku*)

葛城猪石岡天下神天破命之後也。六世孫吉足日命、磯城瑞籬宮御宇〈諡崇神。〉天皇御世、天下有_災。因遣_吉足日命_、令_斎_祭大物主神_、災異即止。天皇詔曰、消_天下災_、百姓得_福。自_今以後、可_為_宮能売神_。仍賜_姓宮能売公_。然後庚午年籍注_神宮部造_也。

In this article, in the era of Emperor Sujin[28] (崇神天皇), Etaruhi (吉足日命) worshipped Ōmononushi-no-Kami (大物主神), so his clan was granted the name Miyanome-no-Kimi (宮能売公). Later, his clan was recorded as the Miwa-no-Miyabe clan in *Kōgo-Nenjaku*[29] (庚午年籍). The contents of this article resemble the legend of Ōtataneko in *Kojiki* and *Nihonshoki*.[30] According to Arikiyo Saeki (佐伯有清), "Miyanome" referred to a female Shintō priest, so the Miyanome clan was the Hafuri[31] (祝) of the Ōmiwa-jinja Shrine (Saeki 1982b).

It is accepted that this clan took charge of the religious service conducted at Mt. Miwa in one way or another.

Furthermore, according to an ancient document,[32] Miwa-no-Miyabe-no-Yasuhito (神宮部造安比等) was appointed Shusei[33] (主政), in charge of Uji County, Yamashiro Province[34] (山城国宇治郡). Therefore, the Miwa-no-Miyabe clan's stronghold was Uji County, Yamashiro Province.

The legend of Etaruhi was recorded in a historical document of later ages. For example, in *Ōmiwashinsansha-Chinzanoshidai*[35] (大三輪神三社鎮座次第), Etaruhi erected a Mizukaki[36] (瑞籬) on Mt. Miwa and worshipped Ōnamuchi-no-Kami (大己貴神) and Ōmononushi-no-Kami in the era of Emperor Kōgen[37] (孝元天皇). Furthermore, in *Ōmiwasūhisho*[38] (大神崇秘書), Yoshikawa-Hiko (吉川比古), who was thought to be the same person as Etaruhi, was appointed as the priest of the Kōnomiya-jinja Shrine[39] (髙宮神社). The contents of the legend of Etaruhi became more detailed in subsequent ages. It is thought that the legend was embellished in later ages, based on the legend of *Nihonshoki* and *Kogoshūi*[40] (古語拾遺) (Saeki 1982b).

Furthermore, I examine the Takamiya-jinja Shrine in this legend. As I explain in detail in Chapter 5, the sun god was eagerly worshipped at the Ōmiwa-jinja Shrine in the Middle Ages. However, the sun god was not worshipped in the ancient ages. The posterity of the Ōmiwa clan reinterpreted the legend of *Shinsenshōjiroku* (Article 10), connected it with the worship of the sun, and created the legend of *Ōmiwashinsansha-Chinzanoshidai* and *Ōmiwasūhisho*.

Next, the Ōmiwa-no-Ōyosami clan appears in the following article.

### Article 11: 『続日本紀』文武元年（六九七）九月丙申条
(Heishin, September, the first year of Emperor Monmu[41] [697], *Shokunihongi*)

京人大神大網造百足家、生_嘉稲_。

In this article, Ōmiwa-no-Ōyosami-no-Momotari presented an auspicious rice plant to the emperor. According to the law,[42] an auspicious rice plant was a good omen. The old name of this clan is not clear, but this clan was originally a different clan from either the Ōmiwa clan or the Ōmiwa-no-Shimotota clan, which was mentioned later. Furthermore, Article 11 states that Ōmiwa-no-Ōyosami-no-Momotari lived in Fujiwara-Kyō (藤原京) at that time. However, the Ōyosami-jinja Shrine (大依羅神社) is listed in *Engishiki-Jinmyōchō*. This shrine was in Sumiyoshi County, Settsu Province[43] (摂津国住吉郡). This shows that the Ōmiwa-no-Ōyosami clan's stronghold was located there.

## 3.4 The cognate clans that lived in Izumo and Buzen Provinces

As observed earlier, many Ōmiwa cognate clans were based in the territories nearest the capital, such as Yamato, Yamashiro, and Settsu Provinces. However, some cognate clans were based outside of these territories. These were the Ōmiwa-no-Hakishi and Ōmiwa-no-Shimotota clans.

A member of the Ōmiwa-no-Hakishi clan appears in the following article.

### Article 12: 『続日本紀』神護景雲二年八月癸卯条
(Kibō, October, the second year of the Jingokeiun [768], *Shokunihongi*)

出雲国嶋根郡人外従六位上神掃石公文麻呂・意宇郡人外少初位上神人公人足・同郡人神人公五百成等廿六人、賜‗姓大神掃石朝臣‗。

In this article, twenty-six people, including Miwa-no-Hakishi-no-Kuimaro (神掃石公久比麻呂), who lived in Shimane County, Izumo Province[44] (出雲国嶋根郡), were granted the clan name Ōmiwa-no-Hakishi-no-Ason (大神掃石朝臣). This article shows that this clan's stronghold was Izumo Province.

*Miwa-Takamiya-Kakeizu* (三輪髙宮家系図) states that the little brother of Iwatoko (石床) was Mujiko (牟自古), and Mujiko was the ancestor of the Kanimori clan (掃部氏). The Ōmiwa-no-Ishi clan (大神石氏) appears in *Ōmiwa-no-Ason-Honkeichōryaku* (大神朝臣本系牒略). These notations are thought to be mistakes. To be correct, these are the Hakishi clan (掃石氏) and the Ōmiwa-no-Hakishi clan (大神掃石氏). I explained in Chapter 2 that the head lineage of the Ōmiwa clan and the cognate clans diverged from Iwatoko.

Finally, I examine the Ōmiwa-no-Shimotota clan. This clan's stronghold was in Shimotota Village, Usa County, Buzen Province[45] (豊前国宇佐郡楉田村). Ōmiwa-no-Shimotota clan members Semaro (勢麻呂) and Ehi (愛比) appear in the following articles.

### Article 13: 『続日本紀』天平十二年（七四〇）九月己酉条
(Kiyū, September, the twelfth year of Tenpyō [740], *Shokunihongi*)

豊前国京都郡大領外従七位上楉田〔勝〕[46]勢麻呂将‗兵五百騎、仲津郡擬少領无位膳東人兵八十人、下毛郡擬少領无位勇山伎美麻呂・築城郡擬少領外大初位上佐伯豊石兵七十人‗、来‗帰官軍‗。

### Article 14: 『続日本紀』天平十三年（七四一）閏三月乙卯条
(Itsubō, intercalary March, the thirteenth year of Tenpyō [741], *Shokunihongi*)

外従七位上楉田勝〔勢〕[47]麻呂（略）並外従五位下。

### Article 15: 『続日本紀』宝亀七年（七七六）十二月庚戌条
(Kōjutsu, December, the seventh year of Hōki [776], *Shokunihongi*)

豊前国京都人正六位上楉田勝愛比、賜‗姓大神楉田朝臣‗。

### Article 16: 『続日本紀』延暦三年（七八四）十二月己巳条
(Kishi, December, the third year of the Enryaku [784], *Shokunihongi*)

正六位上（略）大神楉田朝臣愛比（略）並外従五位下。

In Article 13, Semaro participated in the suppression of the Rebellion of Fujiwara-no-Hirotsugu (藤原広嗣の乱). At that time, Semaro was Dairyo[48] (大領) in Miyako County, Buzen Province[49] (豊前国京都郡). In Article 14, he was promoted to Gejugoige (外従五位下) from Gejushichiijō (外従七位上). This promotion was probably the result of his activity in the suppression of the rebellion.

In Article 15, Ehi lived in Miyako County, Buzen Province, as did Semaro, and Ehi was granted the clan name Ōmiwa-no-Shimotota-no-Ason (大神楮田朝臣). In Article 16, he was promoted to Gejugoige (外従五位下) from Shorokuijō (正六位上). According to Articles 13–15, Ehi originally belonged to the Shimotota clan (楮田氏). This shows that this clan was originally called the Shimotota clan, which later built a political and genealogical relationship with the Ōmiwa clan, eventually joining the cognate clans of the Ōmiwa clan.

## 3.5 Conclusion

In this chapter, I analyzed the cognate clans of the Ōmiwa clan. The processes by which the name of each clan changed are represented below.

- Miwa-no-Hikita clan → Ōmiwa-no-Hikita clan → Ōmiwa clan
- Ōmiwa-no-Kisaibe clan → Ōmiwa clan
- Ōmiwa-no-Hata clan → Ōmiwa clan
- Miwa clan → Miwa-no-Makamuta clan → Ōmiwa-no-Makamuta clan → Ōmiwa clan
- Miwa clan → Miwa-no-Kurukuma clan
- Miyanome clan → Miwa-no-Miyabe clan
- Ōyosami clan → Ōmiwa-no-Ōyosami clan
- Miwa-no-Hakishi clan → Ōmiwa-no-Hakishi clan
- Shimotota clan → Ōmiwa-no-Shimotota clan

Based on this pattern, I make three points. The first is that changes to the names of cognate clans mostly happened in the late eighth century. According to Article 2, the Ōmiwa-no-Hikita, Ōmiwa-no-Kisaibe, and Ōmiwa-no-Hata clans changed their name to Ōmiwa in 768. According to Article 12, the Miwa-no-Hakishi clan changed its name to Ōmiwa-no-Hakishi in the same year. According to Article 15, the Shimotota clan changed its name to Ōmiwa-no-Shimotota in 776.

As I mentioned in Chapter 2, the movement to reorganize many ancient clans was very active from the early eighth century to the early ninth century. Drawing on this historical background, the head lineages of the Ōmiwa clan, its cognate clans, and other clans were reorganized in this period.

For example, the government commanded clans to submit *Honkeichō*[50] (本系帳) before the era of Tenpyōshōhō[51] [749–757] and commanded the same again in 799.[52] Based on these, *Shinsenshōjiroku* was edited in 815. As part of this movement, the relationship of the head lineage of the Ōmiwa clan to the cognate clans and the constitution of these clans were reorganized in politics and genealogies. This period was the greatest epoch for many ancient clans. The Ōmiwa clan was no exception.

The second point is that there is a pattern in the distribution of cognate clans. The Ōmiwa-no-Hikita clan's stronghold was Hikita Village, Shikinokami County, Yamato Province. The Ōmiwa-no-Hata clan's stronghold was Hata Village, Takaichi County, Yamato Province. The Ōmiwa-no-Makamuta clan's stronghold was Makamuhara Region, Takaichi County, Yamato Province. The Miwa-no-Kurukuma clan's stronghold was Kurukuma Village, Kuze County, Yamashiro Province. The Miwa-no-Miyabe clan's stronghold was Uji County, Yamashiro Province. The Ōmiwa-no-Ōyosami clan's stronghold was Sumiyoshi County, Settsu Province. The Ōmiwa-no-Shimotota clan's stronghold was Shimotota Village, Usa County, Buzen Province.

These clans' strongholds were distributed in the territories adjacent to the capital and western Japan. In particular, the strongholds of the Ōmiwa-no-Hikita, Ōmiwa-no-Hata, and Ōmiwa-no-Makamuta clans were very near the stronghold of the head lineage of the Ōmiwa clan. The same is probably true of the Ōmiwa-no-Kisaibe clan. These clans connected with each other through a territorial relationship.

The third point is that the distribution of clans was related to sea traffic. The Ōmiwa-no-Ōyosami clan's stronghold was at the estuary of the Yamato River (大和川). Many people in the Ōmiwa clan and its cognate clans played significant roles in diplomacy. As mentioned earlier, Miwa-no-Hikita-no-Naniwamaro was dispatched to Kokuryo. Miwa-no-Kurukuma-no-Azumahito was dispatched to Baekje and Mimana, Ōmiwa-no-Shikobu was dispatched to Silla,[53] and Ōmiwa-no-Nemaro was dispatched to the Korean Peninsula.[54] In later ages, Ōmiwa-no-Suetari and Ōmiwa-no-Muneo were dispatched to the Tang dynasty[55] (唐).

As I explain in detail in Chapter 4, it is thought that before the seventh century, when a member of the head lineage of the Ōmiwa clan or its cognate clans was dispatched to a foreign country and participated in the overseas dispatch of troops, many related clans in various places were mobilized. Therefore, the relationship between the Ōmiwa clan and its cognate clans was strengthened. Furthermore, as a result, the Ōmiwa clan built new relationships with its cognate clans, which did not previously have close relationships.

The Ōmiwa-no-Ōyosami clan's stronghold was a strategically important place for the Ōmiwa clan. Therefore, the Ōmiwa clan was based in that place, so those two clans began to interact with each other and build a political and genealogical relationship. As a result, the Ōmiwa-no-Ōyosami clan joined the group of Ōmiwa clans as a cognate clan.

Similarly, the Ōmiwa-no-Hakishi and Ōmiwa-no-Shimotota clans were based in coastal areas in western Japan. Therefore, the Ōmiwa clan built political and genealogical relationships with them through sea traffic.[56]

# Notes

1. Some researchers insist that the Miwa-no-Yorita clan (神依田氏) should be included among the Ōmiwa cognate clans (Maeda 2006). However, the Miwa-no-Yorita clan did not have a direct relationship with the Ōmiwa clan.
2. In present-day Shirakawa, Sakurai City, Nara Prefecture (奈良県桜井市白河).
3. *Engishiki-Jinmyōchō* (延喜式神名帳) is a record of Shintō shrines in ancient Japan. It was edited in 927.
4. Tenmu (天武天皇) was the fortieth emperor.
5. In present-day Kyōto Prefecture (京都府).
6. *Dainihon-Komonjyo* (大日本古文書) 4–81.
7. Kōsin, February, the sixth year of Emperor Bidatsu [577], *Nihonshoki*. Bidatsu (敏達天皇) was the thirtieth emperor.
8. In present-day Fuyuno, Asuka Village, Takaichi County, Nara Prefecture (奈良県高市郡明日香村冬野).
9. In present-day Nara Prefecture (奈良県).
10. The first year of Emperor Sushun [588], *Nihonshoki*. Sushun (崇峻天皇) was the thirty-second emperor.
11. In present-day Asuka, Asuka Village, Takaichi County, Nara Prefecture (奈良県高市郡明日香村飛鳥).
12. In present-day Mie Prefecture (三重県).
13. Prince Ōama later became Emperor Tenmu.
14. Jikifu (食封), also known as Fuko (封戸), was a vassal household allotted a courtier, shrines, and temples.
15. The part of Kofu-jō in Roku-Ryō (禄令).
16. *Nihonsandaijitsuroku* (日本三代実録) is a history of the era of Emperors Seiwa (清和天皇), Yōzei (陽成天皇), and Kōkō (光孝天皇). It was edited in 901. Emperor Seiwa was the fifty-sixth emperor. Emperor Yōzei was the fifty-seventh emperor. Emperor Kōkō was the fifty-eighth emperor.
17. Kōgo, January, the fifth year of Jōgan [863], *Nihonsandaijitsuroku*. Kibō, February, the fifth year of Jōgan, *Nihonsandaijitsuroku*. Kōgo, March, the sixth year of Jōgan [864], *Nihonsandaijitsuroku*. Itsuyū, January, the eighth year of Jōgan [866], *Nihonsandaijitsuroku*. Shinshi, February, the tenth year of Jōgan [868], *Nihonsandaijitsuroku*.
18. Teibi, January, the second year of Ninna [886], *Nihonsandaijitsuroku*. Heishin, January, the second year of Ninna, *Nihonsandaijitsuroku*. Shinbi, February, the second year of Ninna, *Nihonsandaijitsuroku*.
19. Gei (外位) was a court rank given to the clans based outside of the vicinal territories of the capital. In contrast, Naii (内位) was a court rank given to clans based in the vicinal territories of the capital.
20. *Kojiki* (古事記) is a record of ancient matters in Japan. It was edited in 712.
21. *Nihonshoki* (日本書紀) is a chronicle of ancient Japan. It was edited in 720.
22. In present-day Ōsaka Prefecture (大阪府).
23. In present-day Ōkubo, Uji City, Kyōto Prefecture (京都府宇治市大久保).
24. October, the twelfth year of Emperor Nintoku, *Nihonshoki*. Nintoku (仁徳天皇) was the sixteenth emperor.
25. The fifteenth year of Emperor Suiko, *Nihonshoki*. Suiko (推古天皇) was the thirty-third emperor.
26. Boshi, October, the first year of Jōwa [834], *Shokunihonkōki* (続日本後紀). *Shokunihonkōki* was the history book that recorded the period after *Nihonkōki*. It was edited in 869.
27. Shinbetsu (神別) refers to the social status of a clan whose members were descended from a god. Shin means "god."

46   *The constitution of the Ōmiwa clan*

28 Sujin (崇神天皇) was the tenth emperor.
29 *Kōgo-Nenjyaku* (庚午年籍) was the nationwide family register. It was created in 670.
30 I explain these legends in detail in Chapter 7.
31 Hafuri (祝) refers to a lower-ranking Shintō priest.
32 *Dainihon-Komonjyo* 15–127.
33 Shusei (主政) was the third-highest official rank of Gunji (郡司). Gunji was the district manager in ancient Japan.
34 In present-day Uji City, Kyōto Prefecture (京都府宇治市).
35 *Ōmiwashinsansha-Chinzanoshidai* (大三輪神三社鎮座次第) is a historical chronicle of the Ōmiwa-jinja Shrine. This is included in *Ōmiwajinja-shiryō* (大神神社史料) *Volume* 1.
36 A Mizukaki (瑞籬) is a Shintō shrine fence establishing the limits of the sanctuary.
37 Kōgen (孝元天皇) was the eighth emperor.
38 *Ōmiwasūhisho* (大神崇秘書) is a historical record of the Ōmiwa-jinja Shrine. It was edited in 1119.
39 In Miwa, Sakurai City, Nara Prefecture.
40 *Kogoshūi* (古語拾遺) is a historical record of the Inbe clan (忌部氏). It was edited in 807.
41 Monmu (文武天皇) was the forty-second emperor.
42 The part of Shōzui-jō in Engi-Jibushō-Shiki (延喜治部省式).
43 In present-day Sumiyoshi Ward, Ōsaka City, Ōsaka Prefecture (大阪府大阪市住吉区).
44 In present-day Matsue City, Shimane Prefecture (島根県松江市).
45 In present-day Wake, Usa City, Ōita Prefecture (大分県宇佐市和気).
46 In this article, 勝 was not written. This is thought to be a mistake. For the notation to be correct, 勝 should be supplemented.
47 In this article, 勢 was not written. This is thought to be a mistake. For the notation to be correct, 勢 should be supplemented.
48 Dairyo (大領) was a chief district official.
49 In the eastern part of present-day Fukuoka Prefecture (福岡県).
50 *Honkeichō* (本系帳) was the genealogy of the clan. Many clans submitted a genealogy, of which only fragments survive today.
51 The introduction of *Kōninshiki* (弘仁私記). *Kōninshiki* is an annotation of *Nihonshoki*. It was edited in 813.
52 Bojutsu, December, the eighteenth year of Enryaku, *Nihonkōki* (日本後紀). *Nihonkōki* is the history book that records the period after *Shokunihongi*. It was edited in 840.
53 Kibō, May, the fifth year of Taika [649], *Nihonshoki*.
54 March, the second year of Tenji [663], *Nihonshoki*. Tenji (天智天皇) was the thirty-eighth emperor.
55 Teibō, December, the seventh year of Hōki [776], *Shokunihongi*. Kishi, August, the sixth year of Jōwa [839], *Shokunihonkōki*.
56 For reference, the Kii clan (紀氏), who played an active part in diplomacy in ancient times, built many relationships with the clans based in the coastal area of western Japan (Suzuki M. 2012).

# 4 The dispersal of the Ōmiwa clan

## 4.1 Introduction

In Chapter 3, I examined the constitution of the Ōmiwa clan. Strictly speaking, the Ōmiwa clan was constructed in the head linage of the Ōmiwa clan, such as the lineages of Sakau and Takechimaro, and the cognate (Fukusei) clans, such as the Ōmiwa-no-Hikita and Ōmiwa-no-Makamuta clans. However, the Ōmiwa clan also had relationships with many other clans. Various clans throughout Japan had "Miwa" (神, 三輪) or "Ōmiwa" (大神, 大三輪) in their name, such as the Miwa clan (神氏), the Miwahito clan (神人氏), the Miwahitobe clan (神人部氏), and the Miwabe clan (神部氏). These clans were an important element constituting the Ōmiwa clan, too. I collectively refer to all of these clans as the Ōmiwa clan.[1] In this chapter, I analyze the dispersal of the Ōmiwa clan, and I investigate the historical background to these clans' distribution throughout the Japanese islands.

## 4.2 Circumstances of dispersal throughout Japan

First, I extracted the following place names thought to be related to "Miwa" or "Ōmiwa" from ancient historical materials.

Kinai[2] (畿内)

- Miwa Village (Shikinokami County, Yamato Province)
- Ōmiwa Village (Shikinokami County, Yamato Province)
- Ōmiwa Village (Arima County, Settsu Province)
- Ōmiwa Village (Kawabe County, Settsu Province)
- Miwa Village (Ōtori County, Izumi Province)
- Kamitsumiwa Village (Ōtori County, Izumi Province)

Tōkaidō[3] (東海道)

- Miwa Village (Nakashima County, Owari Province)
- Miwa Village (Yana County, Mikawa Province)

- Ōmiwa Village (Hamana County, Tōtoumi Province)
- Miwa Village (Abe County, Suruga Province)
- Ōmiwa Village (Niihari County, Hitachi Province)
- Ōmiwa Station (Niihari County, Hitachi Province)
- Miwa Village (Kuji County, Hitachi Province)

Tōsandō[4] (東山道)

- Miwa Village (Kamo County, Mino Province)
- Miwa Village (Mushirota County, Mino Province)
- Miwa Village (Ōno County, Mino Province)
- Ōmiwa Village (Ōno County, Mino Province)
- Miwa Village (Suwa County, Shinano Province)
- Miwa Village (Nasu County, Shimotsuke Province)

Sanindō[5] (山陰道)

- Miwa Village (Hikami County, Tanba Province)
- Miwa Village (Ōmi County, Inaba Province)
- Kazuwa Village (Kume County, Hōki Province)
- Shimotsuwa Village (Kume County, Hōki Province)

Sanyodō[6] (山陽道)

- Miwa Village (Kamo County, Harima Province)
- Ōmiwa Village (Kamo County, Harima Province)
- Miwa Village (Tomahigashi County, Mimasaka Province)
- Miwa Village (Ōba County, Mimasaka Province)
- Miwa Village (Kuboya County, Bicchū Province)
- Miwa Village (Kumage County, Suō Province)

Saikaidō[7] (西海道)

- Ōmiwa Village (Yamato County, Chikushi Province)
- Ōmiwa Village (Hayami County, Bungo Province)

Next, I extracted the following Shintō shrines thought to be related to the "Miwa" or "Ōmiwa" from *Engishiki-Jinmyōchō*[8] (延喜式神名帳) and other historical materials.

Kinai (畿内)

- The Ōmiwa-jinja Shrine (Shikinokami County, Yamato Province)
- The Sai-jinja Shrine (Shikinokami County, Yamato Province)
- The Miwanimasuhimuka-jinja Shrine (Shikinokami County, Yamato Province)
- The Isagawa-jinja Shrine (Sōnokami County, Yamato Province)
- The Isagawaawa-jinja Shrine (Sōnokami County, Yamato Province)
- The Miwatakayasu-jinja Shrine (Kawachi Province)
- The Tōsen-jinja Shrine (Arima County, Settsu Province)

Tōkaidō (東海道)

- The Kuni-jinja Shrine (Ōtori County, Izumi Province)
- The Ōwa-jinja Shrine (Iitaka County, Ise Province)
- The Ōmiwa-jinja Shrine (Asake County, Ise Province)
- The Ōmiwa-jinja Shrine (Nakashima County, Owari Province)
- The Ōmiwa-jinja Shrine (Hamana County, Tōtoumi Province)
- The Miwayama-jinja Shrine (Hamana County, Tōtoumi Province)
- The Miwabe-jinja Shrine (Abe County, Suruga Province)
- The Miwa-jinja Shrine (Mashizu County, Suruga Province)
- The Miwabe-jinja Shrine (Yamanashi County, Kai Province)
- The Miwabe-jinja Shrine (Koma County, Kai Province)

Tōsandō (東山道)

- The Ōmiwa-jinja Shrine (Tagi County, Mino Province)
- The Miwa-jinja Shrine (Minochi County, Shinano Province)
- The Miwa-jinja Shrine (Yamada County, Kōzuke Province)
- The Miwa-jinja Shrine (Nasu County, Shimotsuke Province)
- The Ōmiwa-jinja Shrine (Tsuge County, Shimotsuke Province)

Hokurikudō[9] (北陸道)

- The Miwa-jinja Shrine (Onyū County, Wakasa Province)
- The Ōmiwanoshimosaki-jinja Shrine (Tsuruga County, Echizen Province)
- The Miwa-jinja Shrine (Kaga County, Kaga Province)
- The Ōmiwa-jinja Shrine (Kubiki County, Echigo Province)

Sanindō (山陰道)

- The Awaga-jinja Shrine (Asako County, Tajima Province)
- The Ōmiwa-jinja Shrine (Kono County, Inaba Province)
- The Ōgamiyama-jinja Shrine (Aimi County, Hōki Province)
- The Miwa-jinja Shrine (Aimi County, Hōki Province)

Sanyodō (山陽道)

- The Ōyamatonomonoshironushi-jinja Shrine (Shisawa County, Harima Province)
- The Miwa-jinja Shrine (Ōku County, Bizen Province)
- The Ōmiwa-jinja Shrine (Kamitsumichi County, Bizen Province)
- The Miwa-jinja Shrine (Shimotsumichi County, Bicchū Province)
- The Ōmiwa-jinja Shrine (Bingo Province)

Nankaidō[10] (南海道)

- The Ōmiwa-jinja Shrine (Nakata County, Awa Province)

Saikaidō (西海道)

- The Ōnamuchi-jinja Shrine (Yasu County, Chikuzen Province)

## 50  *The dispersal of the Ōmiwa clan*

Finally, I extracted the names of the following clans thought to be related to the "Miwa" or "Ōmiwa" from ancient historical materials.

Kinai (畿内)

- The Miwa clan (Shikinokami County, Yamato Province)
- The Ōmiwa clan (Shikinokami County, Yamato Province)
- The Miwa-no-Hikita clan (Shikinokami County, Yamato Province)
- The Ōmiwa-no-Hikita clan (Shikinokami County, Yamato Province)
- The Ōmiwa-no-Hata clan (Takaichi County, Yamato Province)
- The Ōmiwa-no-Makamuta clan (Takaichi County, Yamato Province)
- The Miwa clan (Otagi County, Yamashiro Province)
- The Miwa-no-Kurukuma clan (Kuze County, Yamashiro Province)
- The Miwa-no Miyabe clan (Uji County, Yamashiro Province)
- The Miwahito clan (Yamashiro Province)
- The Miwahito clan (Nose County, Settsu Province)
- The Ōmiwa-no-Ōyosami clan (Sumiyoshi County, Settsu Province)
- The Miwahito clan (Settsu Province)
- The Miwahito clan (Kawachi Province)
- The Miwa clan (Izumi Province)
- The Miwahito clan (Izumi Province)

Tōkaidō (東海道)

- The Miwahitobe clan (Ano County, Ise Province)
- The Miwahito clan (Hakuri County, Owari Province)
- The Miwabe clan (Chita County, Owari Province)
- The Miwa clan (Hamana County, Tōtoumi Province)
- The Miwahito clan (Hamana County, Tōtoumi Province)
- The Miwahitobe clan (Hamana County, Tōtoumi Province)
- The Miwahitobe clan (Tagata County, Izu Province)
- The Ōmiwa clan (Ōsumi County, Sagami Province)
- The Miwahitobe clan (Musashi Province)
- The Miwabe clan (Hitachi Province)

Tōsandō (東山道)

- The Miwahito clan (Inugami County, Ōmi Province)
- The Miwahito clan (Ōmi Province)
- The Miwahito clan (Kamo County, Mino Province)
- The Miwahitobe clan (Kamo County, Mino Province)
- The Miwa clan (Ōno County, Mino Province)
- The Miwahito clan (Ōno County, Mino Province)
- The Miwa clan (Yamagata County, Mino Province)
- The Miwahito clan (Yamagata County, Mino Province)
- The Miwa clan (Kagamu County, Mino Province)
- The Miwahito clan (Kagamu County, Mino Province)

- The Ōmiwa clan (Anpachi County, Mino Province)
- The Miwahito clan (Takai County, Shinano Province)
- The Miwahitobe clan (Hanishina County, Shinano Province)
- The Miwahito clan (Tone County, Kōzuke Province)
- The Miwahito clan (Kuruma County, Kōzuke Province)
- The Miwahito clan (Kōzuke Province)
- The Miwahito clan (Mutsu Province)
- The Miwahito clan (Dewa Province)
- The Miwahitobe clan (Dewa Province)

Hokurikudō (北陸道)

- The Ōmiwa clan (Tsuruga County, Echizen Province)
- The Miwa clan (Tsuruga County, Echizen Province)
- The Miwahito clan (Tsuruga County, Echizen Province)
- The Ōmiwabe clan (Tsuruga County, Echizen Province)
- The Miwa clan (Enuma County, Kaga Province)
- The Miwahito clan (Enuma County, Kaga Province)
- The Ōmiwa clan (Kaga Province)
- The Miwa clan (Ecchū Province)
- The Miwa clan (Echigo Province)
- The Miwahito clan (Echigo Province)
- The Miwahitobe clan (Echigo Province)
- The Miwahito clan (Kamo County, Sado Province)

Sanindō (山陰道)

- The Miwahito clan (Hikami County, Tanba Province)
- The Miwa clan (Tanba Province)
- The Miwahito clan (Tanba Province)
- The Miwahitobe clan (Tanba Province)
- The Miwahito clan (Kumano County, Tango Province)
- The Miwabe clan (Asako County, Tajima Province)
- The Miwabe clan (Izushi County, Tajima Province)
- The Miwabe clan (Keta County, Inaba Province)
- The Miwa clan (Takakusa County, Inaba Province)
- The Miwabe clan (Takakusa County, Inaba Province)
- The Miwabe clan (Inaba Province)
- The Miwahitobe clan (Kando County, Izumo Province)
- The Miwa-no-Hakishi clan (Shimane County, Izumo Province)
- The Ōmiwa-no-Hakishi clan (Shimane County, Izumo Province)
- The Ōmiwa-no-Hakishi clan (Ou County, Izumo Province)
- The Miwahito clan (Ou County, Izumo Province)
- The Miwa clan (Ōchi County, Iwami Province)
- The Ikuwa-no-Ōmiwa clan (Ōchi County, Iwami Province)

Sanyodō (山陽道)

- The Miwahito clan (Shisawa County, Harima Province)
- The Miwahitobe clan (Shisawa County, Harima Province)
- The Miwahito clan (Ibo County, Harima Province)
- The Miwahito clan (Ako County, Harima Province)
- The Ōmiwa clan (Harima Province)
- The Miwa clan (Ōba County, Mimasaka Province)
- The Miwa clan (Kuboya County, Bicchū Province)
- The Miwahitobe clan (Kuboya County, Bicchū Province)
- The Miwabe clan (Asakuchi County, Bicchū Province)
- The Miwahito clan (Naka County, Suō Province)
- The Ōmiwa clan (Nagato Province)
- The Ōmiwabe clan (Nagato Province)
- The Miwabe clan (Nagato Province)
- The Shimotsumiwabe clan (Nagato Province)

Nankaidō (南海道)

- The Miwahitobe clan (Mihara County, Awaji Province)
- The Miwahito clan (Yamada County, Sanuki Province)

Saikaidō (西海道)

- The Ōgabe clan (Shima County, Chikuzen Province)
- The Ōga clan (Naka County, Chikuzen Province)
- The Ōgabe clan (Naka County, Chikuzen Province)
- The Ōgabe clan (Yasu County, Chikuzen Province)
- The Miwabe clan (Chikuzen Province)
- The Ōgabe clan (Nakatsu County, Buzen Province)
- The Ōmiwa-no-Shimotota clan (Miyako County, Buzen Province)
- The Ōga clan (Usa County, Buzen Province)
- The Miwabe clan (Usa County, Buzen Province)
- The Ōga clan (Bungo Province)
- The Miwa clan (Takaku County, Hizen Province)
- The Ōgabe clan (Hizen Province)
- The Miwahito clan (Hizen Province)
- The Miwabe clan (Taki County, Satsuma Province)

Others

- The Miwa clan (Locations unknown)
- The Miwahitobe clan (Locations unknown)

Based on these lists, I make two observations. First, the place names, shrine names, and clan names thought to be related to the "Miwa" or "Ōmiwa" were distributed throughout the Japanese islands rather than limited to a specific district. This is related to the migration of the Ōmiwa clan to various places and to the spread of faith in the Ōmiwa god.

Second, some place names, shrine names, and clan names overlap. For example, in Hamana County, Tōtoumi Province[11] (遠江国浜名郡), there was an Ōmiwa Village (大神郷). In addition, the Ōmiwa-jinja Shrine (大神神社) and the Miwayama-jinja Shrine (弥和山神社) were located in this county. Furthermore, the Miwa, Miwahito, and Miwahitobe clans lived in this county, too. Considering these examples, the distributions of place names, shrine names, and clan names were likely related (Ikebe 1972). Even if only the place name remains now, it means the Ōmiwa clan is likely to have resided there in ancient times. In the same way, even if only the shrine remains, the shrine was likely erected by the Ōmiwa clan, whose members lived there in ancient times.

## 4.3 Advancement to western Japan and to foreign countries

How did the Ōmiwa clan disperse across the Japanese islands? In regard to this point, previous researchers have made much of the distribution of shrines. Takehiko Abe (阿部武彦) argues that, when the Yamato Kingdom sent troops to eastern and western Japan and to the Korean Peninsula (朝鮮半島), the soldiers worshipped the Ōmiwa god. Therefore, the Ōmiwa clan was dispatched to various places (Abe 1975). Atsumu Wada (和田萃) makes this point, as well. He notes that the Ōmiwa god was a "war god," so the Ōmiwa god was enshrined when the Yamato Kingdom sent troops to eastern Japan. Accordingly, the Ōmiwa clan was dispatched to worship the Ōmiwa god in various places (Wada 1985). Many researchers support this theory (Maekawa 1986, Maeda 2006). Below, I confirm the legends that are the basis for this theory.

First, I examine the legends about the advancement of the Yamato Kingdom to western Japan and to foreign countries.

### Article 1: 『日本書紀』神功皇后摂政前紀
(The record before the enthronement of Empress Jingū,[12] *Nihonshoki*[13])

令＿諸国＿、集＿船舶＿練＿兵甲＿。時軍卒難↓集。皇后曰、必神心焉、則立＿大三輪社＿、以奉＿刀矛＿矣。軍衆自聚。

### Article 2: 『筑前国風土記』逸文
(The surviving fragments of *Chikuzennokuni-Fudoki*[14])

気長足姫尊、欲↓伐＿新羅＿。整＿理軍士＿、発行之間、道中遁亡。占＿求其由＿、即有＿崇神＿。名曰＿大三輪神＿。所以樹＿此神社＿、遂平＿新羅＿。

In Article 1, Empress Jingū (神功皇后) tried to send troops to Silla (新羅) but could not gather the soldiers. She blamed her failure on the curse of the Ōmiwa god. After she worshipped the Ōmiwa god and dedicated a sword and a pike, she succeeded in gathering soldiers.

The contents of Article 2 are similar to those of Article 1. In this article, Empress Jingū sent troops to Silla, but her soldiers escaped. Then, she worshipped the Ōmiwa god, so she succeeded in conquering Silla.

Empress Jingū established the Ōnamuchi-jinja Shrine[15] (於保奈牟智神社) at the place where she had worshipped the Ōmiwa god. It is listed in *Engishiki-Jinmyōchō*. Researchers have said that the Ōmiwa god had the following characterizations (Ikeda 1971, Wada 1985).

- The mountain and forest god
- The god of light
- The thunder god
- The god of snakes
- The god of curses
- The god who marries a human woman
- The clan deity
- The war god
- The national guardian deity

Of course, I acknowledge that one of the characterizations – that of the war god – attracted attention and worship from ancient people during wartime. However, these multiple characterizations are indivisible from each other. Ancient people viewed the god as multilayered.

In Article 2, the Ōmiwa god is obviously presented as a god of curses. However, settling the curse led the troops to success. Therefore, the Ōmiwa god was both the god of curses and the war god. It is clear that the Ōmiwa god is presented as a war god in this article, even if the characterization is not clearly explained.

No member of the Ōmiwa clan appears in this article. However, in another legend, when Empress Jingū sent troops to Silla, the Suminoe gods[16] (住吉神) haunted the empress. At that time, Tamoni-no-Sukune (田裳見宿禰), the ancestor of the Tsumori clan (津守氏), suggested that she conduct a religious service.[17] The Tsumori clan provided the priest for the Sumiyoshi-taisha Shrine[18] (住吉大社) and worshipped the Suminoe gods.

In addition, when Prince Kume (来目皇子) was dispatched to Silla in the era of Empress Suiko[19] (推古天皇), Mononobe-no-Wakamiyabe (物部若宮部) enshrined Futsunushi-no-Kami (経津主神) on the way. Futsunushi was the god that the Mononobe clan (物部氏) worshipped.

In these legends, when a Shintō shrine was established or a religious service was conducted, a member of the clan that worshipped that god took charge. Recent research suggests that Empress Jingū was a fictional character, so the precise date of sending troops is unknown. However, the people of the Ōmiwa clan participated in the sending of troops at a certain ancient date, and they established the Ōnamuchi-jinja Shrine in Chikuzen Province.

## Article 3:『続日本紀』天平九年（七三七）四月乙巳条
(Isshi, April, the ninth year of Tenpyō [737], *Shokunihongi*)

遣_使於伊勢神宮、大神社、筑紫住吉・八幡二社及香椎宮_、奉_幣、以告_新羅无_礼之状_。

In Article 3, the government offered Heihaku[20] (幣帛) to the Ise-jingū Grand Shrine[21] (伊勢神宮), the Ōmiwa-jinja Shrine, the Suminoe-jinja Shrine[22] (住吉神社), the Usa-jingū Shrine[23] (宇佐神宮), and the Kashii-gū Shrine[24] (香椎宮). Then the government reported Silla's disrespect of these shrines. Before this, Silla had restored its diplomatic relationship with the Tang dynasty (唐) and insisted on equal diplomatic relations with Japan. The Kentōshi[25] (遣唐使) reported Silla's disrespect to the emperor.[26] The government discussed diplomatic policy. Some government officials insisted that the government dispatch a messenger to Silla and question them closely or severely. Some government officials insisted that the government send troops to Silla.[27] In response, the government dedicated Heihaku to these shrines.

Among the shrines listed in Article 3, the Ise-jingū Grand Shrine enshrined Amaterasu-Ōmikami (天照大神), regarded as the ancestor of the imperial family. The Ōmiwa-jinja Shrine and the Suminoe-jinja Shrine appear in the legend of sending troops in the era of Empress Jingū. The Usa-jingū Shrine and Kashii-gū Shrine enshrined Empress Jingū. Ancient people believed that these shrines could provide a miracle for the dispatch of troops. The Ōmiwa-jinja Shrine was included among those shrines.

## Article 4:『粟鹿大明神元記』太多彦命尻付
(The part of Ōtatahiko in *Awagadaimyōjinganki*[28])

右多太彦、磯城瑞籬宮御宇初国所知御間城入彦五十瓊殖天皇御世、国々荒振人等令_平服_。以_大国主神術魂・荒(魂脱ヵ)_、召著_於桙・楯・大刀・鏡_、遣_於西国_。于時、初貢_男女之調物_。即但馬国朝来郡粟鹿村宿住矣也。

## Article 5:『粟鹿大明神元記』奥書
(The postscript of *Awagadaimyōjinganki*)

右、根閇氏大明神天美佐利命者、神氏最初之天降人、皇治化之崇基也。此境山陰道、但馬州朝来郡粟鹿郷也。尒時、山海混沌、煙雲闇靄。庶民漸事二人王一、神霊未レ入_皇帰_。吾親皇命、振固洲天下御坐。名曰_粟鹿大明神_也。花夷未_頒之時、荊樹点_瑞之処、天下俄陰、霖雨久洪水、饑餓疾癘、生者流亡。時焉、朝廷驚奇、便下勅_宣天文陰(陽脱ヵ)家_、勘奏占諮。大田彦(大国主命ヵ)子天美佐利、依_未_受_公祟_、忽致_此怪災_也云々。仍下_勅宣_、忽建_宝殿_、十二箇所別社、神戸二烟、神田七十五町五段百八十歩、則定_神立(直ヵ)氏_、并祝部氏請_下大和国大神明神氏人等_也。

In Article 4, Emperor Sujin[29] (崇神天皇) dispatched Ōtatahiko (太多彦命) to conquer western Japan. Ōtatahiko brought with him a pike, a shield, a sword, and a mirror that were possessed by the Sumemitama (術魂) and Aramitama[30] (荒魂) of Ōkuninushi-no-Kami[31] (大国主神). (In ancient legends, many troops carried holy treasures possessed by gods,[32] and in fact it was a widely practiced custom.) After the campaign, Ōtatahiko lived in Awaga Village, Asako County, Tajima Province[33] (但馬国朝来郡粟鹿郷). He became the ancestor of the Miwabe clan based in Tajima Province, and he was enshrined in the Awaga-jinja Shrine[34] (粟鹿神社).

In Article 5, a natural disaster had occurred and plague was rife. A fortune-teller said that the god Amemisari-no-Mikoto (天美佐利命), who was enshrined in the Awaga-jinja Shrine, had cursed the people because the government had not conducted religious services for him. After receiving this report, the government mended the main hall of the shrine, dedicated parishioners and rice fields to the shrine, and appointed and settled the priest of the shrine. Furthermore, the government commanded the Ōmiwa clan to dispatch parishioners from the Ōmiwa-jinja Shrine in Yamato Province[35] (大和国) to the Awaga-jinja Shrine. It is important that parishioners were dispatched from the Ōmiwa-jinja Shrine, not another shrine. The Ōmiwa-jinja Shrine was chosen from among many other Shintō shrines to quiet the curse.

These legends of *Awagadaimyōjinganki* may partially include fiction created by succeeding generations. However, these legends are not regarded as complete fictions. That the ancestor of the Miwabe clan was dispatched to western Japan, brought the holy treasures possessed by gods, and lived in Tajima Province and that the Ōmiwa clan dispatched parishioners from the Ōmiwa-jinja Shrine to the Awaga-jinja Shrine are thought to be historical facts.

Considering the above-mentioned articles, the Ōmiwa god was considered a war god, and ancient people worshipped the Ōmiwa god when troops were dispatched.

## 4.4 Advancement to eastern Japan

Next, I examine the legends regarding the Yamato Kingdom's expansion into eastern Japan.

### Article 6: 『日本書紀』崇神四十八年正月戊子条
(Boshi, January, the forty-eighth year of Emperor Sujin, *Nihonshoki*)

天皇勅＿豊城命・活目尊＿曰、汝等二子、慈愛共斎。不＿知、曷為＿嗣。各宜＿夢。朕以＿夢占之。二皇子、於是、被＿命、浄沐而祈寐。各得＿夢也。会明、兄豊城命以＿夢辞＿奏＿于天皇＿曰、自登＿御諸山＿向＿東、而八廻弄槍、八廻撃刀。弟活目尊以＿夢辞＿奏言、自登＿御諸山之嶺＿、縄絚＿四方＿、逐＿食粟雀＿。則天皇相夢、謂＿二子＿曰、兄則一片向＿東。当治＿東国＿。弟是悉臨＿四方＿。宜継＿朕位＿。

Article 6 is a legend about divination through the interpretation of dreams. Emperor Sujin had two children. The older brother was Toyoki-no-Mikoto (豊城命), and the younger brother was Ikume-no-Mikoto (活目尊). The emperor could not decide which of the two to designate as his successor. To help him choose, he decided he would conduct a divination through an interpretation of dreams. The brothers performed a purification ceremony and slept. The next morning, each reported the dream that he had had. Toyoki said that he climbed Mt. Miwa (三輪山), faced east, thrusted a spear to the east eight times, and brandished a sword to the east eight times. Ikume said that he climbed to the top of Mt. Miwa, stretched a rope in all directions, and chased away sparrows. The emperor decided that, because Toyoki faced east in his dream, Toyoki should dominate eastern Japan. In contrast, Ikume faced in all directions in his dream, so Ikume should succeed to the imperial throne.

Although the stage was Mt. Miwa, the Ōmiwa clan and the Ōmiwa god did not appear in the legend. However, the emperor commanded Toyoki to dominate eastern Japan. This shows that thrusting a spear and brandishing a sword to the east at Mt. Miwa signalled the legitimacy of dominating eastern Japan. The Ōmiwa god and eastern Japan were related, and the Ōmiwa god played an important role in the advance to eastern Japan.

### Article 7:『日本書紀』景行五十一年八月壬子条
(Jinshi, August, the fifty-first year of Emperor Keikō,[36] *Nihonshoki*)

於是、所_献神宮_蝦夷等、晝夜喧譁、出入無_礼。時倭姫命曰、是蝦夷等、不_可_近_就於神宮_。則進_上於朝庭_。仍令_安_置御諸山傍_。未_経_幾時_、悉伐_神山樹_、叫_呼隣里_、而脅_人民_。天皇聞之、詔_群卿_曰、其置_神山傍_之蝦夷。是本有_獸心_。難_住_中国_。故隨_其情願_、令_班_邦畿之外_。是今播磨・讃岐・伊予・安芸・阿波、凡五国佐伯部之祖也。

In Article 7, the Emishi[37] (蝦夷) were dedicated to the Ise-jingū Grand Shrine. However, they made noise day and night and disrespected the shrine. Therefore, the emperor moved them to the foot of Mt. Miwa. However, they immediately cut down the trees of the mountain and threatened the neighborhood residents. Therefore, the emperor moved them to the outskirts of the capital. Eventually, they became the ancestors of the Saekibe (佐伯部), whose members lived in Harima Province[38] (播磨国), Sanuki Province[39] (讃岐国), Iyo Province[40] (伊予国), Aki Province[41] (安芸国), and Awa Province[42] (阿波国).

According to this article, the Emishi had savage souls. However, such a description is not historical fact. In order to explain the origins of the Saekibe clan, who were distributed across several provinces, the editor of *Nihonshoki* depicted the Emishi in this way. I prefer to note that the Emishi were moved to the foot of Mt. Miwa, where the Ōmiwa-jinja Shrine was. This means that the Emishi were dedicated to the Ōmiwa god. Ancient people believed that the Ōmiwa god had the miracle power to subdue the Emishi, and that is why the emperor moved them to the foot of Mt. Miwa.

### Article 8: 『日本書紀』敏達十年（五八一）閏二月条
(Intercalary February, the tenth year of Emperor Bidatsu,[43] [581] *Nihonshoki*)

蝦夷数千、寇_於辺境_。由_是、召_其魁帥綾糟等_。〈魁帥者、大毛人也。〉詔曰、惟、爾蝦夷者、大足彦天皇之世、合_殺者斬、応_原者赦。今朕遵_彼前例_、欲_誅_元悪_。於是、綾糟等懼然恐懼、乃下_泊瀬中流_、面_三諸岳_、歃_水而盟曰、臣等蝦夷、自_今以後、子々孫々、〈古語云_生児八十綿連_。〉用_清明心_、事_奉天闕_。臣等若違_盟者、天地諸神及天皇霊、絶二滅臣種一矣。

In Article 8, thousands of Emishi crossed the border. Emperor Bidatsu summoned Ayakasu (綾糟), the leader of the Emishi. The emperor declared that he would kill the ringleader of the rebellion, as in the era of Emperor Keikō. Ayakasu was afraid of being killed. He advanced to the midstream of the Hatsusegawa River[44] (初瀬川), looked toward Mt. Miwa, and swore that the Emishi would serve the Yamato Kingdom without treacherous thoughts until the following generation. If they were to break the vow, "the gods of heaven and earth" (天地諸神) and "Tennōrei"[45] (天皇霊) would destroy their descendants.

This legend is very important for analyzing the Emishi's ritual of obedience before the seventh century (Kumagai 1985, Kumagai 1991). I focus on "Tennōrei" in this article. Many researchers have considered this case. Seishi Okada (岡田精司) states that Tennōrei was the root of the emperor's prestige, and Mt. Miwa was the sacred place where Tennōrei existed (Okada Seishi 1966). Kimio Kumagai (熊谷公男) argues that Tennōrei was the mysterious power of the soul of the successive emperors; the ancient people believed that "the gods of heaven and earth" and Tennōrei descended from Mt. Miwa, and Ayakasu swore by these gods (Kumagai 1988).

In this way, many researchers related Tennōrei to Mt. Miwa. However, some dispute this theory. Takashi Tanaka (田中卓) argues that it is strange that "the gods of heaven and earth" and Tennōrei all existed on Mt. Miwa. He compared this with other examples. He argues that Tennōrei did not stay in one place; it was originally unrelated to Mt. Miwa, and Ayakasu swore by the Ōmiwa god, who lived in Mt. Miwa (Tanaka 1987). Toshio Kobayashi (小林敏男) argues that it is unnecessary to relate Tennōrei with Mt. Miwa. Furthermore, Tennōrei was distinguished from the souls of the successive emperors in *Nihonshoki*, and Ayakasu swore by the Ōmiwa god as the god of curses (Kobayashi 1994).

Therefore, if Tennōrei existed in Mt. Miwa or descended from Mt. Miwa, the relations between Tennōrei and the Ōmiwa god cannot be explained logically. It is clear that Ayakasu swore by the Ōmiwa god. In other words, ancient people believed that the Ōmiwa god had the magical power to conquer not only Ayakasu but also the Emishi as a whole. This shows that the Ōmiwa god was worshipped as a war god.

When the Yamato Kingdom advanced to eastern Japan, as with the advancement into western Japan and foreign countries, the Ōmiwa god was worshipped as a war god. It is thought that the Ōmiwa clan spread across Japan, the Ōmiwa god gained worshippers, and then the Ōmiwa-jinja Shrines were established.

## 4.5 Local ruling systems of the Yamato Kingdom

As mentioned earlier, researchers associate the distribution of the Ōmiwa clan with that of the Ōmiwa-jinja Shrines. I agree with this theory, although it does not always apply. I present two points.

First, based on the list of clans above, the Miwahito, Miwahitobe, and Miwabe clans were in the majority over the others. This shows that the distribution of the Ōmiwa clan was deeply related to the Hito system[46] (人制) and the Bemin system[47] (部民制), two of the Yamato Kingdom's local ruling systems which were enforced from approximately the fifth century to the seventh century.

Until recently, scholars believed that the Hito system was enforced after the Bemin system (Naoki 1958). However, according to recent research, the Hito system was enforced prior to the Bemin system, and the Hito system was absorbed into the Bemin system (Yoshimura 1993). Strictly speaking, in the early stage of the late fifth century, the government frequently classified government officials as civil officers, called Tensōjin (典曹人), and military officers, called Jōtōjin (杖刀人). In this stage, Tensōjin and Jōtōjin were written as three characters. In the later stage of the late fifth century, the government classified government officials in more detail into concrete roles, such as Kurahito (倉人), Sakahito (酒人), and Shishihito (宍人). In this stage, they were written as two characters. In other words, the period when the Hito system was enforced is divided into two stages (Shinokawa 1996). "Miwahito," whom I pick up here, belonged to the latter. Therefore, it is thought that the Miwahito clan was organized in the late stage of the late fifth century.

Although the Hito system has not been studied much, studies of the Bemin system are numerous (Takemitsu 1981, Kanō 1993). According to the commonly accepted theory, under the influence of the Bushi system (部司制) and the Gobu system (五部制) in Baekje (百済), the Bemin system was in effect from the end of the fifth century to the early sixth century. Therefore, it is thought that the Miwabe clan was organized in this period, at the earliest.

"Miwahitobe" has elements of both the Hito system and the Bemin system. The title Miwahitobe is constructed from "Miwa" (神), "Hito" (人), and "Be" (部). "Miwa" means to belong to the Ōmiwa clan. However, if it were organized after the Bemin system was introduced, "Hito" would not be added to the name. Therefore, Miwahitobe was organized before the introduction of the Bemin system, and "Be" was added to the name after the introduction of the Bemin system.

The shift from the Hito system to the Bemin system did not only mean a change in names. In the Hito system, only those who served the emperor in the capital were organized as government officials. By contrast, in the Bemin system, not only those who served the emperor in the capital but also those who stayed in their hometowns and fed others were organized. Therefore, in the Hito system, Miwahito was restricted to the capital. With the introduction of the Bemin system, people living in various places were organized as Miwahitobe or Miwabe.

Of course, these titles were sometimes used flexibly. In *Nihonshoki*, there is a notation that one need not pronounce, "Be."[48] Based on this notation, Takehiko Yoshimura (吉村武彦) wrote that "Be," which is derived from the Hito system, was not pronounced (Yoshimura 1993). For example, Shishihitobe (宍人部) was pronounced "Shishihito," so it was often written as "Shishihito." In regard to the Ōmiwa clan, Miwabe-no-Ushimaru (神部牛丸) was paraphrased as Miwa-no-Ushimaru (神牛丸) in the same ancient document.[49] In this case, "Be" was omitted.

Therefore, the Miwahito, listed above, were actually the Miwahitobe, but both Miwahito and Miwahitobe were pronounced "Miwahito," as "Be" was often omitted when written. The Miwahitobe and Miwabe clans took their names from the Hito system; they were influenced by the introduction of the Bemin system, and, as a result, they were distributed in various places. This lasted until the end of the fifth century.

The second point is that, in the list of clans above, many clans had the Kabane[50] (姓) "Atai" (直), such as the Miwa-no-Atai clan (神直氏) and the Miwabe-no-Atai clan (神部直氏). These were the senior clans that administrated the Miwahitobe and Miwabe clans in the local areas (Naoki 1958, Ōyama 1975). This shows that the distribution of the Ōmiwa clan was related to the Kokuzō system[51] (国造制). This system was one of the Yamato Kingdom's local ruling systems, which were enforced from approximately the sixth century to the seventh century. It is well known that many clans that were appointed as Kokuzō had the Kabana "Atai" (Abe 1950, Inoue 1951, Shinokawa 1996). For example, the Ōyamato-no-Atai (大倭直) clan was appointed as the Ōyamato-Kokuzō (大倭国造), the Katsuragi-no-Atai clan (葛城直) was appointed as the Katsuragi-Kokuzō (葛城国造), and the Kii-no-Atai (紀直) was appointed as the Kii-Kokuzō (紀伊国造).

According to *Nihonshoki*, Sotōri-no-Iratsume (衣通郎姫) lived in Fujiwara Palace (藤原宮). After she died, Emperor Ingyō[52] (允恭天皇) wanted to commemorate her. Therefore, the emperor commanded the Kokuzō in each region to organize Fujiwarabe[53] (藤原部). In another legend, Ōyamato-Kokuzō dedicated Shishihitobe to the emperor. Then, other Kokuzōs dedicated Shishihitobe to the emperor in the same way.[54] Based on these examples, Ken Shinokawa (篠川賢) notes that the Kokuzō often organized Be (Shinokawa 2009).

This tendency applies to the Miwahitobe and Miwabe clans. I list the following clans with the Kabane "Atai."

- Yamashiro Province     Miwa-no-Atai (神直)
- Izumi Province     Miwa-no-Atai (神直)
- Tōtoumi Province     Miwa-no-Atai (神直)

*The dispersal of the Ōmiwa clan* 61

- Mino Province         Miwa-no-Atai (神直)
- Tanba Province        Miwa-no-Atai (神直)
- Tajima Province       Miwabe-no-Atai (神部直)
- Inaba Province        Miwabe-no-Atai (神部直)
- Iwami Province        Miwa-no-Atai (神直)
                        Ōmiwa-no-Atai (大神直)
- Mimasaka Province     Miwa-no-Atai (神直)
- Nagato Province       Ōmiwa-no-Atai (大神直)

In contrast, the names of clans appointed as Kokuzō in these provinces were as follows.

- Yamashiro Province    Yamashiro-no-Atai[55] (山代直)
- Izumi Province        Ōshikōchi-no-Atai[56] (凡河内直)
- Tōtoumi Province      Unknown
- Mino Province         Mino-no-Atai[57] (美濃直)
- Tanba Province        Tanba-no-Atai[58] (丹波直)
                        Amabe-no-Atai[59] (海部直)
- Tajima Province       Miwabe-no-Atai[60] (神部直)
- Inaba Province        Inaba-no-Kokuzō[61] (因幡国造),
                        Iokibe-no-Omi[62] (伊福部臣)
- Iwami Province        Unknown
- Mimasaka Province     Did not exist
- Nagato Province       Anato-no-Atai[63] (穴門直)

As before, many Ōmiwa clans distributed across various provinces had "Atai" in their name, and Kokuzō, which were established in various provinces, had "Atai" as well. Inaba Province is the only exception. However, there was the Miwabe-no-Atai clan in Keta County, Inaba Province[64] (因幡国気多郡). The county of the same name was in Tajima Province[65] (但馬国). The Miwabe-no-Atai clan in Inaba Province emigrated from Tajima Province. Therefore, Inaba Province is not an exception.

It is thus clear that the distribution of the Ōmiwa clan was related to the Kokuzō system in the same way as with the Hito system and the Bemin system. The Miwa-no-Atai and Miwabe-no-Atai clans were organized by the Kokuzō in the province in order to administrate the Miwahitobe and Miwabe clans, which were antecedently organized. In this process, Kokuzō had the Kabane "Atai," so the Miwa-no-Atai and Miwabe-no-Atai clans called themselves the same Kabane.

Many researchers have discussed the timing of the establishment of the Kokuzō system.[66] I agree with Ken Shinokawa, who argues that the Kokuzō system was established in western Japan in the mid-sixth century and spread to eastern Japan in the late sixth century (Shinokawa 1996). Therefore, it is thought that the period of the organization of the Miwa-no-Atai and Miwabe-no-Atai clans was from the mid-sixth century to the late sixth century.

Haruto Maeda (前田晴人) disagrees with Shinokawa's theory (Maeda 2006). He argues that the Ōmiwa clan admitted Kokuzō from various provinces into "the fictitious blood relationship." Then, the Ōmiwa clan gave the name Miwa-no-Atai or Miwabe-no-Atai clan to Kokuzō. Furthermore, the Ōmiwa clan gave the name of the Miwabe clan to the people controlled by Kokuzō. In this way, the Ōmiwa clan spread to various places by using local vertical relationships. This process applies to Mino[67] (美濃), Suruga[68] (駿河), Kai[69] (甲斐), Shinano[70] (信濃), Tajima, Tanba[71] (丹波), Inaba, Iwami[72] (石見), Mimasaka[73] (美作), Bingo[74] (備後), Nagato[75] (長門), Chikuzen, and Buzen[76] (豊前) Provinces.

However, based on the existing historical materials, only the Miwabe-no-Atai clan living in Tajima Province was established to build "the fictitious blood relationship" with the Ōmiwa clan. It is highly unlikely that the Ōmiwa clan had the power to change freely the genealogy and name of Kokuzō. Of course, in some cases, the Ōmiwa clan strongly influenced Kokuzō. However, as I mentioned earlier, it seems likely that the Miwa-no-Atai and Miwabe-no-Atai clans were organized by Kokuzō, and they administrated the Miwahitobe and Miwabe clans in each province. As a result of these processes, the Ōmiwa clan was scattered across the Japanese islands.

## 4.6 Conclusion

I have analyzed the dispersal of the Ōmiwa clan and investigated its historical background.

First, I extracted the place names, Shintō shrine names, and clan names thought to be related to the "Miwa" or "Ōmiwa" from ancient historical materials. They were distributed throughout almost all the Japanese islands and were not limited to a specific district. Furthermore, some names of places, shrines, and clans overlapped. Therefore, the places, shrines, and clans were related to each other. Wherever a place or shrine with "Miwa" or "Ōmiwa" in its name is found today, the Ōmiwa clan was likely to have lived in that place in ancient times.

Next, I examined the Ōmiwa god's characterization as a war god. Because researchers have made much of the distribution of Shintō shrines, I analyzed the legends that are the basis for these studies. According to my analysis, when the Yamato Kingdom sent troops to or advanced into western Japan, eastern Japan, or foreign countries, people viewed the Ōmiwa god as a war god. Therefore, they worshipped the god and established Ōmiwa-jinja Shrines. As a result, the Ōmiwa clan was distributed to various places in Japan to worship the god.

Finally, I address the relationship between the distribution of the Ōmiwa clan and the local ruling systems of the Yamato Kingdom. In the list of clans above, the Miwahito, Miwahitobe, and Miwabe clans are in the majority. This shows that these clans were influenced by the introduction of the Hito and Bemin systems, which were in effect in the late fifth century. Furthermore, there were many clans called Miwa-no-Atai or Miwabe-no-Atai. Many clans that were appointed as Kokuzōs had the Kabane "Atai," as well. This shows that the distribution of the Ōmiwa clan was related to the Kokuzō system. In concrete terms, the Miwahitobe and Miwabe clans were organized based on the Hito and Bemin systems, so the Miwa-no-Atai and Miwabe-no-Atai clans were organized by Kokuzō in order to administrate the Miwahitobe and Miwabe clans. Because Kokuzō had the Kabane "Atai," the Miwa-no-Atai and Miwabe-no-Atai clans also had the Kabane "Atai" in their names. This took place during the mid-to-late sixth century.

There were two patterns by which the Ōmiwa clan spread to various places in the Japanese islands. One was by the expansion of the faith in the "war god" interpretation of the Ōmiwa god, and the other was by the advancement of the local ruling systems of the Yamato Kingdom. These two patterns were intertwined. For example, local people who worshipped the Ōmiwa god might later be organized as the Miwabe clan. Alternatively, if the Miwabe clan existed locally, they might later come to worship the Ōmiwa god.

Previous research emphasizes the Ōmiwa god's characterization as a war god, thus clearly explaining the process by which Shintō shrines were distributed. However, the process of the Ōmiwa clan's dispersal is explained only vaguely. I add the influence of the local ruling systems to the previous theory. From both the perspective of faith and that of systems, I explain the process of the Ōmiwa clan's dispersal more clearly and concretely as compared to previous research.

## Notes

1 Some researchers include the Kamo clan (賀茂氏) and the Munakata clan (宗像氏) among the cognate clans of the Ōmiwa clan. Certainly, these clans had "the fictitious blood relationship" with the Ōmiwa clan. However, as the names suggest, these clans were obviously different from the Ōmiwa clan. Therefore, I exclude these clans from the Ōmiwa clan.
2 Kinai (畿内) refers to the territories near the capital in ancient Japan.
3 Tōkaidō (東海道) refers to the area along the Pacific coastline in eastern Japan.
4 Tōsandō (東山道) refers to the inland area in eastern Japan.
5 Sanindō (山陰道) refers to the north side of the Chūgoku Region (中国地方) in western Japan.
6 Sanyodō (山陽道) refers to the south side of the Chūgoku Region in western Japan.
7 Saikaidō (西海道) is almost equivalent to present-day Kyūshū District (九州地方).
8 *Engishiki-Jinmyōchō* (延喜式神名帳) is a record of Shintō shrines in ancient Japan. It was edited in 927.
9 Hokurikudō (北陸道) refers to the area along the Sea of Japan coastline in eastern Japan.
10 Nankaidō (南海道) is almost equivalent to present-day Wakayama Prefecture (和歌山県) and Shikoku District (四国地方).
11 In present-day Kosai City, Shizuoka Prefecture (静岡県湖西市).
12 Jingū (神功皇后) was the wife of Chūai (仲哀天皇), the fourteenth emperor.
13 *Nihonshoki* (日本書紀) is a chronicle of ancient Japan. It was edited in 720.
14 *Chikuzennokuni-Fudoki* (筑前国風土記) is the topography of Chikuzen Province. In 713, the government ordered each province to edit its *Fudoki* (風土記).

64  *The dispersal of the Ōmiwa clan*

*Chikuzennokuni-Fudoki* was one of these. Chikuzen Province (筑前国) was in the northern part of present-day Fukuoka Prefecture (福岡県).

15  The Ōnamuchi-jinja Shrine (於保奈牟智神社) is in present-day Iyanaga, Chikuzen Cho, Asakura County, Fukuoka Prefecture (福岡県朝倉郡筑前町弥永).
16  The Suminoe gods were Uwatsustunoo-no-Mikoto (表筒男命), Nakatsutsunoo-no-Mikoto (中筒男命), and Sokotsutsunoo-no-Mikoto (底筒男命). They are enshrined in the Sumiyoshi-taisha Shrine.
17  The record before the enthronement of Empress Jingū, *Nihonshoki*.
18  In present-day Sumiyoshi Ward, Ōsaka City, Ōsaka Prefecture (大阪府大阪市住吉区).
19  Suiko (推古天皇) was the thirty-third emperor.
20  Heihaku (幣帛) refers to papers, silk cuttings, and cloth dedicated to a god or shrine.
21  In present-day Ise City, Mie Prefecture (三重県伊勢市).
22  In present-day Sumiyoshi, Hakata Ward, Fukuoka City, Fukuoka Prefecture (福岡県福岡市博多区住吉).
23  In present-day Usa County, Ōita Prefecture (大分県宇佐市).
24  In present-day Kashii, Higashi Ward, Fukuoka City, Fukuoka Prefecture (福岡県福岡市東区香椎).
25  The Kentōshi (遣唐使) was a team of envoys to the Tang dynasty. They were dispatched from the seventh century to the ninth century and brought Japan much advanced culture.
26  Kibi, February, the ninth year of Tenpyō [737], *Shokunihongi*.
27  Heiin, February, the ninth year of Tenpyō [737], *Shokunihongi*.
28  *Awagadaimyōjinganki* (粟鹿大明神元記) was the genealogy of the Miwabe clan living in Tajima Province.
29  Sujin (崇神天皇) was the tenth emperor.
30  Aramitama (荒魂) means the "savage soul" of a god. The meaning of Sumemitama (術魂) is not precisely known, although it is thought to be the "marvellous soul" of a god.
31  Ōkuninushi-no-Kami (大国主神) was another name for Ōmononushi-no-Kami (大物主神), who lived in Mt. Miwa, or the Ōmiwa god.
32  Jingo, January, the eighth year of Emperor Chūai, *Nihonshoki*.
33  In present-day Asako County, Hyōgo Prefecture (兵庫県朝来市).
34  In present-day Asako County, Hyōgo Prefecture.
35  In present-day Nara Prefecture (奈良県).
36  Keikō (景行天皇) was the twelfth emperor.
37  Emishi (蝦夷) were people who did not belong to the Yamato Kingdom. Most lived in northeastern Japan.
38  In the southern part of present-day Hyōgo Prefecture (兵庫県).
39  In present-day Kagawa Prefecture (香川県).
40  In present-day Ehime Prefecture (愛媛県).
41  In the western part of present-day Hiroshima Prefecture (広島県).
42  In present-day Tokushima Prefecture (徳島県).
43  Bidatsu (敏達天皇) was the thirtieth emperor.
44  The Hatsusegawa River (初瀬川) has flowed past the foot of Mt. Miwa since ancient times.
45  Literally, Tennōrei (天皇霊) means "the soul of the emperor."
46  In the Hito system (人制), the government organized the movement of people to the capital to serve the emperor as government officials according to their business and gave them the title of Hito (人). Hito means "person."
47  In the Bemin system (部民制), the government organized the movement of people to the capital to serve the emperor as government officials according to

*The dispersal of the Ōmiwa clan* 65

their business and gave them the title of Be (部). Be means "group." The government also gave the title of Be (部) to people who stayed in their hometowns and supported the people who came to the capital to serve the emperor. Bemin was strictly called Be-no-Tami in Japanese. However, in recent works, it is common to call it by the sound of the Chinese character, "Bemin."

48 The seventh year of Emperor Yūryaku, *Nihonshoki*. Yūryaku (雄略天皇) was the twenty-first emperor.
49 *Dainihon-Komonjyo* (大日本古文書), *Tōnaninmonjo* (東南院文書) 2–537.
50 Kabane (姓) was the hereditary title owned by ancient clans. It roughly represented the hierarchy in the Yamato Kingdom.
51 In the Kokuzō system (国造制), the government appointed a powerful local clan as the chief officer of a region or the Kokuzō (国造) and granted them local rule. In return, the Kokuzō was required to supply goods, workers, and military power to the government. For example, in Kii Province, the Kii-uji clan was appointed as Kii-Kokuzō (紀伊国造) by the Yamato Kingdom. The Kokuzō was strictly called Kuni-no-Miyatsuko in Japanese. However, in recent research, it is common to call it by the sound of the Chinese character, "Kokuzō."
52 Ingyō (允恭天皇) was the nineteenth emperor.
53 Heigo, March, the eleventh year of Emperor Ingyō, *Nihonshoki*.
54 Heishi, October, the second year of Emperor Yūryaku, *Nihonshoki*.
55 The body (本文) of the sixth part of Jindaiki, *Nihonshoki*. Jindaiki (神代紀) is part of the myth in *Nihonshoki*.
56 The body of the sixth part of Jindaiki, *Nihonshoki*.
57 Boin, June, the second year of Jingokeiun [768], *Shokunihongi*.
58 Kigai, January, the fourth year of Enryaku [785], *Shokunihongi*.
59 *The Genealogy of the Amabe clan* (海部氏系図).
60 *Awagadaimyōjinganki*.
61 Heishin, February, the second year of Hōki [771], *Shokunihongi*.
62 *The Genealogy of the Iokibe clan* (因幡国伊福部臣古志).
63 The record before the enthronement of Empress Jingū, *Nihonshoki*.
64 In present-day Tottori City, Tottori Prefecture (鳥取県鳥取市).
65 Tajima Province (但馬国) was in the northern part of present-day Hyōgo Prefecture.
66 Naoyoshi Niino (新野直吉) and Ken Shinokawa have described the history of such studies in detail (Niino 1974, Shinokawa 1996).
67 Mino Province (美濃国) was in the southern part of present-day Gifu Prefecture (岐阜県).
68 Suruga Province (駿河国) was in the central part of present-day Shizuoka Prefecture.
69 Kai Province (甲斐国) was in present-day Yamanashi Prefecture (山梨県).
70 Shinano Province (信濃国) was in present-day Nagano Prefecture (長野県).
71 Tanba Province (丹波国) was in the central part of present-day Kyōto Prefecture (京都府).
72 Iwami Province (石見国) was in the western part of present-day Shimane Prefecture (島根県).
73 Mimasaka Province (美作国) was in the northern part of present-day Okayama Prefecture (岡山県).
74 Bingo Province (備後国) was in the western part of present-day Okayama Prefecture.
75 Nagato Province (長門国) was in present-day Yamaguchi Prefecture (山口県).
76 Buzen Province (豊前国) was in the eastern part of present-day Fukuoka Prefecture and the northern part of Ōita Prefecture.

# 5 Characterizations of the Ōmiwa god

## 5.1 Introduction

Ancient people believed that the Ōmiwa god (大三輪神) resided in Mt. Miwa and, hence, they worshipped the mountain devoutly. Many myths about the Ōmiwa god are recorded in the *Kojiki*[1] (古事記) and *Nihonshoki*[2] (日本書紀) legends. Many remains and relics that were used for religious services have been discovered at the foot of this mountain. In this chapter, by analyzing these historical documents and archaeological materials, I will explain the characterizations of the Ōmiwa god.

Previous researchers have studied this theme from different perspectives, including research of historical documents, archaeology, literature, and mythology. Atsumu Wada (和田萃) is one of the most famous of these researchers.

Wada proposes that there were two periods of religious services at Mt. Miwa. According to Wada, from the fourth century to the mid-fifth century, the imperial family worshipped the sun god there. They also conducted the Kunimi ceremony[3] (国見儀礼) there. Wada hypothesizes that religious services at Mt. Miwa were discontinued in the late fifth century, around the time that people came to regard the Ōmiwa god as a god of curses.[4] When religious services were resumed by the Ōmiwa clan in the mid-sixth century, the Ōmiwa god was worshipped as a god of curses (Wada 1979, Wada 1985).

Before Wada's work was published, the main arguments about the Ōmiwa god were based on the change of dynasties theory[5] (王朝交替説). Wada's research departed from this theory. I have a high opinion of his research, because he explained the process of the developing religious services at Mt. Miwa in chronological order. However, as I will mention below, there are some points in his argument that lack sufficient evidence.

To develop this argument critically, it is necessary to reexamine whether the imperial family conducted the Kunimi ceremony and worshipped the sun god at Mt. Miwa from the fourth century to the mid-fifth century. It is also necessary to reexamine whether religious services at Mt. Miwa were interrupted from the late fifth century to the mid-sixth century and whether that led ancient people to regard the Ōmiwa god as a god of curses.

## 5.2 Reexamining the Kunimi ceremony

First, I will reexamine whether the imperial family conducted the Kunimi ceremony at Mt. Miwa from the fourth century to the mid-fifth century. The main evidence for this is the legend from *Nihonshoki*.

### Article 1:『日本書紀』崇神四十八年正月戊子条
(Boshi, January, the forty-eighth year of Emperor Sujin,[6] *Nihonshoki*)

天皇勅_豊城命・活目尊_曰、汝等二子、慈愛共斎。不╷知、曷為╷嗣。各宜╷夢。朕以╷夢占之。二皇子、於是、被╷命、浄沐而祈寐。各得╷夢也。会明、兄豊城命以_夢辞_奏_于天皇_曰、自登_御諸山_向╷東、而八廻弄槍、八廻撃刀。弟活目尊以_夢辞_奏言、自登_御諸山之嶺_、縄絚_四方_、逐_食╷粟雀_。則天皇相夢、謂_二子_曰、兄則一片向╷東。当治_東国_。弟是悉臨_四方_。宜継_朕位_。

This article describes the legend of divination through the interpretation of dreams. It notes that Emperor Sujin had two children. The older brother was Toyoki-no-Mikoto (豊城命) and the younger brother was Ikume-no-Mikoto (活目尊). The emperor could not decide which of the two to make his successor. He conducted a divination through the interpretation of dreams. The brothers performed a purification ceremony and slept. The next morning, they reported their dreams. Toyoki said that he climbed Mt. Miwa, faced east, thrusted a spear to the east eight times, and brandished a sword to the east eight times. Ikume said that he climbed to the top of Mt. Miwa in the same way, stretched a rope in all directions, and chased away the sparrows that ate foxtail millet. The emperor heard the two reports and decided that, because Toyoki had faced east, he would command eastern Japan. In contrast, Ikume had faced in all directions, so the emperor commanded Ikume to succeed to the imperial throne.

Wada argues that the Kunimi ceremony was conducted on the top of Mt. Miwa, because in this article Ikume was said to stand at the top of this mountain and face in all directions. Further, Wada states that the Kunimi ceremony was probably conducted in the fourth century, because at this time the imperial palaces were located at the foot of Mt. Miwa. He concludes that the imperial family conducted the Kunimi ceremony at the top of Mt. Miwa in the fourth and fifth centuries.

In fact, the imperial family conducted the Kunimi ceremony in various places in ancient times. For example, the following poem and legends are well known.

### Article 2:『万葉集』1–2
(*Manyōshū* 1–2)

高市岡本宮御宇天皇代、天皇登_香具山_望国之時御製歌。
　山常庭 村山有等 取与呂布 天乃香具山 騰立 国見乎為者 国原波 煙立龍 海原波 加萬目立多都 怜国曽 蜻嶋 八間跡能国者

In this article, Emperor Jhomei[7] (舒明天皇) climbed Mt. Ama-no-Kaguyama[8] (天香久山), conducted the Kunimi ceremony, and composed a poem. This confirms that the Kunimi ceremony was conducted on Mt. Kaguyama during the era of Emperor Jhomei [629–642].

### Article 3: 『日本書紀』神武即位前紀戊午年九月戊辰条
(Boshin, September, the year of Bogo, before the enthronement of Emperor Jinmu[9], *Nihonshoki*)

天皇陟_彼菟田高倉山之嶺_、瞻_望域中_。時国見丘上則有_八十梟帥_。〈梟帥、此云_多稽屢_。〉又於女坂置_女軍_。男坂置_男軍_。墨坂置_焃炭_。其女坂、男坂、墨坂之号、由_此而起也。復有_兄磯城軍_、布_満於磐余邑_。〈磯、此云_志。〉賊虜所_拠、皆是要害之地。故道路絶塞、無_処_可_通。天皇悪之。是夜、自祈而寝。夢有_天神、訓之曰、宜取_天香山社中土_。〈香山、此云_介遇夜摩_。〉以造_天平瓮八十枚_。〈平瓮、此云_毘邏介_。〉并造_厳瓮_、而敬_祭天神地祇_。〈厳瓮、此云_怡途背_。〉亦為_厳呪詛_。如此、則虜自平伏。〈厳呪詛、此云_怡途能伽辞離_。〉天皇、祇承_夢訓_、依以将_行。(略)乃使_椎根津彦_、著_弊衣服及簑笠_、為_老父貌_。又使_弟猾_被_箕、為_老嫗貌_、而勅之曰、宜汝二人、到_天香山_、潜取_其巓土_、而可来旋矣。基業成否、当以_汝為_占。努力慎歟。是時、虜兵満_路、難_以往還_。(略)時群虜見_二人_、大咲之曰、大醜乎。〈大醜、此云_鞅奈瀰爾勾_。〉老父老嫗、則相与闘_道使_行。二人得_至_其山_、取_土来帰。於是天皇甚悦、乃以_此埴_、造_作八十平瓮・天手抉八十枚_。〈手抉、此云_多衢餌離_。〉・厳瓮_、而陟_于丹生川上_、用_祭天神地祇_。(略)

This article is a part of the legend of the expedition of Emperor Jinmu (神武天皇) to the central district of Japan. The emperor surveyed the whole country from Mt. Takakura (高倉山) in Uda County, Yamato Province (大和国宇陀郡).[10] The enemy military troops were in the Sumisaka[11] (墨坂) and Iware areas[12] (磐余), so the emperor could not advance against them. The emperor conducted a divination through the interpretation of dreams. A god appeared in his dream and said that the enemy would surrender if the emperor made an earthenware pot from the soil of Mt. Kaguyama and conducted religious services using it. The next morning, the emperor commanded Shiinetsuhiko (椎根津彦) and Otoukashi (弟猾) to take soil from the mountain: they made the pot and conducted religious services. After this article, it is written that the emperor succeeded in defeating the enemies as a result of his actions.

### Article 4: 『日本書紀』崇神十年九月壬子条
(Jinshi, September, the tenth year of Emperor Sujin, *Nihonshoki*)

於是、天皇姑倭迹迹日百襲姫命、聡明叡智、能識_未然_。乃知_其歌怪_、言_于天皇_、是武埴安彦将_謀反_之表者也。吾聞、武埴安彦之妻吾田媛、密来之、取_倭香山土_、裹_領巾頭_、而祈曰、是倭国之物実、乃反之。〈物実、此云_望能志呂_。〉是以、知_有_事焉。非_早図_、必後之。於是、更留_

諸将軍_、而議之。未_幾時_、武埴安彦与_妻吾田媛_、謀反逆興_師忽至。
(略)

This article describes the legend of the rebellion of Takehani-no-Yasuhiko (武埴安彦). In the era of Emperor Sujin (崇神天皇), Ata-hime (吾田媛), who was the wife of Yasuhiko, came to Mt. Kaguyama, took some soil from the mountain, said that it was the symbol of Yamato, and went back to her home. In addition, a mysterious girl appeared and composed a strange poem. After this, Princess Yamatototohimomoso-hime[13] (倭迹迹日百襲姫命), who had the ability to foresee the future, heard and interpreted the event and the poem. She said to the emperor that they were ill omens predicting a rebellion by Yasuhiko and that the emperor should deal with it as soon as possible. The emperor discussed the issue with his generals. Immediately, Yasuhiko and Ata-hime raised a rebellion against the emperor.

Wada highlights the fact that Article 3 describes the soil of Mt. Kaguyama as having the power to defeat the enemy and that Article 4 describes the soil of the mountain as the symbol of Yamato. Wada insists that Mt. Kaguyama was the center of the rule of the Yamato Kingdom and that the imperial family conducted the Kunimi ceremony at this mountain.

It is accepted that ancient people worshipped Mt. Kaguyama, and some emperors conducted the Kunimi ceremony at this mountain. However, Emperor Jinmu and Emperor Sujin are thought to be fictional characters. According to Article 2, the period when the Kunimi ceremony was conducted at Mt. Kaguyama was during the era of Emperor Jhomei in the early seventh century. There is no evidence showing that the Kunimi ceremony was conducted at Mt. Miwa before the era of Emperor Jhomei.

As above, Wada cites the idea that the imperial palace was located at the foot of Mt. Miwa in the fourth century as evidence. However, the description of the location of the imperial palace in *Nihonshoki* is hard to believe. Even if the imperial palace was located at the foot of Mt. Miwa, this does not prove that the Kunimi ceremony was conducted there.

According to Kaoru Terasawa (寺澤薫), who assisted in Wada's research, the legend about a divination through the interpretation of dreams (Article 1) was also evidence that the emperor conducted the Kunimi ceremony there. However, Terasawa states that the top of Mt. Miwa was not suitable for observing the outlying country because of trees and ridges. He points out that no remains and relics used for religious services have been discovered at the top of Mt. Miwa. However, he insists that the place around the Hibara-jinja Shrine[14] (檜原神社) was a suitable spot for conducting the Kunimi ceremony (Terasawa 1988).

However, the Hibara-jinja Shrine is located at the foot of Mt. Miwa, whereas Ikume is described as climbing the "Mine" (嶺) of Mt. Miwa. This word, "Mine," obviously means the mountaintop. Ikume was able to face in all directions because he climbed to the top of the mountain. He would not have been able to face in all directions at the foot of the mountain. Terasawa also searched for a place that would have been suitable for conducting the Kunimi ceremony, on the presupposition that it was conducted at Mt. Miwa. But before searching for a suitable specific place, it is necessary to confirm whether the ceremony was actually conducted on Mt. Miwa.

I now present two points. First, in Article 1, Toyoki and Ikume climbed Mt. Miwa in their dreams. They did not actually climb the mountain. Furthermore, Emperor Sujin conducted a divination through the interpretation of dreams and decided his successor when he heard the reports of their dreams. They did not describe actually climbing Mt. Miwa, either in their dreams or in the real world. This fact shows that Mt. Miwa was not a place where the Kunimi ceremony was actually conducted. Rather, it shows that the mountain was thought to be a sanctuary where people could not usually enter.

I will cite a relevant example here. In *Nihonshoki*,[15] Ahe-no-Kunimi (阿閇国見) was afraid of the revenge of Iokibe-no-Kikoyu[16] (廬城部枳莒喩) and fled to the Isonokami-jingū Shrine[17] (石上神宮). In the same way, in *Shokunihongi*[18] (続日本紀), Prince Wake (和気王) planned a rebellion, but after his plan was uncovered, he fled to the Isagawa-jinja Shrine[19] (率川神社). Based on these examples, it can be said that the place where religious services were conducted was believed to be a sanctuary, which was free from common law (Wada 1989).

*Nihonshoki*[20] describes a similar event occurring at Mt. Miwa. When Emperor Bidatsu[21] (敏達天皇) died, Ōmiwa-no-Sakau (三輪逆) took charge of guarding the funeral ceremony place. Prince Anahobe (穴穂部皇子) tried to break into the ceremony place, but Sakau had a subordinate guard the gate and prevented Anahobe from passing through. Anahobe demanded seven times that Sakau open the gate, but Sakau would not open it. Anahobe became angry and commanded Mononobe-no-Moriya (物部守屋) to kill Sakau. Moriya approached Sakau with an army. Sakau knew that Moriya's forces were coming, and he fled to Mt. Miwa.

In this story, Sakau fled to Mt. Miwa, because it was densely forested and the enemy army would struggle to find him. However, this is thought not to be the only reason for his fleeing there. In addition to the Isonokami-jingū Shrine and the Isagawa-jinja Shrine, Mt. Miwa was another place where religious services were conducted, and it had a sanctuary where people could not go, so Sakau fled there. Based on this religious faith, the Ōmiwa-jinja Shrine was established at the foot of Mt. Miwa.

Therefore it is important that Toyoki and Ikume climbed Mt. Miwa in their dreams, rather than actually climbing the mountain. This does not show that the Kunimi ceremony was conducted at the top of Mt. Miwa.

Second, the legend of the rebellion of Takehani-no-Yasuhiko was described during the era of Emperor Sujin. This emperor had a close relationship with Mt. Miwa. As I mentioned in Chapter 2, according to *Kojiki*[22] and *Nihonshoki*,[23] the religious services at Mt. Miwa were begun by Ōtataneko (大田田根子) during the era of Emperor Sujin. However, in Article 4, the symbol of Yamato is described as the soil of Mt. Kaguyama, not Mt. Miwa. This is strange. If the Kunimi ceremony was conducted at Mt. Miwa during the era of Emperor Sujin, the soil of Mt. Miwa should have been described as the symbol of Yamato.

Therefore, there is no evidence that the Kunimi ceremony was conducted at the top of Mt. Miwa, before it was conducted at Mt. Kaguyama during the era of Emperor Jhomei, in the early seventh century.

## 5.3 Reexamining the worship of the sun god

Next, I will reexamine the possibility that the imperial family worshipped the sun god at Mt. Miwa from the fourth century to the mid-fifth century. The grounds of this assumption are in the following two facts:

The Ōmiwa-no-Ōmononushi-jinja Shrine (大神大物主神社) and the Miwanimasu-Himuka-jinja Shrine (神坐日向神社) are listed in *Engishiki-Jinmyōchō*[24] (延喜式神名帳). The former shrine is the Ōmiwa-jinja Shrine. There are two present-day candidates for the latter shrine. One is the Himuka-jinja Shrine, which is to the south of the Ōmiwa-jinja Shrine. Another is the Kōnomiya-jinja Shrine[25] (髙宮神社), which is at the top of Mt. Miwa.[26]

Regarding this point, Wada pays attention to pictorial materials. In the old image of Mt. Miwa[27] (三輪山古図), "Miwanimasu-Himuka-jinja Shrine" is labelled as being at the top of Mt. Miwa. Wada insists that the Himuka-jinja Shrine was located at the top of Mt. Miwa in ancient times. Just as the name Himuka[28] (日向) suggests, the service for the sun god was conducted in that place.

The important point is where the Himuka-jinja Shrine was located in ancient times. This shrine was listed in *Engishiki-Jinmyōchō*, as described above. In addition, it appears in the following article.

### Article 5: 『日本三代実録』貞観元年（八五九）正月甲申条
(Kōshin, January, the first year of Jōgan [859], *Nihonsandaijitsuroku*[29])

京畿七道諸神進〓階及新〓叙。惣二百六十七社。(略)従五位下(略)〔神〕坐日向神。(略)並従五位上。

In this article, the Himuka-jinja Shrine was ranked as Jugoige (従五位下) and was awarded Jugoijō[30] (従五位上). This shrine appears only in this article; it does not appear in any ancient history books.

In *Ōmiwasūhisho*[31] (大神崇秘書), "Kōnomiya" (髙宮・上宮) is labelled as being at the top of Mt. Miwa, and the Himuka-jinja Shrine is identified with this "Kōnomiya." In the same way, in *Ōmiwabunshinruishashō*[32] (大神分身類社抄), "Miwa-no-Kami-no-jinja Shrine" (三輪上神社) is described as being at the top of the mountain, and the Himuka-jinja Shrine is identified with this shrine.

The insistence that the Himuka-jinja Shrine was located at the top of Mt. Miwa only appeared between the twelfth and the thirteenth centuries. Furthermore, in the two books described above, "Kōnomiya" or "Miwa-no-Kami-no-jinja Shrine" is said to be at the top of Mt. Miwa. The Himuka-jinja Shrine is described as being at the top of the mountain. This shows that the location of the Himuka-jinja Shrine was unknown in the twelfth and thirteenth centuries.

Regarding this point, I will describe the relevant pictures, except the above-mentioned old image of Mt. Miwa. There are seven pictures that depict Mt. Miwa, as follows.[33]

(a) The illustration of Mt. Miwa[34] (三輪山絵図)
(b) The illustration of the Miwa-jinja Shrine[35] (三輪社絵図)
(c) The old image of Mt. Miwa (三輪山古図)
(d) The figure of the Miwa-jinja Shrine in Yamato Province[36] (大和国三輪神社図)
(e) The illustration of Miwa-Daimyōjin in Yamato Province[37] (和州三輪大明神絵図)
(f) The illustration of the Ōmiwa-jinja Shrine in Yamato Province[38] (和州大三輪社絵図)
(g) The figure of the Miwa-jinja Shrine in Yamato Province[39] (大和国三輪神社之図)

As I mentioned above, in (c), the shrine at the top of Mt. Miwa is called Miwanimasu-Himuka-jinja Shrine (神在日向社), but it is also written as "Kōnomine" (高峯) in (a), "Kōnomiya" (髙宮) in (b), "Kōnomiya" (上ノ宮) in (d) and (f), and "Miwa-no-Kōnomiya" (神上ノ宮) in (e). It is not described in (g). Kōnomine means "the top of the mountain." Kōnomiya and Miwa-no-Kōnomiya are thought to mean "the shrine located at the top of the mountain."

(a) was painted in the Muromachi period (室町時代), approximately from the early fourteenth century to the late sixteenth century. (b) was painted in 1645, (c) was painted in 1830, and (d) was painted in 1868. The years of composition of (e), (f), and (g) are unknown. However, Haruki Kageyama (景山春樹) analyzed all of them and pointed out that (a) is the oldest of these pictures and that the others were painted based on (a) (Kageyama 1971).

The only pictorial material that indicates a relationship between Mt. Miwa and the Himuka-jinja Shrine is (c). In contrast, (a), which was painted earlier than (c), does not indicate such a relationship. According to Kageyama's research, (c) was based on (a). This suggests that the notation of "Kōnomine" was intentionally changed to "Miwanimasu-Himuka-jinja Shrine" by the painter of (c).

The reason why the painter did this is unknown. However, in *Yamatohime-nomikotoseiki*[40] (倭姫命世記), Princess Toyosukiiri-hime (豊鍬入姫命) worshipped Amaterasu-Ōmikami[41] (天照大神), wandered through various countries, went back to Mt. Miwa, and stayed there for two years. Based on this history book from the Middle Ages, some people insisted that in ancient times the Himuka-jinja Shrine was located at the top of Mt. Miwa. It is thought that the Himuka-jinja Shrine fell into ruin or merged with another shrine after the shrine was awarded Jugoijō in 859. In the twelfth and thirteenth centuries, the location of the shrine was unknown, thus leading to the search for its location. From the available clues, it is at best difficult to prove that the Himuka-jinja Shrine was located at the top of Mt. Miwa in ancient times.

In addition, as Wada and Terasawa have mentioned, I pay attention to the fact that no remains and relics used for religious services have been discovered at the top of Mt. Miwa. Of course, in modern times, it is necessary to obtain the Ōmiwa-jinja Shrine's permission to climb Mt. Miwa. Excavation and research are prohibited on the mountain. However, many remains and relics have been discovered on the surface of the earth around the mountain. It is said that it is easy for people to go into the tabooed land of the Ōmiwa-jinja Shrine and collect some relics from the old days (Higuchi K. 1990). Nevertheless, no remains or relics have been discovered at the top of the mountain. This shows that religious services were not conducted there in ancient times.

I will now reexamine another ground for the assumption that the imperial family worshipped the sun god at Mt. Miwa from the fourth century to the mid-fifth century. This is the legend about Kasanui Village, Yamato Province[42] (倭笠縫邑).

### Article 6:『日本書紀』崇神五年条
(The fifth year of Emperor Sujin, *Nihonshoki*)

国内多_疾疫_。民有_死亡者_。且大半矣。

### Article 7:『日本書紀』崇神六年条
(The sixth year of Emperor Sujin, *Nihonshoki*)

百姓流離。或有_背叛_。其勢難_以_徳治_之。是以、晨興夕惕、請_罪神祇_。先_是、天照大神・倭大国魂二神、並_祭於天皇大殿之内_。然畏_其神勢_、共住不_安。故以_天照大神_、託_豊鍬入姫命_、祭_於倭笠縫邑_。仍立_磯堅城神籬_。〈神籬、此云_比莽呂岐_。〉亦以_日本大国魂神_、託_淳名城入姫命_令_祭。然淳名城入姫命、髪落体痩而不_能_祭。

In these articles, the following narrative is presented: in the era of Emperor Sujin, many people died because of an epidemic. Before this, Amaterasu-Ōmiwakmi and Yamato-no-Ōkunitama-no-Kami (倭大国魂神) were worshipped together in the imperial palace. The emperor commanded Princess Toyosukiiri-hime to worship Amaterasu in Kasanui Village. The emperor commanded Princess Nunakiiri-hime (淳名城入姫命) to worship Ōkunitama, but Nunakiiri-hime was very debilitated and could not worship the god. The presumed location of Kasanui Village is around the above-mentioned Hibara-jinja Shrine. Based on these articles, according to Wada, ceremonial sites were established at the foot of Mt. Miwa and services for the sun god were conducted there.

However, this opinion is questionable. As I mentioned above, Wada identified the Kōnomiya-jinja Shrine, which is now at the top of Mt. Miwa, as the Himuka-jinja, which is listed in *Engishiki-Jinmyōchō*, and insisted that the religious services for the sun god were conducted at Mt. Miwa. In contrast, the Hibara-jinja Shrine is at the foot of Mt. Miwa. Therefore, the location of the services for the sun god seems inconsistent with the evidence.

In addition, as I stated in the beginning of this chapter, Wada insisted that the imperial family worshipped the sun god at Mt. Miwa from the fourth century to the mid-fifth century and that the religious services were discontinued in the late fifth century and resumed in the mid-sixth century. However, the ages of the remains and relics that were discovered around Mt. Miwa do not correspond to Wada's research. I will explain this point in detail in Chapter 6 but describe it briefly here.

Iwao Ōba (大場磐雄), Kiyoyuki Higuchi (樋口清之), Mikio Sasaki (佐々木幹雄), Kaoru Terasawa (寺沢薫), and Kazue Koike (小池香津江) have analyzed and arranged the remains and relics that were discovered around Mt. Miwa (Ōba 1951, Higuchi K. 1971, Higuchi K. 1972, Higuchi K. 1975, Higuchi K. 1977, Sasaki 1975, Sasaki 1976, Sasaki 1979a, Sasaki 1979b, Sasaki 1984, Sasaki 1986, Terasawa 1988, Terasawa 1984, Koike 1997). According to this previous research, the remains and relics included talc instruments (滑石製模造品), clay instruments (土製模造品), comma-shaped beads with decorations (子持勾玉), and Sue ware (須恵器). Talc instruments and clay instruments[43] were mainly used for religious services. These were made from the late fifth century to the early sixth century. Comma-shaped beads with decorations were made from the late fifth century to the sixth century. Sue ware was made approximately from the late fifth century to the late seventh century. In particular, Mikio Sasaki investigated seventy-four pieces of Sue ware that were owned by the Ōmiwa-jinja Shrine and made in the now-ruined Suemura kilns[44] (陶邑窯跡群). He reported that Sue ware that was made in the late fifth century accounted for 21 per cent; 35 per cent was from the early sixth century, 24 per cent was from the late sixth century, 3 per cent was from the late seventh century, and 17 per cent was from unknown time periods.

Of the remains and relics that have been discovered around Mt. Miwa, relatively few date from the late sixth century onward. Most date from the late fifth century to early sixth century. Of course, this dating does not show the actual situation of the religious services, but it is considered to be a fair index of them. We can see that religious services were continuously conducted from the late fifth century to the late sixth century.

If the religious services at Mt. Miwa were discontinued in the late fifth century and resumed in the mid-sixth century, as Wada says, the remains and relics should demonstrate this change in one way or another. However, we cannot discern any changes in their quantity and quality. If anything, a larger number of remains and relics from the early sixth century have been discovered. This shows that, far from being discontinued, the religious services were flourishing during this period.

Therefore, the ground of the assumption that the imperial family worshipped the sun god at Mt. Miwa from the fourth century to the mid-fifth century should be denied. Based on the legend about Kasanui Village (Articles 6 and 7), it is difficult to insist that religious services for the sun god were conducted at Mt. Miwa.

## 5.4 Characterizations of the Ōmiwa god

As above, we can see that the Kunimi ceremony and the religious services for the sun god were not conducted at Mt. Miwa during the fourth and fifth centuries. Then what kind of religious services would have been conducted on the mountain in ancient times?

Ancient people believed that this mountain was the home of a god, and they worshipped this god devoutly. History books call this god the Ōmiwa god or Ōmononushi-no-Kami (大物主神). Previous research describes this god as having many characterizations. Genta Ikeda (池田源太) analyzed the characterizations of the Ōmiwa god, classified them as follows, and insisted that they evolved in turn (Ikeda 1971, Ikeda 1975, Ikeda 1990).

- The mountain and forest god
- The thunder god
- The snake god
- The Sakimitama (幸魂) and Kushimitama (奇魂) of Ōmononushi[45]
- The god of light
- The god who marries a human woman
- The clan deity

Later, Wada followed Ikeda's research and added some characterizations (Wada 1985).

- The mountain and forest god
- The thunder god
- The snake god
- The god of curses
- The Sakimitama and Kushimitama of Ōmononushi
- The war god
- The god of light
- The god who marries a human woman
- The clan deity

Ikeda and Wada extracted individual elements from the characterizations of the Ōmiwa god, which had only been described vaguely up to that point. Their research is very important. Based on their important research, I rearrange the characterizations of the Ōmiwa god as follows.[46]

1  The mountain and forest god
2  The god of light
3  The thunder god
4  The snake god
5  The god of curses

6   The god who marries a human woman
7   The clan deity
8   The war god
9   The national guardian deity[47]

Based on this classification, I will consider the myths and legends in which the Ōmiwa god appears and reexamine the kinds of characterizations of the god that these articles describe. I excluded the legends in which the Ōmiwa god does not appear, such as a legend in which only Mt. Miwa or the Ōmiwa-jinja Shrine appears.

### Article 8: 『古事記』上巻
### (The first part of *Kojiki*)

故、自爾。大穴牟遲与少名毘古那、二柱神相並、作堅此国。然後者、其少名毘古那神者、度于常世国也。(略)於是、大国主神、愁而告、吾独何能得作此国。孰神与、吾能相作此国耶。是時、有光海依来之神。其神言、能治我前者、吾能共与相作成。若不然者、国難成。爾、大国主神曰、然者治奉之状奈何。答言、吾者、伊都岐奉于倭之青垣東山上。此者、坐御諸山上神也。

This myth is about the creation of the ancient country by Ōkuninushi-no-kami (大国主神). Ōkuninushi and Sukunabikona (少名毘古那) created the ancient country, but Sukunabikona died during the creation. Ōkuninushi grieved at the death of Sukunabikona. Someone approached Ōkuninushi, shining from the distant sea. He said that he would cooperate with Ōkuninushi if Ōkuninushi worshipped him. Ōkuninushi asked him how to worship him. He said that Ōkuninushi should worship him at the top of Mt. Miwa. This god was in fact the Ōmiwa god.

In this article, the Ōmiwa god shone as he approached, was worshipped at Mt. Miwa, and created the ancient country alongside Ōkuninushi. These descriptions show that the Ōmiwa god was characterized as a mountain and forest god (see 1 above), the god of light (see 2 above), and the national guardian deity (see 9 above).

### Article 9: 『日本書紀』神代上第八段一書第六
### (The first book of the eighth part of Jindaiki,[48] *Nihonshoki*)

大国主神、亦名大物主神、亦号国作大己貴命(略)夫大己貴命、与少彦名命、戮力一心、経営天下。(略)其後、少彦名命行、至熊野之御碕。遂適於常世郷矣。亦曰、至淡嶋、而縁粟茎者、則弾渡而至常世郷矣。自後、国中所未成者、大己貴神、独能巡造。遂到出雲国、乃興言曰、夫葦原中国、本自荒芒。至及磐石草木、咸能強暴。然吾已摧伏、莫不和順。遂因言、今理此国、唯吾一身而已。其可与吾共理天下者、盖有之乎。于時、神光照海、忽然有浮来者。曰、如吾不在者、汝何能平此国乎。由吾在故、汝得建其大造之績矣。是時、大己貴神問曰、然則汝是誰耶。対曰、吾是汝之幸魂奇魂也。大己貴神曰、唯然。廼知汝是吾之幸魂奇魂。今欲〓何処住〓耶。対曰、吾欲〓住〓於日本国之三諸山〓。故即営〓宮彼所〓、使〓就而居〓。此大三輪之神也。此神之子、甘茂君等・大三輪君等。

This myth is also about the creation of the ancient country by Ōkuninushi. In this article, it is written that Ōmononushi and Onamuchi-no-kami (大己貴神) were alternative names for Ōkuninusi. When Ōmononushi was grieving at the death of Sukunabikona, someone approached, shining from the sea. Ōmononushi asked him about his real nature. He answered that he was the Sakimitama and Kushimitama of Ōmononushi. Ōmononushi asked where he wanted to live. He answered that he would live at Mt. Miwa in Yamato Province. Ōmononushi built the shrine and let him live at Mt. Miwa. This article states that this god was the Ōmiwa god and his descendants were the Ōmiwa clan.

In this article, as in Article 8, the Ōmiwa god approached as a shining figure and was worshipped at Mt. Miwa. Furthermore, the god introduced himself as the Sakimitama and Kushimitama of Ōmononushi, and he became the ancestor of the Ōmiwa clan. These descriptions show that the Ōmiwa god was characterized as a mountain and forest god (see 1 above), the god of light (see 2 above), the clan deity (see 7 above), and the national guardian deity (see 9 above).

### Article 10: 出雲国造神賀詞
(*Izumo-Kokusō-Kamuyogoto*[49])

乃大穴持命〈乃〉申給〈久〉、皇御孫命〈乃〉静坐〈牟〉大倭国申〈天〉、己命和魂〈乎〉八咫鏡〈尓〉取託〈天〉、倭大物主櫛𤭖玉命〈登〉名〈乎〉称〈天〉、大御和〈乃〉神奈備〈尓〉坐、(略)皇孫命〈能〉近守神〈登〉貢置〈天〉、八百丹杵築宮〈尓〉静坐〈支〉。

This article is part of the *Izumo-Kokusō-Kamuyogoto*. *Izumo-Kokusō-Kamuyogoto* was an explanation of the origin of a ritual imperial greeting to the emperor. In this article, Ōmononushi was worshipped at Mt. Miwa and is described as the Nigimitama[50] (和魂) of Onamuchi and as the guardian deity of the imperial family. These descriptions show that the Ōmiwa god was characterized as a mountain and forest god (see 1 above) and the national guardian deity (see 9 above).

### Article 11: 『古事記』神武段
(The part of Emperor Jinmu in *Kojiki*)

(略)然更求〓為〓大后〓之美人〓時、大久米命曰、此間有〓媛女〓。是謂〓神御子〓。其所〓以謂〓神御子〓者、三嶋湟咋之女、名勢夜陀多良比売、其容姿麗美。故、美和之大物主神見感而、其美人為〓大便〓之時、化〓丹塗矢、自〓其為〓大便〓之溝〓流下、突〓其美人之富登〓。〈此二字以〓音。下効〓此。〉爾其美人驚而、立走伊須須岐伎。〈此五字以〓音。〉乃将〓来其矢、置〓於〓床辺〓、忽成〓麗壮夫〓。即娶〓其美人〓生子、名謂〓富登多多良伊須須岐比売命‗。亦名謂‗比売多多良伊須気余理比売‗。〈此者悪‗其富登云事‗、後改‗名者也。〉故是以謂神御子也。

This legend is about the "red arrow" (丹塗矢). Ōmononushi fell in love with Seyadatara-hime (勢夜陀多良比売), who was very beautiful. He transformed into a red arrow, fell down a ditch, and stuck in her abdomen. He then married her, and she gave birth to Hototataraisusuki-hime (富登多多良伊須須岐比売命). Seyadatara-hime's other name was Himetataraisukeyori-hime (比売多多良伊須気余理比売). She later married Jinmu, the first emperor.

In this article, the red arrow that Ōmononushi transformed into is said to be the symbol of thunder. Furthermore, Ōmononushi married Seyadatara-hime. These descriptions show that the Ōmiwa god was characterized as a thunder god (see 3 above) and the god who marries a human woman (see 6 above).

### Article 12:『古事記』崇神段
### (The part of Emperor Sujin in *Kojiki*)

此天皇御世、疫病多起、人民死為‗尽。爾天皇愁歎而、坐‗神牀‗之夜、大物主大神、顕‗於‗御夢‗曰、是者我之御心。故、以‗意富多多泥古‗而、令‗祭‗我御前‗者、神気不‗起、国安平。是以駅使班‗于‗四方‗、求下謂‗意富多多泥古‗人上之時、於‗河内之美努村‗、見‗得其人‗貢進。爾天皇問‗賜之汝者誰子‗也、答曰、僕者大物主大神、娶‗陶津耳命之女、活玉依毘売‗、生子、名櫛御方命之子、飯肩巣見命之子、建甕槌命之子、僕意富多多泥古白。於‗是天皇大歓以詔之、天下平、人民栄。即以‗意富多多泥古命‗、為‗神主‗而、於‗御諸山‗拝‗祭意富美和之大神前‗、又仰‗伊迦賀色許男命‗、作‗天之八十毘羅訶‗。〈此参字以‗音也。〉定‗奉天神地祇之社‗、又於‗宇陀墨坂神‗、祭‗赤色楯矛‗、又於‗大坂神‗、祭‗墨色楯矛‗、又於‗坂之御尾神及河瀬神‗、悉無‗遺忘‗以奉‗幣帛‗也。因‗此而疫気悉息、国家安平也。(略)〈此意富多多泥古命者、神君・鴨君之祖。〉

此謂‗意富多多泥古‗人、所‗以知‗神子‗者、上所‗云活玉依毘売、其容姿端正。於‗是有‗壮夫‗、其形姿威儀、於‗時無‗比、夜半之時、儵忽到来。故、相感、共婚共住之間、未‗経‗幾時‗、其美人妊身。爾父母怪‗其妊身之事‗、問‗其女‗曰、汝者自妊。无‗夫何由妊身乎。答曰、有‗麗美壮夫‗、不‗知‗其姓名‗、毎‗夕到来、共住之間、自然懐妊。是以其父母、欲‗知‗其人‗、誨‗其女‗曰、以‗赤土‗散‗床前‗、以‗閇蘇〈此二字以‗音。〉紡麻‗貫‗針、刺‗其衣襴‗。故、如‗教而旦時見者、所‗著‗針麻者、自‗戸之鉤穴‗控通而出、唯遺麻者三勾耳。爾即知下自‗鉤穴‗出之状上而、従‗糸尋行者、至‗美和山‗而留‗神社‗。故、知‗其神子‗。故、因‗其麻之三勾遺‗而、名‗其地‗謂‗美和‗也。〈此意富多多泥古命者、神君・鴨君之祖。〉

The legend of Ōtataneko in *Kojiki* was mentioned in Chapter 2, and I describe it in detail in Chapter 7. In the era of Emperor Sujin, many people died due to an epidemic. The emperor anxiously sought to have his fortune told. On the advice of an oracle, the emperor found Ōtataneko in Mino Village, Kawachi Province[51] (河内之美努村), and commanded him to worship the god at Mt. Miwa. After this, the epidemic ceased.

This legend also has another part, known as the legend of Odamaki[52] (苧環伝承). A beautiful woman named Ikutamayori-bime (活玉依毘売) married a certain man and became pregnant soon after. However, she did not know her husband's name. After a suggestion by her parents, she sprinkled red soil on the floor and pricked her husband's clothes with a needle attached to some hemp thread. The next morning, the hemp thread went out through the keyhole of the door. She followed the thread and arrived at the Ōmiwa-jinja Shrine. Eventually, she realized that her husband was the Ōmiwa god. Only three rolls of hemp thread were left in her house. After this event, this place was named Miwa.[53] Furthermore, the child of the Ōmiwa god and Ikutamayori-bime was Ōtataneko, the ancestor of the Ōmiwa clan.

In the former article, the Ōmiwa god cursed people and was worshipped at Mt. Miwa. In the latter article, the god married Ikutamayori-bime and lived in the Ōmiwa-jinja Shrine, at the foot of Mt. Miwa. He was also the ancestor of the Ōmiwa clan. The fact that the hemp thread went out through the keyhole also suggests that the real nature of the god was a snake. These descriptions show that the Ōmiwa god was characterized as the mountain and forest god (see 1 above), the snake god (see 4 above), the god of curses (see 5 above), the god who marries a human woman (see 6 above), and the clan deity (see 7 above).

### Article 13: 『日本書紀』崇神七年二月辛卯条
(Shinbō, February, the seventh year of Emperor Sujin, *Nihonshoki*)

詔曰、昔我皇祖、大啓⌐鴻基⌐。其後、聖業逾高、王風転盛。不⌐意、今当⌐朕世⌐、数有⌐災害⌐。恐朝無⌐善政⌐、取⌐咎於神祇⌐耶。蓋下命神亀、以極中致上災之所由⌐也。於是、天皇乃幸⌐于神浅茅原⌐、而会⌐八十万神⌐、以卜問之。是時、神明憑⌐倭迹々日百襲姫命⌐曰、天皇、何憂⌐国之不⌐治也。若能敬⌐祭我⌐者、必当自平矣。天皇問曰、教⌐如此⌐者誰神也。答曰、我是倭国域内所居神、名為⌐大物主神⌐。時得⌐神語⌐、随⌐教祭祀。然猶於⌐事無験。天皇乃沐浴斎戒、潔⌐浄殿内⌐、而祈之曰、朕礼⌐神尚未⌐尽耶。何不⌐享之甚也。冀亦夢裏教之、以畢⌐神恩⌐。是夜夢、有⌐一貴人⌐。対⌐立殿戸⌐、自称⌐大物主神⌐曰、天皇、勿⌐復為⌐愁。国之不⌐治、是吾意也。若以⌐吾児大田々根子⌐、令⌐祭吾⌐者、則立平矣。亦有⌐海外之国⌐、自当帰伏。

### Article 14: 『日本書紀』崇神七年八月己酉条
(Kiyū, August, the seventh year of Emperor Sujin, *Nihonshoki*)

倭迹速神浅茅原目妙姫・穂積臣遠祖大水口宿禰・伊勢麻績君、参人共同⌐夢、而奏言、昨夜夢之、有⌐一貴人⌐、誨曰、以⌐大田々根子命⌐、為下祭⌐大物主大神⌐之主上、亦以⌐市磯長尾市⌐、為下祭⌐倭大国魂神⌐主上、必天下太平矣。天皇得⌐夢辞⌐、益歓⌐於心⌐。布告⌐天下、求⌐大田々根子⌐、即於⌐

茅渟県陶邑_得_大田々根子_而貢之。天皇、即親臨_于神浅茅原_、会_諸王卿及八十諸部_、而問_大田々根子_曰、汝其誰子。対曰、父曰_大物主大神_。母曰_活玉依媛_、陶津耳之女。亦云、奇日方天日方武茅渟祇之女也。天皇曰、朕当栄楽。乃卜┬使_物部連祖伊香色雄_、為中神班物者上、吉之。又卜=便祭_他神_、不レ吉。

### Article 15:『日本書紀』崇神七年十一月己卯条
(Kibō, November, the seventh year of Emperor Sujin, *Nihonshoki*)

命_伊香色雄_、而以_物部八十平瓮_、作_祭神之物_。即以_大田々根子_、為下祭_大物主大神_之主上。又以_長尾市_、為下祭_倭大国魂神_之主上。然後、卜レ祭_他神_、吉焉。便別祭_八十万群神_。仍定_天社・国社、及神地・神戸_。於是、疫病始息、国内漸謐。五穀既成、百姓饒之。

### Article 16:『日本書紀』崇神八年十二月乙卯条
(Itsubō, December, the eighth year of Emperor Sujin, *Nihonshoki*)

天皇、以_大田々根子_、令レ祭_大神_。是日活日自挙神酒。献天皇。(略)所謂大田々根子、今三輪君等之始祖也。

The legend of Ōtataneko in *Nihonshoki* was also mentioned in Chapter 2, and I describe it in detail in Chapter 7. The summary of the story is similar to that in *Kojiki*. In the era of Emperor Sujin, many people died of an epidemic. On the advice of an oracle, the emperor looked for Ōtataneko and found him in Sue Village, Chinu Region[54] (茅渟県陶邑). The emperor asked Ōtataneko about his lineage. Ōtataneko answered that he was a son of Ōmononushi and Ikutamayori-bime. The emperor was pleased and commanded Ōtataneko to worship the god at Mt. Miwa. As a result, the epidemic came to an end. The next year, the emperor again commanded Ōtataneko to worship the god at Mt. Miwa. Ōtataneko was the ancestor of the Ōmiwa clan.

In this article, the Ōmiwa god cursed people and married Ikutamayori-bime. Ōtataneko was the ancestor of the Ōmiwa clan. These descriptions show that the Ōmiwa god was characterized as the god of curses (see 5 above), the god who marries a human woman (see 6 above), and the clan deity (see 7 above).

### Article 17:『日本書紀』崇神十年九月条
(September, the tenth year of Emperor Sujin, *Nihonshoki*)

是後、倭迹々日百襲姫命、為_大物主神之妻_。然其神常昼不レ見。而夜来矣。倭迹々姫命語_夫曰、君常昼不レ見者、分明不レ得レ視其_尊顔_。願暫留之。明旦仰欲レ観_美麗之威儀_。大神対曰、言理灼然。吾明旦入_汝櫛笥_而居。願無レ驚_吾形_。爰倭迹々姫命、心裏密異之。待レ明以見_櫛笥_、遂有_美麗小蛇_。其長大如_衣紐_。即驚之叫啼。時大神有恥、忽化_人形_。謂_其妻_曰、汝不レ忍令レ羞レ吾。吾還令レ羞レ汝。仍践_大虚_、登_御諸山_。

爰倭迹々姫命仰見、而悔之急居。〈急居、此云_菟岐于_。〉則箸撞╷陰而薨。乃葬_於大市_。故時人号_其墓_、謂箸墓也。是墓者、日也人作、夜也神作。故運╷大坂山石╷而造。則自╷山至_于墓_、人民相踵、以手遞伝而運焉。(略)

This was called the legend of Hashihaka (箸墓伝承). In this legend, Princess Yamatototohimomoso-hime married a certain man, but she did not look at his face because he only came at night. She asked him to stay until the morning. He agreed to her proposal, said that he would be in her toiletries case the next morning, and asked her not to be surprised when she looked at him. She wondered why he said this. The next morning, she opened her toiletries case. A beautiful little snake was there. She was surprised and screamed. The snake quickly transformed into the figure of a human. Because she had been shocked by his true figure, he was angry with her. He said that he would take revenge on her for shaming him. He returned to Mt. Miwa, walking through the air. She regretted what she had done and sat on the floor. At that moment, chopsticks fell to the floor there. Unfortunately, the chopsticks stuck into her abdomen, and she died. Her tomb was named Hashihaka.[55]

It is clear that the man who married the princess was the Ōmiwa god, because he returned to Mt. Miwa walking through the air. In this legend, the Ōmiwa god was married to a princess. The real nature of the god was a snake. The god lived in Mt. Miwa. Furthermore, it indicates the antagonism between the Ōmiwa god and the imperial family and that their marriage came to a tragic end. These descriptions show that the Ōmiwa god was characterized as a mountain and forest god (see 1 above), the snake god (see 4 above), the god of curses (see 5 above), and the god who marries a human woman (see 6 above).

### Article 18: 『筑前国風土記』逸文
### (The surviving fragments of *Chikuzennokuni-Fudoki*[56])

気長足姫尊、欲╷伐_新羅_。整╷理軍士_、発行之間、道中遁亡。占╷求其由_、即有_崇神_。名曰╷大三輪神_。所以樹╷此神社_、遂平_新羅_。

In this article, Empress Jingū[57] (神功皇后) tried to send troops to Silla (新羅) but could not gather the soldiers. She blamed her failure on being cursed by the Ōmiwa god. She then worshipped the Ōmiwa god in Chikuzen Province (筑前国). As a result, she succeeded in gathering soldiers.

In this article, the Ōmiwa god cursed the empress. Her eventual worship of the god led to the successful dispatch of troops. These descriptions show that the Ōmiwa god was characterized as the god of curses (see 5 above) and the war god (see 8 above).

The Ōmiwa god appears in the following legend about Chiisakobe-no-Sugaru (少子部蜾蠃).

### Article 19: 『日本書紀』雄略七年七月丙子条
(Heishi, July, the seventh year of Emperor Yūryaku, *Nihonshoki*)

天皇詔_少子部連蜾蠃_曰、朕欲﹅見三諸岳神之形_。〈或云、此山之神為_大物主神_也。或云、菟田墨坂神也。〉汝膂力過﹅人。自行捉来。蜾蠃答曰、試往捉之。乃登_三諸岳_、捉_取大蛇_、奉﹅示_天皇_。天皇不_齋戒_。其雷虺虺、目精赫赫。天皇畏、蔽﹅目不﹅見、却_入殿中_。使﹅放_於岳_。仍改賜﹅名為﹅雷。

In this article, Emperor Yūryaku (雄略天皇) wanted to look at the god of Mt. Miwa, so he commanded Sugaru to capture the god. Sugaru climbed Mt. Miwa and captured a huge snake and gave it to the emperor. However, the emperor did not perform ablutions. Therefore the huge snake summoned thunder, made its eyes shine strangely, and threatened the emperor. The emperor hid for fear of the huge snake and commanded Sugaru to set it free on Mt. Miwa.

In this article, the god lived on Mt. Miwa, its real nature was a huge snake, the snake's eyes shone, and the god threatened the emperor. These descriptions show that the Ōmiwa god was characterized as a mountain and forest god (see 1 above), the god of light (see 2 above), the snake god (see 4 above), and the god of curses (see 5 above).

As above, I have reexamined the different characterizations of the Ōmiwa god. Ikeda and Wada extracted individual elements from the characterizations of the god and systematized them. In contrast, I focused on the relationships between mutual elements from the reverse viewpoint. The results are as follows.

- Article 8 . . . (1), (2), (9)
- Article 9 . . . (1), (2), (7), (9)
- Article 10 . . . (1), (9)
- Article 11 . . . (3), (6)
- Article 12 . . . (1), (4), (5), (6), (7)
- Articles 13–16 . . . (5), (6), (7)
- Article 17 . . . (1), (4), (5), (6)
- Article 18 . . . (5), (8)
- Article 19 . . . (1), (2), (4), (5)

Each text described the Ōmiwa god as having plural characterizations. This fact shows that characterizations of the god were multiple and indivisible. Ancient people worshipped the Ōmiwa god as a multilayered god and conducted religious services for him at Mt. Miwa.

## 5.5 Conclusion

In previous research, the religious services at Mt. Miwa were understood as follows: from the fourth century to the mid-fifth century, the imperial family worshipped the sun god and conducted the Kunimi ceremony at Mt. Miwa. In the late fifth century, the religious services at Mt. Miwa were discontinued. At this point, people began to regard the Ōmiwa god as a god of curses. In the mid-sixth century, the religious services were resumed, and the Ōmiwa god was worshipped as a god of curses. This previous research suggested that the religious services at Mt. Miwa could be divided into two periods, with different characterizations of the Ōmiwa god.

However, there is no evidence that the Kunimi ceremony was conducted at the top of Mt. Miwa from the fourth century to the mid-fifth century. Furthermore, there is no evidence that the imperial family worshipped the sun god at Mt. Miwa during the same period.

A large number of remains and relics from the late fifth century to the early sixth century have been discovered around Mt. Miwa, compared to few from the late sixth century. This shows that the religious services were continuously conducted from the late fifth century to the late sixth century. We cannot discern a gap between or discontinuity in these religious services. In particular, many remains and relics were made in the early sixth century. The religious services are thought to have flourished during this period.

In addition, the Ōmiwa god had plural characterizations. This fact was also noted by previous scholars. However, it is important to note that these plural characterizations did not exist separately: they were indivisible by nature. Ancient people worshipped the Ōmiwa god as a multilayered god.

In research about Shintō (神道), when people neglect to perform religious services, the god of curses creates big problems, but when people worship him carefully he brings peace and an abundant harvest (Masuda 1976). In other words, the curse is both an expression of the will of the god and the essence of the god (Tanaka 1990, Nakamura 1994, Okada Shōji 2005, Ōe 2007). In that light, the mountain and forest god, the god of light, the thunder god, the snake god, the god who marries a human woman, the clan deity, the war god, the national guardian deity, and the sun god all have indivisible relationships with the god of curses.

Therefore, I cannot agree with the argument that there were two periods of religious services at Mt. Miwa and that the Ōmiwa god became the god of curses during the gap between them. Of course, it is possible that specific elements of this god attracted the attention of ancient people in different ways according to historical background, political requests, and the specific group and their purpose for conducting the religious services. However, to ancient people, the many characterizations of the Ōmiwa god were indivisible. The god with all of these characterizations was the object of faith for these people.

## Notes

1 *Kojiki* (古事記) is a record of ancient matters in Japan. It was edited in 712.
2 *Nihonshoki* (日本書紀) is a chronicle of ancient Japan. It was edited in 720.
3 Kunimi (国見) was the ceremony in which the emperor observed the territories under his control from a high place and confirmed that the people lived peacefully.
4 Ancient people believed that the Ōmiwa god brought curses to people.

5 The change of dynasties theory (王朝交替説) was proposed by Yū Mizuno (水野祐). According to this theory, the imperial family in ancient Japan changed several times (Mizuno 1952).
6 Sujin (崇神天皇) was the tenth emperor.
7 Jhomei (舒明天皇) was the thirty-fourth emperor.
8 In present-day Kashihara City, Nara Prefecture (奈良県橿原市).
9 Jinmu (神武天皇) was the first emperor.
10 In present-day Uda City, Nara Prefecture (奈良県宇陀市).
11 In present-day Uda City, Nara Prefecture (奈良県宇陀市).
12 In present-day Sakurai City, Nara Prefecture (奈良県桜井市).
13 Princess Yamatototohimomoso-hime (倭迹迹日百襲姫命) was a daughter of Emperor Kōrei (孝霊天皇), the seventh emperor. She was later the grand-aunt of Emperor Sujin.
14 The Hibara-jinja Shrine (檜原神社) is in Sakurai City, Nara Prefecture (奈良県桜井市).
15 April, the third year of Emperor Yūryaku, *Nhonshoki*. Yūryaku (雄略天皇) was the twenty-first emperor.
16 Iokibe-no-Kikoyu (廬城部枳莒喩) was deceived by Ahe-no-Kunimi (阿閇国見), who had murdered his son. Once Kikoyu knew that he had been deceived by Kunimi, he bore a grudge against Kunimi and planned to murder him.
17 In Tenri City, Nara Prefecture (奈良県天理市).
18 Kōshin, August, the first year of Tenpyō [765], *Shokunihongi*.
19 In Nara City, Nara Prefecture (奈良県奈良市).
20 May, the first year of Emperor Yōmei [586], *Nihonshoki*. Yōmei (用明天皇) was the thirty-first emperor.
21 Bidatsu (敏達天皇) was the thirtieth emperor.
22 The part of Emperor Sujin in *Kojiki*.
23 Shinbō, February, the seventh year of Emperor Sujin, *Nihonshoki*. Kiyū, August, the seventh year of Emperor Sujin, *Nihonshoki*. Kibō, November, the seventh year of Emperor Sujin, *Nihonshoki*. Itsubō, December, the eighth year of Emperor Sujin, *Nihonshoki*.
24 *Engishiki Jinmyōchō* (延喜式神名帳) is a record of Shintō shrines in ancient Japan. It was edited in 927.
25 In Miwa, Sakurai City, Nara Prefecture (奈良県桜井市三輪).
26 According to the record of the Ōmiwa-jinja Shrine, the Himuka-jinja Shrine was located at the top of Mt. Miwa, and the Kōnomiya-jinja Shrine was originally located at the foot of the mountain, although these names were incorrectly swapped. Therefore, in 1885, the Ōmiwa-jinja Shrine requested that the government correct the names. However, the request was rejected (Umeda 1982).
27 The old image of Mt. Miwa is owned by the Ōmiwa-jinja Shrine. This is included in *Ōmiwajinja-shiryō* (大神神社史料) Vol. 2.
28 Himuka means "turning towards the sun."
29 *Nihonsandaijitsuroku* (日本三代実録) is a history of the era of Emperors Seiwa (清和天皇), Yōzei (陽成天皇), and Kōkō (光孝天皇). It was edited in 901. Seiwa was the fifty-sixth emperor, Yōzei was the fifty-seventh emperor, and Kōkō was the fifty-eighth emperor.
30 Jugoijō (従五位上) means "Junior Fifth Rank, Upper Grade." In ancient Japan, ranks were awarded to Shintō shrines in the same way as to the aristocracy and public servants.
31 *Ōmiwasūhisho* (大神崇秘書) is a historical record of the Ōmiwa-jinja Shrine. It was edited in 1119. This is included in *Ōmiwajinja-shiryō* Vol. 1.
32 *Ōmiwabunshinruishashō* (大神分身類社抄) contains the records of the Sessha (摂社, auxiliary shrine) and Massha (末社, affiliated sub-shrines) of the Ōmiwa-jinja Shrine. It was edited in 1265. This is included in *Ōmiwajinja-shiryō* Vol. 1.

33 All of them are included in *Ōmiwajinja-shiryō* Vol. 2.
34 The illustration of Mt. Miwa (三輪山絵図) is owned by the Ōmiwa-jinja Shrine.
35 The illustration of the Miwa-jinja Shrine (三輪社絵図) is owned by the Ōmiwa-jinja Shrine.
36 The figure of the Miwa-jinja Shrine in Yamato Province (大和国三輪神社図) is owned by the Imperial Household Archives (宮内庁書陵部).
37 The illustration of Miwa-Daimyōjin in Yamato Province (和州三輪大明神絵図) is owned by the Ōmiwa-jinja Shrine.
38 The illustration of Ōmiwa-jinja Shrine in Yamato Province (和州大三輪社絵図) is owned by the Ōmiwa-jinja Shrine.
39 The figure of the Miwa-jinja Shrine in Yamato Province (大和国三輪神社之図) is owned by the Tenri Library, which is attached to Tenri University (天理大学付属天理図書館).
40 *Yamatohimenomikotoseiki* (倭姫命世記) is a record of the Ise-jingū Grand Shrine (伊勢神宮). It was edited in the Kamakura period (鎌倉時代), sometime from the end of the twelfth century to the early fourteenth century.
41 Amaterasu-Ōmikami (天照大神) was regarded as the ancestor of the imperial family.
42 In present-day Sakurai City, Nara Prefecture (奈良県桜井市).
43 Talc instruments (滑石製模造品) and clay instruments (土製模造品) were made from talc and clay, imitating the instruments that were used for religious services such as treasures and vessels.
44 In present-day Sakai, Ōsakasayama, Izumi, and Kishiwada City, Ōsaka Prefecture (大阪府堺市, 大阪狭山市, 和泉市, 岸和田市).
45 Sakimitama (幸魂) means "the spirit of happiness." Kushimitama (奇魂) means "the spirit of wisdom." They have various interpretations.
46 I do not think that the characterizations of the Ōmiwa god changed in order from (1) to (9). However, it is necessary to distinguish the symbolization of a natural entity or phenomenon (1–5) from the symbolization of a relationship with humans (6–9). Of course, various standards can be set to analyze the different characterizations of the god, so the above-mentioned classifications are provisional.
47 According to Ikeda, "the Sakimitama and Kushimitama of Ōmononushi" means "the guardian spirit" or "the national guardian deity" (Ikeda 1971). I have adopted the phrase "the national guardian deity."
48 Jindaiki (神代紀) is part of the myth in *Nihonshoki*.
49 *Izumo-Kokusō-Kamuyogoto* (出雲国造神賀詞) was a ritual greeting performed by the highest priest of the Izumo-taisha Shrine (出雲大社) to the emperor. This is described in *Engishiki*, a statute book edited in 927.
50 Nigimitama (和魂) means "the spirit of peace." It has various interpretations.
51 In present-day Sakai, Osakasayama, Izumi, and Kishiwada City, Osaka Prefecture.
52 Odamaki (苧環) means "ball of hemp threads."
53 Miwa (三勾, 三輪) means "three rolls."
54 In present-day Sakai, Osakasayama, Izumi, and Kishiwada City, Osaka Prefecture.
55 Hashi means "chopsticks," and Haka means "tomb."
56 *Chikuzennokuni-Fudoki* (筑前国風土記) is the topography of Chikuzen Province. In 713, the government ordered each province to edit *Fudoki* (風土記). *Chikuzennokuni-Fudoki* was one of these edits. Chikuzen Province was in the northern part of present-day Fukuoka Prefecture (福岡県).
57 Jingū (神功皇后) was the wife of Chūai (仲哀天皇), the fourteenth emperor.

# 6 The transition of religious services at Mt. Miwa

## 6.1 Introduction

I considered the legend of Ōtataneko (大田田根子) in some detail in the previous chapters. This legend explains the origin of the religious services at Mt. Miwa and also explains the legitimacy of the Ōmiwa clan, whose members were Ōtataneko's descendants, in serving the Yamato Kingdom (大和王権). In order to elucidate the actual situation of the Ōmiwa clan in ancient times, it is necessary to analyze how the religious services were conducted at Mt. Miwa and how the imperial family and the Ōmiwa clan participated in the religious services there. Furthermore, this consideration leads us to explore the relationships between the imperial family and the ancient clans, which led to the formation of the ancient Japanese nation.

From the above perspectives, in this chapter, I will reexamine the arguments in previous research relating to religious services at Mt. Miwa, and I will investigate the way in which the religious services were structured and how they developed, while paying attention to how the Ōmiwa clan participated in these developments.

## 6.2 The change of dynasties theory

In *Kojiki*[1] (古事記) and *Nihonshoki*[2] (日本書紀), the Ōmiwa god (大三輪神) was characterized as a god of curses. In previous research, one of the main points of contention was how the nature of this god could be recognized and explained. Kōjiro Naoki (直木孝次郎) considers this point using the change of dynasties theory[3] (王朝交替説) and analyzes the nature of the Ōmiwa god as the god of curses (Naoki 1964, Naoki 1977). He pays attention to three legends, but I have already explained these in the previous chapters, so I will briefly review them in this chapter.

First: the legend of Ōtataneko in *Kojiki*[4] and *Nihonshoki*.[5] In *Kojiki*, in the era of Emperor Sujin[6] (崇神天皇), when people were dying from an epidemic, Ōmononushi appeared to the emperor in a dream. The god said that the epidemic was his curse and that it would be settled if the emperor commanded Ōtataneko to worship him. The emperor looked for Ōtataneko, found him in

Mino Village, Kawachi Province[7] (河内之美努村), and commanded him to worship the god at Mt. Miwa. In this way, the epidemic was ended.

The contents of *Nihonshoki* were similar to that of *Kojiki*. In the era of Emperor Sujin, at the time of the epidemic, Ōmononushi-no-Kami (大物主神) was haunting the Princess Yamatototohimomoso-hime (倭迹迹日百襲姫命).[8] She said that the epidemic was a curse from the god. The emperor conducted a religious service according to her instructions, but he was unsuccessful. The god then appeared in the emperor's dream and said that the emperor must command Ōtataneko to worship the god. The emperor looked for Ōtataneko and found him in Sue Village, Chinu Region[9] (茅渟県陶邑). The emperor asked Ōtataneko about his lineage. Ōtataneko answered that he was the child of Ōmononushi and Ikutamayori-bime (活玉依毘売). The emperor was pleased and commanded Ōtataneko to worship the god at Mt. Miwa. As a result, the epidemic came to an end. The next year, the emperor again commanded Ōtataneko to worship the god at Mt. Miwa. Ōtataneko became the ancestor of the Ōmiwa clan.

Second: the legend of Hashihaka (箸墓伝承) in *Nihonshoki*.[10] Princess Yamatototohimomoso-hime married a certain man, but she had not seen his face, because he came only at night and stayed during night. One night, she asked him to stay until the morning. He agreed to her proposal, said that he would be in her toiletries case, and told her not to be surprised when she looked at his true figure. She wondered why he said this. The next morning, when she opened her toiletries case, there was a beautiful little snake. Yamatototohimomoso-hime screamed in surprise. The snake quickly transformed into a human figure. Because she had been shocked to see his true form, he became angry with her. He said that he would take revenge on her because she had shamed him. He returned to Mt. Miwa, walking through the air. She sat on the floor in regret. At that moment, chopsticks fell to the floor. Unfortunately, the chopsticks pierced her abdomen, and she died. Her tomb was named Hashihaka.[11]

Third: the legend of Chiisakobe-no-Sugaru (少子部蜾蠃) in *Nihonshoki*.[12] In this legend, Emperor Yūryaku (雄略天皇) wanted to look at the god of Mt. Miwa, and so he commanded Sugaru to capture the god. He climbed Mt. Miwa, captured a huge snake, and gave it to the emperor. However, the emperor did not perform the necessary ablutions. Therefore, the snake summoned thunder, made its eyes shine strangely, and threatened the emperor. The emperor hid for fear of the snake and commanded Sugaru to set it free on Mt. Miwa.

Naoki analyzed these three legends, referring to the change of dynasties theory. As a result, he argues that the Ōmiwa god was opposed to the imperial family, because these legends described him as the god of curses. Naoki explains the historical background as follows. In the fifth century, the Kawachi dynasty (河内政権) arose in Kawachi Province[13] (河内国) and invaded Yamato Province[14] (大和国). The Kawachi dynasty destroyed the early Yamato dynasty (初期大和政権) that had ruled over Yamato Province and conducted religious services at Mt. Miwa since the fourth century; the Kawachi dynasty seized the right to rule over Yamato Province and the right to conduct religious services at Mt. Miwa.

Naoki argues that this is how the Ōmiwa god became opposed to the imperial family.

In the 1960s and 1970s, Masaaki Ueda (上田正昭), Seishi Okada (岡田精司), Iwao Yoshii (吉井巌), Takeshi Matsumae (松前健), Katsumi Masuda (益田勝美), Mikio Sasaki (佐々木幹雄), and many other researchers based their arguments about the religious services at Mt. Miwa on the change of dynasties theory, just as Naoki did (Ueda 1967, Okada Seishi 1968, Yoshii 1974, Matsumae 1975, Masuda 1976, Sasaki 1975, Sasaki 1976, Sasaki 1979a, Sasaki 1979b, Sasaki 1984, Sasaki 1986).

However, recent research has challenged this theory (Suzuki Y. 1980, Kadowaki 1984, Maenosono 1986, Kumagai 2001). In particular, Jūichirō Inobe (伊野部重一郎), Atsumu Wada (和田萃), and Takashi Tanaka (田中卓) have criticized this earlier research in detail (Inobe 1983, Wada 1973, Tanaka 1987). Their criticism is rational. Regarding the nature of the Ōmiwa god as the god of curses, many recent researchers have insisted that a curse is an expression of the will of a god, so it is not necessary to consider the Ōmiwa god and the imperial family as having an antagonistic relationship (Tanaka 1990, Nakamura 1994, Okada Shōji 2005, Ōe 2007).

Furthermore, as Naoki holds, if the cause of the curse was the invasion of Yamato Province by the Kawachi dynasty, the Ōmiwa god should have cursed the Kawachi dynasty. However, in the legends of Ōtataneko and Hashihaka, the Ōmiwa god performed his curses during the era of Emperor Sujin, and Naoki argues that this emperor belonged to the early Yamato dynasty. Thus Naoki's opinion is inconsistent. We have to separate the discussion of the religious services at Mt. Miwa from the change of dynasties theory.

Atsumu Wada and Fumihiko Matsukura (松倉文比古) have analyzed the development of the religious services at Mt. Miwa from a viewpoint that was not dependent on the change of dynasties theory. I will reexamine Matsukura's research later, but first I focus on the research of Wada.

Wada proposed that there were two periods of religious services at Mt. Miwa. From the fourth century to the mid-fifth century, the imperial family conducted the Kunimi ceremony[15] (国見儀礼) and worshipped the sun god at Mt. Miwa. According to Wada, in the late fifth century, the religious services at Mt. Miwa were discontinued, and soon afterwards people began to regard the Ōmiwa god as a god of curses. In Wada's theory, when the religious services were resumed by the Ōmiwa clan in the mid-sixth century, the Ōmiwa god was worshipped as a god of curses (Wada 1979, Wada 1985).

However, as I mentioned in Chapter 5, there is no evidence that the Kunimi ceremony was conducted at the top of Mt. Miwa. The point at which the sun god came to be related to Mt. Miwa was after the twelfth century at the earliest. I cannot agree that Mt. Miwa was the site of the Kunimi ceremony and sun god worship in ancient times.

In addition, ancient people recognized that there were multiple characterizations of the Ōmiwa god: the mountain and forest god, the god of light, the thunder god, the snake god, the god who marries a human woman, the clan deity, the war god, the national guardian deity, and also the god of curses. These elements were essentially indivisible. Therefore, it seems problematic to argue that there were two periods of religious services at Mt. Miwa and that the Ōmiwa god became the god of curses during the interruption of religious services between the two periods. I will now reexamine these points of contention from an archaeological viewpoint.

## 6.3 Archaeological ruins and relics

Before modern historical science and archaeology began to be practiced in Japan, from the Edo period[16] (江戸時代) to the Meiji period[17] (明治時代), many researchers stated that many items used for religious services had been discovered around Mt. Miwa. In the Shōwa period[18] (昭和時代), Iwao Ōba (大場磐雄) and Kiyoyuki Higuchi (樋口清之) conducted pioneering studies (Ōba 1951, Higuchi K. 1971, Higuchi K. 1972, Higuchi K. 1975, Higuchi K. 1977).

Although the archaeological relics that the previous researchers had introduced had been collected from the surface of the ground, many of the relics had become mixed up over time so that the place from which they had been collected was unclear (Archaeological Institute of Kashihara 1984). In an attempt to clarify this situation, Kaoru Terasawa (寺澤薫) and Kazue Koike (小池香津江) reinvestigated the archaeological ruins and relics that had been excavated and discovered around Mt. Miwa. This enabled a study of the religious services at Mt. Miwa from the viewpoint of both historical science and archaeology. In recent years, a large amount of research has been based on the survey by Terasawa and Koike (Hashimoto 2002, Ōhira 2007, Furuya 2010, Hozumi 2013).

Based on the survey and the results of the recent excavations, I arrange the archaeological ruins and relics again as follows:[19]

1. Name: The site of Katayashiki (カタヤシキ)

    Location: Anashi, Sakurai City, Nara Prefecture
    Relics: talc instruments[20] (滑石製模造品)

2. Name: The Hibara-jinja Shrine (檜原神社)

    Location: Miwa, Sakurai City, Nara Prefecture
    Relics: Iwakura[21] (磐座), clay instruments (土製模造品), Haji pottery[22] (土師器)

3. Name: The Genpindani ruins (玄賓谷遺跡)

    Location: Chihara, Sakurai City, Nara Prefecture
    Relics: Sue ware[23] (須恵器)

4. Name: The Ōkamidani Iwakura unit (オーカミ谷磐座群)

    Location: Miwa, Sakurai City, Nara Prefecture
    Relics: Iwakura

## 90　*The transition of religious services*

5  Name: The Yamanokami ruins (山ノ神遺跡)

   Location: Miwa, Sakurai City, Nara Prefecture
   Relics: Iwakura, a pit, a mirror, a scrap of iron, comma-shaped beads (勾玉), comma-shaped beads with decorations (子持勾玉), talc instruments, clay instruments, Haji pottery, Sue ware

6  Name: The tabooed land Iwakura unit (禁足地裏磐座群)

   Location: Miwa, Sakurai City, Nara Prefecture
   Relics: Iwakura

7  Name: The Minokurayama ruins (箕倉山遺跡)

   Location: Chihara, Sakurai City, Nara Prefecture
   Relics: talc instruments, clay instruments, clay horse figurines[24] (土馬)

8  Name: The site of Chihara-Gensui-Hotta (茅原源水・堀田)

   Location: Chihara, Sakurai City, Nara Prefecture
   Relics: comma-shaped beads with decorations

9  Name: The Okugaito ruins (奥垣内遺跡)

   Location: Baba, Sakurai City, Nara Prefecture
   Relics: Iwakura, talc instruments, clay instruments, Haji pottery, Sue ware, earthenware (陶質土器)

10 Name: The Baba ruins (馬場遺跡)

   Location: Chihara, Sakurai City, Nara Prefecture
   Relics: clay instruments, mortar-shaped beads (臼玉)

11 Name: The Kagami-ike pond (鏡池) of the Sai-jinja Shrine (狭井神社)

   Location: Baba, Sakurai City, Nara Prefecture
   Relics: Haji pottery, Sue ware

12 Name: The Iwakura-jinja Shrine (磐座神社)

   Location: Miwa, Sakurai City, Nara Prefecture
   Relics: Iwakura

13 Name: The Wakamiya-jinja Shrine[25] (若宮神社)

   Location: Baba, Sakurai City, Nara Prefecture
   Relics: Iwakura, talc instruments, Sue ware

14 Name: The Ninotorii[26] (二の鳥居) of the Ōmiwa-jinja Shrine

   Location: Miwa, Sakurai City, Nara Prefecture
   Relics: clay instruments, Haji pottery, Sue ware

15 Name: The site of Meotoiwa[27] (夫婦岩)

   Location: Miwa, Sakurai City, Nara Prefecture
   Relics: Iwakura

16  Name: The Mitsutorii[28] (三ツ鳥居) of the Ōmiwa-jinja Shrine

   Location: Miwa, Sakurai City, Nara Prefecture
   Relics: comma-shaped beads with decorations, clay instruments, Sue ware

17  Name: The tabooed land (禁足地) of the Ōmiwa-jinja Shrine

   Location: Miwa, Sakurai City, Nara Prefecture
   Relics: Iwakura, a square mound, comma-shaped beads with decorations, talc instruments, Haji pottery, Sue wares, earthenware, earthen cups

18  Name: The Susanoo-jinja Shrine (素戔嗚神社)

   Location: Miwa, Sakurai City, Nara Prefecture
   Relics: Iwakura, talc instruments, Haji pottery

19  Name: The site of playground of Miwa Elementary School (三輪小学校)

   Location: Kanaya, Sakurai City, Nara Prefecture
   Relics: Haji pottery, Sue ware, talc instruments, clay instruments, comma-shaped beads, mortar-shaped beads

20  Name: The Shikinomiagatanimasu-jinja Shrine (志貴御県坐神社)

   Location: Kanaya, Sakurai City, Nara Prefecture
   Relics: Iwakura

21  Name: The site of Tenrikyō Shikishima Church (天理教敷島教会)

   Location: Kanaya, Sakurai City, Nara Prefecture
   Relics: talc instruments

22  Name: The Kunitsu-jinja Shrine (国津神社)

   Location: Hashinaka, Sakurai City, Nara Prefecture
   Relics: clay instruments, Haji pottery, Sue ware, stone products

23  Name: The site of Oda Elementary School (織田小学校)

   Location: Shiba, Sakurai City, Nara Prefecture
   Relics: talc instruments

24  Name: The Kunichi-jinja Shrine (九日神社)

   Location: Shiba, Sakurai City, Nara Prefecture
   Relics: Iwakura

25  Name: The Shiba ruins (芝遺跡)

   Location: Shiba, Sakurai City, Nara Prefecture
   Relics: relics of rice fields, comma-shaped beads with decorations

26  Name: The site of Chihara-Maruta (茅原丸田)

   Location: Chihara, Sakurai City, Nara Prefecture
   Relics: comma-shaped beads with decorations

27  Name: The confluence of the Hatsuse-gawa River (初瀬川) and the Makimuku-gawa River (巻向川)

> Location: Shiba, Sakurai City, Nara Prefecture
> Relics: comma-shaped beads with decorations

28  Name: The Matsunomoto ruins (松之本遺跡)

> Location: Ōtono, Sakurai City, Nara Prefecture
> Relics: Haji pottery, Sue ware, comma-shaped beads with decorations, stone products

I will discuss the main archaeological ruins from the above list, explain them based on previous research, and reexamine the periods during which these relics were produced and used.

Initially, Iwakura were scattered in and around Mt. Miwa, as described in the following article.

### Article 1: 『大三輪神三社鎮座次第』 (*Ōmiwashinsansha-Chinzanoshidai*[29])

当社古来無_宝倉_、唯有_三箇鳥居_而已。奥津磐座大物主命、中津磐座大己貴命、辺津磐座少彦名命。

In this article, Okutsu Iwakura (奥津磐座), Nakatsu Iwakura (中津磐座), and Hetsu Iwakura (辺津磐座) were located on Mt. Miwa. Okutsu means "the depths," Nakatsu means "the middle," and Hetsu means "the front." In the Edo period, when *Chinzanoshidai* was edited, the Iwakura on Mt. Miwa were classified according to altitude. The Iwakura at the top of the mountain were called Okutsu Iwakura. Those halfway up the mountain were called Nakatsu Iwakura. Those at the foot of the mountain were called Hetsu Iwakura. The people at that time believed that Ōmononushi-no-Mikoto (大物主命) lived in Okutsu Iwakura, Ōnamuchi-no-Mikoto (大己貴命) lived in Nakatsu Iwakura, and Sukunabikona-no-Mikoto (少彦名命) lived in Hetsu Iwakura.

Kiyoyuki Higuchi also explored Mt. Miwa, discovering that there were two ways in which the Iwakura were connected on the mountain. One set of remains was distributed from the top of the mountain to the Hibara-jinja Shrine. Another was distributed from the top of the mountain to the Ōmiwa-jinja Shrine. Higuchi named the first of these the Ōkamidani Iwakura unit (see 4 above) and the latter as the tabooed land Iwakura unit (see 6 above) (Higuchi K. 1927).

At the foot of Mt. Miwa, in front of the tabooed land Iwakura unit, the Ōmiwa-jinja Shrine was established. Strictly speaking, the Mitsutorii (see 16 above) is equipped on the site of the Haiden[30] (拝殿) of the Ōmiwa-jinja Shrine. The tabooed land Iwakura unit was 200 meters to the east of the Mitsutorii. The tabooed land of the Ōmiwa-jinja Shrine (see 17 above) extends from the worship hall to the Iwakura unit.[31]

In 1958, repair work was conducted on the worship hall and the Mitsutorii. At that time, comma-shaped beads with decorations, clay instruments, and Sue ware were excavated from under the Mitsutorii. In 1961, disaster prevention work was conducted. At that time, talc instruments, Haji pottery, Sue ware, earthenware, and earthen cups were excavated. From a spot 20 meters southeast of the worship hall, comma-shaped beads with decorations were excavated. In 1983, from a spot 100 meters east-southeast of the worship hall, comma-shaped beads with decorations were also excavated.

It is said that there is a square mound near the Iwakura located on the east side of the tabooed land of the Ōmiwa-jinja Shrine. According to the documents[32] that the Ōmiwa-jinja Shrine submitted to the government in the Meiji period, and the documents[33] that were owned by the family of hereditary priests of the Ōmiwa-jinja Shrine, it is recorded that there was a square mound called "the remaining site of the main shrine building,"[34] (御主殿跡) which was about 20 meters square. It is thought that an existing square mound corresponds to this "remaining site of the main shrine building." Isamu Shirai (白井勇) speculated that this square mound was built in the Yayoi period[35] (弥生時代) (Shirai 1984); Koike speculated that it was built after the fifth century (Koike 1997); and Terasawa speculated that it was built after the seventh century (Terasawa 1988). Because no conclusive investigations have been conducted, it is unclear whether any of these guesses is correct. However, up to this point, there have been no reports that archaeological relics have been discovered around the square mound. Therefore, I would argue that the square mound was built after the time when the religious services at Mt. Miwa began to be conducted frequently. This was probably after the late seventh century.

Yamanokami ruins (5) are located to the northwest of the Ōmiwa-jinja Shrine and the Sai-jinja Shrine. The Iwakura are maintained at this place, but they are not in the same condition as they were when they were discovered, because they have been restored for display at the Kokugakuin University Museum (国学院大学博物館) in Tōkyō. In 1918, a boulder 1.5 meters in diameter, a boulder 1.0 meters in diameter, and four stones that were 0.5 meter in diameter were excavated. Many pebbles were found spread out under them. At first, these findings were thought to comprise the stone chamber (石室) of a tumulus (古墳), but they were later thought to be an Iwakura (Takahashi and Nishizaki 1920, Higuchi K. 1928). Over three months from the time when they were discovered to the time when the investigation began, the boulders were moved, and unfortunately many relics were stolen.

Still, some relics remained. According to Higuchi's report, there were mirrors, a scrap of iron, comma-shaped beads, comma-shaped beads with decorations, talc instruments, clay instruments, Haji pottery, Sue ware, and other items. There were more than 100 items in total (Higuchi K. 1928). Some researchers have pointed out that these relics were common tools for brewing rice wine, which were recorded in *Engishiki*[36] (延喜式) (Ōba 1951).

Incidentally, in 1999, a pit, a rock arrangement, Haji pottery, and Sue ware were also excavated around these boulders. This pit (2.3 meters in diameter and 1.2 meter in depth) is thought to be a well. It is thought that some kind of religious service was conducted here before these relics were discarded.

The Okugaito ruins (see 9 above) were discovered when a project to dig a hot spring was begun in 1965. The ruins were preserved as a park named Ōmiwa no Mori (大美和の杜, "the forest of Ōmiwa"). A monument that models the Iwakura is now installed. In this place, boulders that are thought to be the Iwakura, talc instruments, clay instruments, Haji pottery, Sue ware, and earthenware were excavated. The precise excavation spot of the boulders has not been identified, but they were discovered gathered together in one place, just as with the Yamanokami ruins. A big Sue ware pot, 50 centimeters in diameter, was excavated from the east side of the Iwakura, and many small pieces of Sue ware were placed in this big pot. Some talc instruments and Haji pottery were scattered around the pot. These relics are thought to have been placed in the big pot together.

Here, I have only briefly introduced the main archaeological ruins. Out of the ruins, as I mentioned above, the Yamanokami ruins contained the oldest relics. These included mirrors, scraps of iron, and comma-shaped beads. These are estimated to have been made from the late fourth century to the early fifth century. Haji pottery and earthenware, which were excavated from the Okugaito ruins, are also estimated to have been made from the end of fourth century to the beginning of the fifth century. However, there were very few of these early relics. It is possible that some relics that were made longer ago were inherited by people later, and some relics were buried several hundred years after they were made. It would be careless to argue that religious services were conducted at Mt. Miwa from the fourth century to the early fifth century, simply based on these relics.

In contrast, many relics were made after the late fifth century. In particular, talc instruments and clay instruments were used for religious services at Mt. Miwa. The former were excavated from ten ruins in total, while the latter were excavated from nine ruins in total. These relics were made from the late fifth century to the early sixth century.

Mikio Sasaki has analyzed the Sue ware in detail (Sasaki 1975, Sasaki 1976, Sasaki 1979a, Sasaki 1979b, Sasaki 1984, Sasaki 1986). Over seventy-four pieces of Sue ware have now been found at the Ōmiwa-jinja Shrine. Out of these, ten items were excavated from the Yamanokami ruins, twenty-five were excavated from the Okugaito ruins, four were excavated from the Kagami-ike pond of the Sai-jinja Shrine, eight were excavated from the Waka-miya-jinja Shrine, ten were excavated from the Ninotorii of the Ōmiwa-jinja Shrine, and seventeen were excavated from unknown parts of the site. Most of these items were made in the Suemura kilns, which are now ruined[37] (陶邑窯跡群). According to Sasaki's report, 21 per cent of the items were made in the late fifth century, 35 per cent were made in the early sixth century, 24 per cent were made in the late sixth century, 3 per cent were made in the late seventh century, and we do not know when the other 17 per cent were made.

In addition, many comma-shaped beads with decorations have been discovered around Mt. Miwa (Sasaki 1981, Terasawa 1984, Sasaki 1985, Ōhira 2007). To the present day, these beads have been excavated and discovered around the Shiba ruins, the site of Chihara-Maruta, the Yamanokami ruins, the tabooed land of the Ōmiwa-jinja Shrine, the Mitsutorii of the Ōmiwa-jinja Shrine, and the confluence of the Hatsuse-gawa River and the Makimuku-gawa River. In 2012, six items were newly excavated from the Matsunomoto ruins (Archaeological Institute of Kashihara 2012). These items were generally used for religious services from the mid-fifth century to the sixth century.[38] The older items were made with great precision, but the newer items came to be made more simply.

According to Taresaewa's report, the items that were excavated from the Shiba ruins were made in the late fifth century, the items that were excavated from the Yamanokami ruins and the site of Chihara-Maruta were made at the end of the fifth century, and the items that were excavated from the tabooed land of the Ōmiwa-jinja Shrine were made in the sixth century. The items that were excavated from the Mitsutorii of the Ōmiwa-jinja Shrine were broken, but the parts of them that survived were similar to those excavated from the tabooed land of the Ōmiwa-jinja Shrine. The items that were discovered at the confluence of the Hatsuse-gawa River and the Makimuku-gawa River are no longer available, and the survey drawings of them are also lost, but they were said to be old forms (Terasawa 1988). According to the report of the Archaeological Institute of Kashihara, the items that were excavated from the Matsunomonto ruins are thought to have been made in the sixth century (Archaeological Institute of Kashihara 2012).

As I mentioned above, the numbers of archaeological relics that were excavated and discovered around Mt. Miwa increased from the late fifth century, peaked in the sixth century, and decreased from the early seventh century. Of course, these dates do not simply show the actual situation of the religious services that were conducted at the mountain. However, they can be seen as indices of the situation. In short, the religious services at Mt. Miwa were begun in earnest in the late fifth century, conducted most frequently in the sixth century, and gradually declined from the early seventh century.[39]

The results of this analysis are very different from Wada's research, described above. Terasawa has also noted this fact (Terasawa 1988). Wada insisted that the religious services at Mt. Miwa were discontinued from the late fifth century to the early sixth century, resuming in the mid-sixth century. If this is so, the relics should have altered in one way or another. However, we cannot perceive any changes in the quantity or quality of the relics during that period. If anything, more relics that were made in the early sixth century have been discovered around Mt. Miwa. This shows that religious services were conducted very frequently in that period. Therefore, it is problematic to argue that there were two distinct periods of religious services at Mt. Miwa, and that the Ōmiwa God became the god of curses because of the interruption of religious services between the two periods. It is thought that religious services were continuously conducted at Mt. Miwa at least from the late fifth century to the late sixth century.

## 6.4 The notation of "Mt. Miwa" and "Mt. Mimoro"

I will now consider Matsukura's research. Matsukura pays attention to the fact that Mt. Miwa has two different notations in history books. The mountain was usually written as "Mt. Miwa" (三輪山, 美和山), but in some cases it was also written as "Mt. Mimoro"[40] (御諸山, 三諸山). Matsukura argues that the notation "Mt. Mimoro" was used in legends that were related to the imperial family. He also argues that the mountain was originally called "Mt. Mimoro," a sacred place where the imperial family conducted ceremonies, but that its name changed to "Mt. Miwa" after the sixth century, when the Ōmiwa clan took charge of the religious services there (Matsukura 1985, Matsukura 1991).

In the following article, the word Mimoro is used in a context relating to Mt. Miwa.

### Article 2: 『万葉集』七―一〇九五 (Manyōshū[41] 7-1095)

三諸就 三輪山見者 隠口乃 始瀬之桧原 所念鴨

In this article, the word Mimoro was used to modify Mt. Miwa. We can also see the following examples.

### Article 3: 『万葉集』三―四二〇 (Manyōshū 3-420)

石田王卒之時丹生王作歌一首〈并短歌〉

名湯竹乃 十縁皇子 狭丹頬相 吾大王者 隠久乃 始瀬乃山尓 神左備尓 伊都伎坐等 玉梓乃 人曽言鶴 於余頭礼可 吾聞都流 狂言加 我間都流母 天地尓 悔事乃 世間乃 悔言者 天雲乃 曽久敝能極 天地乃 至流左右二 杖策毛 不衝毛去而 夕衢占問 石卜以而 吾屋戸尓 御諸乎立而 枕辺尓 斎戸乎居 竹玉乎 無間貫垂 木綿手次 可比奈尓懸而 天有 左佐羅能小野之 七相菅 手取持而 久堅乃 天川原尓 出立而 潔身而麻之乎 高山乃 石穂乃上尓 伊座都類香物

### Article 4: 『万葉集』七―一三七七 (Manyōshū 7-1377)

木綿懸而 祭三諸乃 神佐備而 齊尓波不在 人目多見許曽

Article 5: 『万葉集』九一一七七〇
(*Manyōshū* 9-1770)

大神大夫任長門守時集三輪河邊宴歌二首三諸乃　神能於婆勢流　泊瀨河水尾之不斷者 吾忘礼米也

Article 6: 『万葉集』一二一二九八一
(*Manyōshū* 12-2981)

祝部等之 斎三諸乃 犬馬鏡 懸而偲 相人毎

Article 7: 『万葉集』一三一三二二七
(*Manyōshū* 13-3227)

葦原笑 水穂之国丹 手向為跡 天降座兼 五百万 千万神之 神代従 云続来在 甘南備乃 三諸山者 春去者 春霞立 秋往者 紅丹穂経 甘甞備乃 三諸乃神之 帯為 明日香之河之 水尾速 生多米難 石枕 蘿生左右二 新夜乃 好去通牟 事計 夢尓令見社 剱刀 斎祭 神二師座者

In these articles, the word Mimoro means "a sacred place." This usage applies to the names of shrines. For example, *Engishiki-Jinmyōchō*[42] (延喜式神名帳) lists the Mimoro-jinja Shrine[43] (御諸神社) and the Moro-jinja Shrine[44] (茂侶神社). Therefore, it is clear that, in ancient times, the word Mimoro meant a sacred place where a god lived or a place where religious services were conducted (Nishimiya 1990, Nishimiya 1999, Ueno 2001). It is thought that the mountain might have been written as "Mt. Mimoro" when the religious services were conducted there.

However, Matsukura discussed the notation of the mountain, the god, and the shrine in the same line, so the characteristics of the notation were unclear in his interpretation. I will extract the notations relating to the mountain from the articles of *Kojiki* and rearrange them. I explained a summary of these articles in previous chapters, so I will only extract the necessary sentences and confirm the notation of the mountain used in them.

Article 8: 『古事記』上巻
(The first part of *Kojiki*)

爾、大国主神曰、然者治奉之状奈何。答言、吾者、伊＿-都-岐-奉于倭之青垣東山上＿。此者、坐＿御諸山上＿神也。

This article relates the myth about the creation of the ancient country by Ōkuninushi-no-Kami (大国主神). Ōkuninushi and Sukunabikona created the ancient country, but Sukunabikona died. Ōkuninushi grieved his death. Then the Ōmiwa god appeared and told Ōkuninushi that Ōkuninushihe should worship the Ōmiwa god at the top of Mt. Miwa. This was the god who lived on the top of "Mt. Mimoro."

### Article 9: 『古事記』崇神段
(The part of Emperor Sujin in *Kojiki*)

即以₋意富多多泥古命₋、為₋神主₋而、於₋御諸山₋拝₋祭意富美和之大神前₋。

This article relates the legend of Ōtataneko, as I mentioned in the first half of this chapter. In the era of Emperor Sujin, many people died because of an epidemic. Therefore, the emperor followed the teachings of Ōmononushi, looked for Ōtataneko, and commanded him to worship the god at "Mt. Mimoro."

### Article 10: 『古事記』崇神段
(The part of Emperor Sujin in *Kojiki*)

故、如ₗ教而且時見者、所ₗ著ₗ針麻者、自₋戸之鉤穴₋控通而出、唯遺麻者三勾耳。爾即知下自₋鉤穴₋出之状上而、従₋糸尋行者、至₋美和山₋而留₋神社₋。故、知₋其神子₋。故、因₋其麻之三勾遺₋而、名₋其地₋謂₋美和₋也。

This article relates the legend of Odamaki[45] (苧環伝承). A beautiful woman named Ikutamayori-bime married a certain man, but she did not know his name. She pricked his clothes with a needle threaded with hemp thread. The next morning, she followed the thread. It led to the Ōmiwa-jinja Shrine at "Mt. Miwa." Ikutamayori-bime realized that her husband was the Ōmiwa god. In her house, only three rolls of hemp thread were left, so this place was named Miwa.[46]

In *Kojiki*, "Mt. Mimoro" appears twice, and "Mt. Miwa" appears once. In Article 8, the Ōmiwa god was worshipped at this mountain. In Article 9, Ōtataneko worshipped the Ōmiwa god and conducted religious services there. This article confirms that "Mt. Mimoro" was a sacred place for religious services, consistent with Matsukura's view.

In contrast, in Article 10, the Ōmiwa-jinja Shrine is described as being on the mountain, so it is clear that this was a sacred place, but this article uses the notation "Mt. Miwa." This contradicts Matsukura's hypothesis. According to Matsukura, the mountain should be called "Mt. Mimoro" in this article because this legend was revised after the Ōmiwa clan took charge of the religious services at the mountain.

However, it would be strange if only Article 10 was revised and Article 9 was left untouched. The legend in Article 9 explains the achievement of Ōtataneko, who was the ancestor of the Ōmiwa clan, and explains the Ōmiwa clan's legitimacy in serving the Yamato Kingdom. If anything, I think that Article 10 was created to explain the origin of "Miwa" as a place name, so the mountain was written down as "Mt. Miwa." It does not matter whether its context was related to the Ōmiwa clan.

In *Kojiki*, the notation "Mimoro" is used to mean a sacred place. In contrast, the notation "Miwa" is used to explain the origin of the place name Miwa, not specifically with reference to the Ōmiwa clan.

I will now rearrange the notation of the mountain in *Nihonshoki*. In the same way as above, I will only extract the relevant sentences.

### Article 11: 『日本書紀』神代上第八段一書第六
(The first book of the eighth part of Jindaiki,[47] *Nihonshoki*)

大己貴神曰、唯然。廼知汝是吾之幸魂奇魂。今欲_何処住_耶。対曰、吾欲‿住_於日本国之三諸山_。故即営_宮彼所_、使_就而居_。此大三輪之神也。

The content of this article is similar to that of Article 8. When Ōmononushi grieved at the death of Sukunabikona, the Ōmiwa god appeared, saying that he would like to live at "Mt. Mimoro." Ōmononushi built the shrine and worshipped the Ōmiwa god at the mountain.

### Article 12: 『日本書紀』崇神十年九月条
(September, the tenth year of Emperor Sujin, *Nihonshoki*)

待‿明以見_櫛笥_、遂有_美麗小蛇_。其長大如_衣紐_。即驚之叫啼。時大神有恥、忽化_人形_。謂_其妻_曰、汝不‿忍乎‿羞_吾。吾還令‿羞_汝。仍踐_大虛_、登_御諸山_。爰倭迹々姫命仰見、而悔之急居。

This article relates the legend of Hashihaka, as I mentioned above. Princess Yamatototohimomoso-hime married the Ōmiwa god, but the god returned to "Mt. Mimoro" by walking through the air.

### Article 13: 『日本書紀』崇神四十八年正月戊子条
(Boshi, January, the forty-eighth year of Emperor Sujin, *Nihonshoki*)

会明、兄豊城命以_夢辞_奏_于天皇_曰、自登_御諸山_向_東、而八廻弄槍、八廻撃刀。弟活目尊以_夢辞_奏言、自登_御諸山之嶺_、縄絚_四方_、逐_食_粟雀_。

This article relates the legend of divination through the interpretation of dreams. In order to decide his successor, Emperor Sujin conducted a divination through the interpretation of dreams. Toyoki-no-Mikoto (豊城命) said that, in his dream, he climbed "Mt. Mimoro," faced east, thrusted a spear, and brandished a sword. Ikume-no-Mikoto (活目尊) said that he climbed to the top of "Mt. Mimoro," stretched a rope in all directions, and chased away sparrows.

### Article 14: 『日本書紀』景行五十一年八月壬子条
(Jinshi, August, the fifty-first year of Emperor Keiko,[48] *Nihonshoki*)

於是、所_献神宮_蝦夷等、晝夜喧譁、出入無‿礼。時倭姫命曰、是蝦夷等、不‿可‿近_就於神宮_。則進_上於朝庭_。仍令‿安_置御諸山傍_。未_経_幾時_、悉伐_神山樹_、叫_呼隣里_、而脅_人民_。天皇聞之、詔_群卿_

曰、其置=神山傍=之蝦夷。是本有=獣心=。難レ住=中国=。故随=其情願=、令レ班=邦畿之外=。

In this article, the Emishi[49] (蝦夷) were dedicated to the Ise-jingū Grand Shrine (伊勢神宮), but they were also noisy and rude, so they were moved to the foot of "Mt. Mimoro."

### Article 15: 『日本書紀』雄略七年七月丙子条
### (Heishi, July, the seventh year of Emperor Yūryaku, *Nihonshoki*)

天皇詔=少子部連蜾蠃=曰、朕欲レ見=三諸岳神之形=。(略)蜾蠃答曰、試往捉之。乃登=三諸岳=、捉=取大蛇=、奉レ示=天皇=。

This article tells the legend of Chiisakobe-no-Sugaru, as I mentioned above. Emperor Yūryaku commanded Sugaru to capture the god of "Mt. Mimoro." Sugaru climbed the mountain, captured a huge snake, and gave it to the emperor.

### Article 16: 『日本書紀』敏達十年（五八一）閏二月条
### (Intercalary February, the tenth year of Emperor Bidatsu[50] [581], *Nihonshoki*)

於是、綾糟等懼然恐懼、乃下=泊瀬中流=、面=三諸岳=、歃水而盟曰、臣等蝦夷、自レ今以後、子々孫々、〈古語云=生児八十綿連=。〉用=清明心=、事=奉天闕=。

In this article, Emperor Bidatsu summoned Ayakasu (綾糟), the leader of the Emishi, and declared that he would kill the ringleader of the rebellion. Ayakasu was afraid, and he stepped into the middle of the river, looked toward "Mt. Mimoro," and swore that the Emishi would obey the Yamato Kingdom.

### Article 17: 『日本書紀』用明元年（五八六）五月条
### (May, the first year of Emperor Yōmei[51] [586], *Nihonshoki*)

穴穂部皇子、欲レ奸=炊屋姫皇后=、而自強入=於殯宮=。寵臣三輪君逆、乃喚=兵衛=、重=璅宮門=、拒而勿レ入。(略)於是、穴穂部皇子、陰謀下王=天下之事上、而口詐在=於殺=逆君。遂与=物部守屋大連=、率=兵囲=繞磐余池辺=。逆君知之、隠=於三諸之岳=。

In this article, Prince Anahobe (穴穂部皇子) tried to break into the venue of Emperor Bidatsu's funeral ceremony. Ōmiwa-no-Sakau (逆) guarded the gate and prevented Anahobe from entering. Anahobe became angry and commanded Mononobe-no-Moriya (物部守屋) to kill Sakau. When Moriya approached Sakau with an army, Sakau fled to "Mt. Mimoro."

### Article 18: 『日本書紀』皇極二年（六四三）是歳条
### (The second year of Emperor Kōgyoku[52] [656], *Nihonshoki*)

百済太子余豊、以=密蜂房四枚=、放=養於三輪山=。而終不=蕃息=。

In this article, Yohō[53] (余豊) tried to undertake beekeeping at "Mt. Miwa," but the bees did not propagate.

### Article 19: 『日本書紀』皇極三年（六四四）六月乙巳条
### (Isshi, June, the third year of Emperor Kōgyoku [657], *Nihonshoki*)

志紀上郡言、有_人、於_三輪山_、見_猿昼睡_、窃執_其臂_、不_害_其身_。猿猶合眼歌曰、

武舸都烏爾　陀底屢制羅我　爾古禰挙曾　倭我底鳴勝羅毎　施我佐基泥　佐基泥曾母野　倭我底勝羅須謀野

其人驚_怪猿歌_、放捨而去。此是、経_歴数年_、上宮王等、為_蘇我鞍作_、囲_於膽駒山_之兆也。

In this article, a man found a monkey that was taking a nap on "Mt. Miwa," so he captured it. The monkey then composed a poem in its sleep. This poem was an ill omen of the disturbances of war that had occurred the previous year.

In *Nihonshoki*, although there are various representations in Chinese characters, there are also two kinds of Japanese pronunciations. "Mt. Mimoro" appears seven times, and "Mt. Miwa" appears twice. When "Mt. Mimoro" is used, the mountain is described as a sacred place where the god lived or where religious services were conducted. In Article 11, Ōmononushi worshipped the Ōmiwa god at this mountain. In Article 12, the Ōmiwa god returned to the mountain. In Article 13, the mountain was the site of the divination. In Article 14, the Emishi were dedicated to the mountain. In Article 15, the Ōmiwa god, who had the true identity of a huge snake, lived on the mountain. In Article 16, the ritual of the Emishi's obedience was conducted at the foot of the mountain. In Article 17, Sakau knew that the armed forces were coming, and he fled to "Mt. Mimoro" due to religious reasons, as well as the difficulty of the enemy finding him on the mountain.

### Article 20: 『日本書紀』雄略三年四月条
### (April, the third year of Emperor Yūryaku, *Nihonshoki*)

阿閇臣国見〈更名磯特牛。〉譖_栲幡皇女与_湯人廬城部連武彦_曰、武彦奸_皇女_而使_任身_。〈湯人、此云_与衛_。〉武彦之父枳莒喩、聞_此流言_、恐_禍_及身、誘_率武彦於廬城河_、偽使鸕鷀没水捕魚、因其不意而打殺之。天皇聞遣_使者_、案_問皇女_。皇女対言、妾不_識也。俄而皇女齎_持神鏡_、詣_於五十鈴河上_、伺_人不_行、埋_鏡経死。天皇疑_皇女不在_、恒使_闇夜東西求覓_。乃於_河上_虹見如_蛇、四五丈者、掘_虹起処_、而獲_神鏡_。移行未遠、得_皇女屍_。割而観之、腹中有_物如_水。水中有_石。枳莒喩、由斯、得_雪_子罪_。還悔_殺_子、報_殺国見_。逃_匿石上神宮_。

### Article 21: 『続日本紀』天平神護元年（七六五）八月庚申条
(Kōshin, August, the first year of Tenpyōjingo [765], *Shokunihongi*)

従三位和気王坐_謀反_誅。(略)和気者、一品舎人親王之孫、正三位御原王之子也。勝宝七歳、賜_姓岡真人_。任_因幡掾_。宝字三年、追_尊舎人親王_、曰_崇道尽敬皇帝_。至_是、復_属籍_、授_従四位下_。八年、至_参議従三位兵部卿_。于╷時、皇統無╷嗣、未╷有_其人_。而紀朝臣益女以_巫鬼著_、得╷幸_和気_。心挟_窺窬_、厚賂_幣物_。参議従四位下近衛員外中将兼勅旨員外大輔式部大輔因幡守粟田朝臣道麻呂・兵部大輔兼美作守従四位上大津宿禰大浦・式部員外少輔従五位下石川朝臣永年等、与_和気_善、数飲_其宅_。道麻呂、時与_和気_密語。而道麻呂佩刀、触_門屛_折。和気、即遣以_装刀_。於╷是、人等心疑、頗泄_其事_。和気知╷之、其夜逃竄。索_獲於率河社中_、流_伊豆国_。到_于山背国相楽郡_、絞╷之埋_于狛野_、又絞_益女於綴喜郡松井村_。

In Article 20, Ahe-no-Kunimi (阿閇国見) gave a slanderous account to the emperor that Iokibe-no-Takehiko (廬城部武彦) had impregnated Princess Takuhata-no-Himemiko (栲幡皇女), who, as a priest serving at the Ise-jingū Grand Shrine, was forbidden from marrying. Iokibe-no-Kikoyu (廬城部枳莒喩), Takehiko's father, was afraid that he would be punished alongside his son, so he killed his son. Emperor Yūryaku questioned Takuhata-no-Himemiko closely, but she insisted on her innocence and then committed suicide on the banks of the Isuzu-gawa River (五十鈴川). The emperor investigated her dead body, and she was not pregnant. Takehiko and Takuhata-no-Himemiko were finally found to be innocent. Kikoyu was aware of this, and he regretted having killed his son, bore a grudge against Kunimi, and tried to take revenge on Kunimi. Kunimi fled to the Isonokami-jingū Shrine[54] (石上神宮).

In Article 21, Prince Wake (和気王) tried to usurp the imperial throne. He commanded Kii-no-Masume (紀益女) to curse Emperor Shōtoku[55] (称徳天皇) and planned a rebellion with Awata-no-Michimaro (粟田道麻呂). However, their plans were exposed. Wake was afraid of being executed, so he fled to the Isagawa-jinja Shrine[56] (率川神社).

In these articles, Kunimi hid in the Isonokami-jingū Shrine, and Wake hid in the Isagawa-jinja Shrine. Based on these examples, it is said that the shrine-like place where religious services were conducted was believed to be a sanctuary that was free from the common law (Wada 1989).

In the same way, in Article 17, Sakau fled to the mountain, not only because it was densely forested and the enemy army would struggle to find him, but also because the mountain, as a place where religious services were conducted, was a sanctuary that people could not enter. That is why the notation "Mt. Mimoro" was used in Article 17.

In contrast, the notation "Mt. Miwa" was used in Articles 11 and 12. These articles were not related to the Ōmiwa clan or to the religious services. This would seem very strange. I will now rearrange the notation of the mountain in the above articles in *Nihonshoki*.

| | | | |
|---|---|---|---|
| Article 11 | Mimoro | (三諸山) | The first book of the eighth part of Jindaiki, *Nihonshoki* |
| Article 12 | Mimoro | (御諸山) | September, the tenth year of Emperor Sujin, *Nihonshoki* |
| Article 13 | Mimoro | (御諸山) | Boshi, January, the forty-eighth year of Emperor Sujin, *Nihonshoki* |
| Article 14 | Mimoro | (御諸山) | Jinshi, August, the fifty-first year of Emperor Keiko, *Nihonshoki* |
| Article 15 | Mimoro | (三諸岳) | Heishi, July, the seventh year of Emperor Yūryaku, *Nihonshoki* |
| Article 16 | Mimoro | (三諸岳) | Intercalary February, the tenth year of Emperor Bidatsu, *Nihonshoki* |
| Article 17 | Mimoro | (三諸之岳) | May, the first year of Emperor Yōmei, *NihonShoki* |
| Article 18 | Miwa | (三輪山) | This month, the second year of Emperor Kōgyoku, *Nihonshoki* |
| Article 19 | Miwa | (三輪山) | Isshi, June, the third year of Emperor Kōgyoku, *Nihonshoki* |

Based on this rearrangement, the moment at which the notation "Mt. Mimoro" changed to "Mt. Miwa" is clear. Article 10 is from the era of Emperor Yōmei [585–587], and Article 11 is from the era of Emperor Kōgyoku [642–645]. Therefore, the notation "Mimoro" was used until the sixth century, and the notation "Miwa" was used in the seventh century.[57]

This fact corresponds with the tendencies of the relics that were discovered around the mountain. As I mentioned above, these relics increased in frequency from the late fifth century, peaked in the sixth century, and decreased from the early seventh century. Therefore, the situation of the religious services on the mountain reflects the distinction between the notations "Mimoro" and "Miwa."

Until the sixth century, religious services were conducted on the mountain, so the mountain was written as "Mt. Mimoro": a sacred place in legends about this period. In contrast, after the seventh century, the religious services declined or changed to a different style, and people's consciousness that the mountain was a site of religious services faded, so the mountain was called "Mt. Miwa." When *Kojiki* and *Nihonshoki* were edited in the eighth century, the notations from these original legends were adopted. In this way, different notations appear in each article.

Matsukura argued that the notation "Mt. Mimoro" was used in the legends that are related to the imperial family, and the notation "Mt. Miwa" was used in the legends that are related to the Ōmiwa clan. He also insisted that the mountain had originally been called Mt. Mimoro, as a sacred place where the imperial family conducted ceremonies, but that its name changed to Mt. Miwa after the Ōmiwa clan took charge of the religious services on the mountain. However, I cannot agree with this hypothesis. Instead, the distinction between the notations "Mimoro" and "Miwa" indicates the conditions of the religious services on the mountain.

## 6.5 The Ōmiwa clan and religious services at Mt. Miwa

My final point here is related to both Wada and Matsukura. In previous research, the religious services at Mt. Miwa have been divided into two periods, and it was said that the Ōmiwa clan took charge of the religious services in the second period. The main basis for this argument is the following legend about Ōmiwa-no-Kotohi (特牛).

> **Article 22:** 『大神朝臣本系牒略』特牛尻付（抜粋）
> (The part of Kotohi in *Ōmiwa-no-Ason-Honkeichōryaku*)
>
> 欽明天皇元年四月辛卯、令₋大神祭₋。之四月祭始乎。〈字類抄。〉

> **Article 23:** 『三輪髙宮家系図』特牛尻付（抜粋）
> (The part of Kotohi in *Miwa-Takamiya-Kakeizu*)
>
> 金刺宮御宇元年四月辛卯、令₋祭₋大神₋。是四月祭之始也。

These articles describe Kotohi as beginning the April festival (四月祭) in the first year of Emperor Kinmei[58] (欽明天皇). According to the provisions of *Engishiki*,[59] the April festival is the Ōmiwa-sai Festival[60] (大神祭), the main festival that was later held at the Ōmiwa-jinja Shrine in April. This article explains the origin of the Ōmiwa-sai Festival and describes when the Ōmiwa clan took charge of the religious services at Mt. Miwa.[61] Wada pays attention to Article 23, insisting that the Ōmiwa clan began to take charge of religious services at Mt. Miwa in the era of Emperor Kinmei, in the mid-sixth century. In other words, the Ōmiwa clan conducted religious services at Mt. Miwa secondly (Wada 1979, Wada 1985). Matsukura supports Wada's opinion (Matsukura 1985, Matsukura 1991).

However, Wada only refers to *Takamiya-Kakeizu*; he does not refer to *Honkeichōryaku*. *Honkeichōryaku* was edited at the end of the eighteenth century, based on *Ōmiwa-no-Ason-Honkeichō* (大神朝臣本系牒), which is thought to have been edited sometime from the end of the eighth century to the early tenth century. In contrast, *Takamiya-Kakeizu* was edited in the late nineteenth century and revised and enlarged the article of *Honkeichōryaku*. Therefore, where the contents of both books are the same, we should consider *Honkeichōryaku* first (Suzuki M. 2012, Suzuki M. 2014). We need to reexamine Article 22.

This article ends with the word *Jiruishō* (字類抄). This article is thought to have been quoted from *Jiruishō* or to have been written based on *Jiruishō*. *Jiruishō* refers either to *Iroha-Jiruishō*[62] (色葉字類抄, 伊呂波字類抄) or

*Sezoku-Jiruishō*[63] (世俗字類抄). The contents of this are quite different in different manuscript copies, so I have not been able to find the specific article about Kotohi. However, in any case, it is clear that the description in Article 22 is not an original description from *Honkeichōryaku*. Furthermore, the following article can be found in *Honkeichōryaku*.

### Article 24:『大神朝臣本系牒略』大田田根子尻付（抜粋）
### (The part of Ōtataneko in *Ōmiwa-no-Ason-Honkeichōryaku*)

崇神天皇八年十二月卯日祭之始。〈書紀。〉

In this article, Ōtataneko began the December festival (十二月祭). This was the Ōmiwa-sai Festival (大神祭), which was held in December at the Ōmiwa-jinja Shrine in ancient times. It was written based on the article in *Nihonshoki*. This article is in parallel with Article 22, which explains the origin of the April festival. It seems that the description of the origin of the April festival was intercalated later to make it correspond with the description of the origin of the December festival. Therefore, the reliability of Article 22 is unclear. We cannot trust this article unquestioningly and assume that the Ōmiwa clan took charge of the religious services at Mt. Miwa during the time of Emperor Kinmei.

How did the Ōmiwa clan participate in the religious services at Mt. Miwa? I look back to the conclusion of Chapter 2. Ōtataneko, Ōtomonushi (大友主), and Iwatoko (石床) were the first people from the Ōmiwa clan to appear in history books and historical documents. However, *Kojiki*[64] and *Nihonshoki*[65] both describe Ōtataneko and Ōtomonushi as "the ancestors" of the clan. Ōtomonushi is one of the four ministers in *Nihonshoki*.[66] However, their constitution of ministers reflected the constitution of the ruling class in the late seventh century. The legend of Ōtomonushi was modified when *Nihonshoki* was edited. Regarding Iwatoko, his name reminds us of the Iwakura, and the head linage of the Ōmiwa clan and its cognate clans diverged from him. These three people are thought to be fictional characters created by descendants of the Ōmiwa clan in order to explain why the Ōmiwa clan served the Yamato Kingdom and to explain "the fictitious blood relationship" with the cognate clans.

In contrast, Musa (身狭) was different from his ancestors. In the era of Emperor Yūryaku, he participated in a fight for succession to the imperial throne. His achievement was handed down in the *Boki*[67] (墓記) of the Ōmiwa clan, as a definite person's name and place name are recorded in the article (Sakamoto 1946). Furthermore, Musa and his descendants are not described as "the ancestors" of the clan. This shows that Musa was the first real person in the Ōmiwa clan.

In the era of Emperors Bidatsu and Yōmei, Sakau held immense power in the Yamato Kingdom. In *Nihonshoki*,[68] Sakau is described as "a favorite retainer of Emperor Bidatsu," and the emperor left all politics to him. When Sogano-Umako (蘇我馬子) heard of Sakau's death, he said that the entire world would be disturbed. This indicates that Sakau had a big influence on politics at that time. He is thought to have gained power by building direct relationships with the emperor and empress (Abe 1975, Nakayama 2002). However, Sakau was killed by Anahobe and Moriya. From Sakau's death to the appearance of Osazaki (小鷦鷯) approximately fifty years later, no member of the Ōmiwa clan appears in a historical manuscript.

As above, the trend of the Ōmiwa clan and the relics that have been discovered around Mt. Miwa correspond completely. In the era of Emperor Yūryaku, in the late fifth century, someone who we are sure was from the Ōmiwa clan appeared in history. In the era of emperors Bidatsu and Yōmei, in the late sixth century, the Ōmiwa clan prospered. This was the golden age of this clan. However, Sakau was involved in political disputes and was murdered. After the early seventh century, the Ōmiwa clan's power declined remarkably. In parallel, the number of archaeological relics that were excavated or discovered around Mt. Miwa increased from the late fifth century, peaked in the sixth century, and decreased from the early seventh century.

In the light of the relationship between these facts, we can see that the religious services at Mt. Miwa were not resumed by the Ōmiwa clan in the mid-sixth century. It seems more likely that the Ōmiwa clan took part in the religious services continuously at least from the fifth century to the mid-sixth century. That is to say, the religious services at Mt. Miwa began in the late fifth century and the Ōmiwa clan officially took charge of them as its duty in the Yamato Kingdom. Throughout the sixth century, religious services were conducted frequently, and the Ōmiwa clan extended its influence and came to the fore. Then, in the early seventh century, the religious services gradually declined or changed to a different style, and the Ōmiwa clan's power diminished.

## 6.6 Conclusion

In this chapter, I reexamined three points of contention that have been stated in previous research.

First, previous researchers have insisted that the religious services at Mt. Miwa were discontinued during the late fifth to the early sixth century, and soon afterwards people began to regard the Ōmiwa god as a god of curses. In this previously stated model, in the mid-sixth century, the religious services were resumed by the Ōmiwa clan. However, the relics that have been excavated and discovered around Mt. Miwa continued to be made from the late fifth century to the sixth century, and no changes in the quality or quantity of the relics has been discerned. Thus there was no interruption of religious services during that period.

Second, it has previously been noted that there were two different notations of the mountain: according to previous research, "Mt. Mimoro" was used as the sacred place name in the period when the imperial family conducted ceremonies on the mountain, and "Mt. Miwa" was used as a place name in the period when the Ōmiwa clan was organizing the religious services on the mountain. However, the notation "Mt. Mimoro" was actually used when the religious services were conducted on the mountain, and "Mt. Miwa" was used when people's consciousness that the mountain was a site of religious services was fading. The distinction in the way that these two notations were written indicates, rather than who conducted the religious services at the mountain, the overall situation of the religious services there.

Third, *Takamiya-Kakeizu* states that the April festival was begun by Kotohi in the era of Emperor Kinmei. Previous researchers have taken up this *Takamiya-Kakeizu* and assumed that the Ōmiwa clan took charge of the religious services at Mt. Miwa at that time. However, this historical document was edited based on *Honkeichōryaku*. In *Honkeichōryaku*, *Jirushō* was ascribed as the source for this article. This description shows that the article that previous researchers had focused on was actually quoted from other historical materials, not originally from the *Honkeichōryaku*. We cannot actually see from this article when the Ōmiwa clan began to conduct religious services at Mt. Miwa.

If anything, the first person from the Ōmiwa clan whose identity we can confirm lived during the era of Emperor Yūryaku. The clan gained power in the era of Emperors Bidatsu and Yōmei. After Sakau was killed, no member of the clan appeared in written history for a long time. In parallel to this, the relics that were excavated or discovered around Mt. Miwa increased in number from the late fifth century, peaked in the sixth century, and decreased from the early seventh century. In this way, the fortunes of the clan and the number of relics correspond, showing that the Ōmiwa clan took continuous charge of the religious services at Mt. Miwa from the fifth century to the mid-sixth century.

The number of relics decreases after the seventh century. This is because Sakau was killed, and the Ōmiwa clan, the main conductor of the religious services, lost its political power. However, this was not the only reason for these changes. From the late sixth century to the early seventh century, the Yamato Kingdom founded a new system of religious services (Naoki 1951, Ueda 1964, Okada Seishi 1960, Okada Seishi 1962). For example, the Ise-jingū Grand Shrine was worshipped, the Saikan[69] system (祭官制) was introduced, the Nakatomi clan (中臣氏) and the Inbe clan (忌部氏) gained more power, and Hiokibe (日置部) and Himatsuribe[70] (日祀部) were established. Furthermore, during the era of Emperors Kinmei, Bidatsu, Yōmei, and Sushun[71] (崇峻天皇), in the sixth century, the imperial palaces were located around Mt. Miwa, but they were moved to the Asuka region[72] (飛鳥地方) after the era of Emperor Suiko[73] (推古天皇). As a result of these changing circumstances, Mt. Miwa's political and religious position in the Yamato Kingdom was altered dynamically, and so the religious services at Mt. Miwa declined or changed gradually. Regarding the Ōmiwa clan, after Sakau's death, they were not able to produce a competent leader, so they were also unable to adapt to the new system. This is why the clan entered a period of decline.

# Notes

1. *Kojiki* (古事記) is a record of ancient matters in Japan. It was edited in 712.
2. *Nihonshoki* (日本書紀) is a chronicle of ancient Japan. It was edited in 720.
3. The change of dynasties theory (王朝交替説) was proposed by Yū Mizuno (水野祐). According to this theory, the imperial family in ancient Japan changed several times (Mizuno 1952).
4. The part of Emperor Sujin in *Kojiki*.
5. Shinbō, February, the seventh year of Emperor Sujin, *Nihonshoki*. Kiyū, August, the seventh year of Emperor Sujin, *Nihonshoki*. Kibō, November, the seventh year of Emperor Sujin, *Nihonshoki*. Itsubō, December, the eighth year of Emperor Sujin, *Nihonshoki*.
6. Sujin (崇神天皇) was the tenth emperor.
7. In present-day Sakai, Ōsakasayama, Izumi, and Kishiwada City, Ōsaka Prefecture (大阪府堺市, 大阪狭山市, 和泉市, 岸和田市).
8. Princess Yamatototohimomoso-hime (倭迹迹日百襲姫命) was a daughter of Emperor Korei (孝霊天皇), the seventh emperor; later she was the grand-aunt of Emperor Sujin.
9. In present-day Sakai, Ōsakasayama, Izumi, and Kishiwada City, Ōsaka Prefecture.
10. September, the tenth year of Emperor Sujin, *Nihonshoki*.
11. Hashi means "chopsticks," and Haka means "tomb."
12. Heishi, July, the seventh year of Emperor Yūryaku (雄略天皇), *Nihonshoki*. Yūryaku was the twenty-first emperor.
13. In the eastern part of present-day Ōsaka Prefecture (大阪府).
14. In present-day Nara Prefecture (奈良県).
15. Kunimi (国見) was the ceremony in which the emperor observed the territories under his control from a high place and confirmed that the people lived peacefully.
16. The Edo period (江戸時代) was approximately from the beginning of the seventeenth century to the beginning of the twentieth century.
17. The Meiji period (明治時代) was from 1868 to 1912.
18. The Shōwa period (昭和時代) was from 1926 to 1989.
19. My arrangement of the archaeological ruins and relics is based on the following research. In addition, there are many little Iwakura in and around Mt. Miwa, but they are omitted for the sake of convenience.

- Archaeological Institute of Kashihara (Kashihara Kōkogaku Kenkyūjo), ed., *Excavation Report of the Ōmiwa-jinja Shrine Precincts (Ōmiwa-jinja Keidaichi Hakkutsuchōsa Hōkokusho)*, the Ōmiwa-jinja Shrine, Nara, Japan, 1984.
- Archaeological Institute of Kashihara (Kashihara Kōkogaku Kenkyūjo), ed., *Summary Report of Ruins of Nara Prefecture (Naraken Iseki Chōsa Gaihō)* 2011–2, Archaeological Institute of Kashihara, Nara, Japan, 2012.
- Kaoru Terasawa, "Ritual Sites at Mt. Miwa and Religious Services (Miwayama no Saishiiseki to sono Matsuri)," Atsumu Wada, ed., *Ōmiwa and Isonokami (Ōmiwa to Isonokami)*, Chikuma-Shobō, Tōkyō, Japan, 1988.
- Kazue Koike, "Ritual Sites around Mt. Miwa (Miwayama Shūhen no Saishi Iseki)," Miwayama Bunka Kenkyūkai, ed., *Sacred Mountains and Ōmiwa and the Miwa-myōjin Shrine (Kannabi Ōmiwa Miwamyōjin)*, Tōhō-Shuppan, Ōsaka, Japan, 1997.
- Masanobu Suzuki, *Study of the Ōmiwa clan (Ōmiwa-Uji no Kenkyū)*, Yūzankaku, Tōkyō, Japan, 2014.
- Sakurai City Center for Archaeological Operations (Sakuraishiritsu Maizōbukaza Center), ed., *Archaeology around Mt. Miwa (Miwayama Shūhen no Kōkogaku)*, Sakurai City Center for Archaeological Operations, Nara, Japan, 2000.

- Sakurai City Institute for Cultural Properties (Sakuraishi Bunkazai Kyōkai), *Excavation report of Sakurai City (Sakuraishinai Maizōbunkazai Hakkutsuchōsa Hōkokusho)* 2, Sakurai City Institute for Cultural Properties, Nara, Japan, 1998.

20 Talc instruments (滑石製模造品) and clay instruments (土製模造品) were made from talc and clay, imitating the instruments that were used for religious services such as treasures and vessels.
21 Iwakura (磐座) refers to boulders in which gods were thought to dwell. Ancient people conducted religious services around Iwakura.
22 Haji pottery (土師器) is a type of unglazed earthenware that evolved from Yayoi-type pottery (弥生土器) and was produced from the Kofun period (古墳時代) to the Heian period (平安時代). The Kofun period was from the fourth century to the seventh century. The Heian period was from the end of the eighth century to the beginning of the twelfth century.
23 Sue ware (須恵器) is a type of unglazed earthenware produced from the latter half of the Kofun period through the Heian period.
24 Clay horse figurines (土馬), in substitution for genuine horses, were used for religious services or ceremonies meant to bring rain.
25 The Wakamiya-jinja Shrine (若宮社) is also known as the Ōtataneko-jinja Shrine (大直禰子神社).
26 The Ninotorii (二の鳥居) is the second gate of the Ōmiwa-jinja Shrine.
27 Motoiwa (夫婦岩) refers to rocks that look like a married couple.
28 The Mitsutorii (三ツ鳥居) is the third gate of the Ōmiwa-jinja Shrine.
29 *Ōmiwashinsansha-Chinzanoshidai* (大三輪神三社鎮座次第) is a historical chronicle of the Ōmiwa-jinja Shrine. This is included in *Ōmiwajinja-shiryō* (大神神社史料) Volume 1.
30 A Haiden (拝殿) is a worship hall of a Shintō shrine.
31 According to *Written Regulation Concerning of the Tabooed Land of the Ōmiwa-jinja Shrine (Miwayama Kinsokuchi Bōji Sadamegaki,* 三輪山禁足牓示定書*)*, very wide areas from the foot of the mountain to the top of the mountain were determined as the tabooed land in the Edo period. This regulation was established in 1666. This is included in *Ōmiwajinja-shiryō* Volume 1.
32 This is included in *Ōmiwajinja-shiryō* Volume 1.
33 This is included in *Ōmiwajinja-shiryō* Volume 7.
34 "The remaining site of the main shrine building" (御主殿跡) is called Goshuden-Ato, Goseiden-Ato, Seiden-Ato, and Kyu-Haiden-Ato. Ato means "remaining site."
35 The Yayoi period (弥生時代) was approximately from the third century BC to the third century AD. Other opinions about this also exist.
36 *Engishiki* (延喜式) was a statute book, edited in 927.
37 The ruins of the Suemura kilns (陶邑窯跡群) are in present-day Sakai, Ōsakasayama, Izumi, and Kishiwada City, Ōsaka Prefecture.
38 In this book, I refer to the reports of Terasawa and the Archaeological Institute of Kashihara (Terasawa 1988, Archaeological Institute of Kashihara 2012). In addition, Ōhira presented another classification standard and published an original report (Ōhira 2007).
39 In regard to the time when the religious services at Mt. Miwa began, some researchers have estimated that this was the mid-fourth century (Terasawa 1988). Some other researchers have estimated that services began in the third century (Higuchi K. 1959, Ishino 1977, Shimizu 1998, Wada 2003). However, there are very few relics that are thought to have been made before the mid-fifth century. As I explained above, it is possible that some relics were inherited in later times and were buried after several hundred years. If anything, the late fifth century, when the quantity of relics increased, might be the most likely era during which these religious services began.

40 In some cases, "Mimoro" is spelt "Mimuro." These two terms have the same meaning.
41 *Manyōshū* (万葉集) was the oldest anthology of classic Japanese poems. It was edited in the mid-eighth century.
42 *Engishiki-Jinmyōchō* (延喜式神名帳) is a record of Shintō shrines in ancient Japan. It was edited in 927.
43 The Mimoro-jinja Shrine (御諸神社) was in Kii County, Yamashiro Province (山城国紀伊郡), which is in present-day Fushimi Ward, Kyōto City, Kyōto Prefecture (京都府京都市伏見区).
44 The Moro-jinja Shrine (茂侶神社) was in Katsushika County, Shimotsuke Province (下総国葛飾郡), which is in present-day Nagareyama City, Chiba Prefecture (千葉県流山市).
45 Odamaki (苧環) means "ball of hemp threads."
46 Miwa (三勾, 三輪) means "three rolls."
47 Jindaiki (神代紀) is part of the myth in *Nihonshoki*.
48 Keiko (景行天皇) was the twelfth emperor.
49 Emishi (蝦夷) refers to people who did not belong to the Yamato Kingdom. Most of them lived in northeastern Japan.
50 Bidatsu (敏達天皇) was the thirtieth emperor.
51 Yōmei (用明天皇) was the thirty-first emperor.
52 Kōgyoku (皇極天皇) was the thirty-fifth emperor.
53 Yohō (余豊) was the prince of Baekje (百済). He visited Japan as a hostage at this time.
54 The Isonokami-jingū Shrine (石上神宮) is in present-day Tenri City, Nara Prefecture (奈良県天理市).
55 Shōtoku (称徳天皇) was the forty-eighth emperor.
56 The Isagawa-jinja Shrine (率川神社) is in present-day Nara City, Nara Prefecture (奈良県奈良市).
57 According to recent research, *Nihonshoki* can be divided into an $\alpha$ part (Volumes 14–21, 24–27) and a $\beta$ part (Volumes 1–13, 22–23, 28–29), and these two parts were written by different authors (Mori 1999). However, both notations "Mt. Mimoro" and "Mt. Miwa" would be found in part $\alpha$. Therefore, the reason why these two notations were distinguished in writing is not that the authors were different.
58 Kinmei (欽明天皇) was the twenty-ninth emperor.
59 The part of Ōmiwasai-jō, Chūgūshiki 17 in *Engishiki*. The part of Ōmiwasai-jō, Tōgūbō 13 in *Engishiki*.
60 In ancient times, the Ōmiwa-sai Festival (大神祭) was held twice a year, in April and December. In modern times, the festival is in April and October.
61 Yoshinobu Tsukaguchi (塚口義信) insisted that the Ōmiwa clan began the religious services at Mt. Miwa, because they were opposed to Buddhism (仏教), which was transmitted to Japan in the era of Emperor Kinmei (Tsukaguchi 2003). However, the description of the Ōmiwa clan as opposed to Buddhism is based on the historical interpretation of the editor of *Nihonshoki* (Shinokawa 2009). The Ōmiwa clan was not actually opposed to Buddhism (Suzuki M. 2014).
62 *Iroha-Jiruishō* (色葉字類抄・伊呂波字類抄) is an ancient Japanese dictionary from the end of the Heian period.
63 *Sezoku-Jiruishō* (世俗字類抄) is an ancient Japanese dictionary that appeared before *Iroha-Jiruishō*.
64 The part of Emperor Sujin in *Kojiki*.
65 Itsubō, December, the eighth year of Emperor Sujin, *Nihonshoki*. March, third year of Emperor Suinin, *Nihonshoki*.

66 Teibi, February, the ninth year of Emperor Chūai, *Nihonshoki*. Emperor Chūai (仲哀天皇) was the fourteenth emperor.
67 *Boki* (墓記) was a genealogy or legend that described how the ancestors of a clan served the Yamato Kingdom from generation to generation (Sakamoto 1970, Noguchi 1992, Katō 2004, Nakamura 2009).
68 May, the first year of Emperor Yōmei [586], *Nihonshoki*.
69 Saikan (祭官) was an official priest who conducted Shintō rituals.
70 Hiokibe (日置部) and Himatsuribe (日祀部) conducted the imperial family's religious services, especially those related to the emperor. Other opinions about this also exist.
71 Sushun (崇峻天皇) was the thirty-second emperor.
72 Near present-day Asuka Village, Takaichi County, Nara Prefecture (奈良県高市郡明日香村).
73 Suiko (推古天皇) was the thirty-third emperor.

# 7 The legend of religious services at Mt. Miwa

## 7.1 Introduction

The legends of Ōtataneko (大田田根子), which were included in *Kojiki*[1] (古事記) and *Nihonshoki*[2] (日本書紀), are well known explanations of the origin of the Ōmiwa clan. I have already considered these articles in earlier chapters, but they are very important for this chapter, so I revisit them here.

> **Article 1:『古事記』崇神段**
> **(The part of Emperor Sujin[3] in *Kojiki*)**
>
> 此天皇御世、疫病多起、人民死為尽。爾天皇愁歎而、坐神牀之夜、大物主大神、顕於御夢曰、是者我之御心。故、以意富多多泥古而、令祭我御前者、神気不起、国安平。是以駅使班于四方、求謂意富多多泥古人之時、於河内之美努村、見得其人貢進。爾天皇問賜之汝者誰子也、答曰、僕者大物主大神、娶陶津耳命之女、活玉依毘売、生子、名櫛御方命之子、飯肩巣見命之子、建甕槌命之子、僕意富多多泥古白。於是天皇大歓以詔之、天下平、人民栄。即以意富多多泥古命、為神主而、於御諸山拝祭意富美和之大神前、又仰伊迦賀色許男命、作天之八十毘羅訶。〈此参字以音也。〉定奉天神地祇之社、又於宇陀墨坂神、祭赤色楯矛、又於大坂神、祭墨色楯矛、又於坂之御尾神及河瀬神、悉無遺忘以奉幣帛也。因此而疫気悉息、国家安平也。(略)〈此意富多多泥古命者、神君・鴨君之祖。〉

In this article, during the era of Emperor Sujin (崇神天皇), many people were dying because of an epidemic. In a dream, Ōmononushi-no-Kami (大物主神), who was the god living in Mt. Miwa, or the Ōmiwa god (大三輪神), told the emperor that the epidemic was his curse and that the curse would be lifted if the emperor commanded Ōtataneko to worship the god. The emperor looked for Ōtataneko, found him in Mino Village, Kawachi Province (河内之美努村), and commanded him to worship the god at Mt. Miwa. This was how the epidemic ended. Furthermore, Ōtataneko was a descendant of the Ōmiwa god and would become the ancestor of the Ōmiwa clan.

## Article 2:『日本書紀』崇神七年二月辛卯条
(Shinbō, February, the seventh year of Emperor Sujin, *Nihonshoki*)

詔曰、昔我皇祖、大啓‿鴻基‿。其後、聖業逾高、王風転盛。不㆑意、今当‿朕世‿、数有‿災害‿。恐朝無㆑善政‿、取㆑咎於神祇‿耶。蓋㆗命神亀、以極㆖致災之所由㆖也。於是、天皇乃幸‿于神浅茅原‿、而会‿八十万神‿、以卜問之。是時、神明憑‿倭迹々日百襲姫命‿曰、天皇、何憂‿国之不㆑治也。若能敬‿祭我‿者、必当自平矣。天皇問曰、教‿如此‿者誰神也。答曰、我是倭国域内所居神、名為‿大物主神‿。時得‿神語‿、随㆑教祭祀。然猶於㆑事無験。天皇乃沐浴斎戒、潔‿浄殿内‿、而祈之曰、朕礼㆑神尚未㆑尽耶。何不㆑享之甚也。冀亦夢裏教之、以畢‿神恩‿。是夜夢、有‿一貴人‿。対‿立殿戸‿、自称‿大物主神‿曰、天皇、勿㆑復為㆑愁。国之不㆑治、是吾意也。若以‿吾児大田々根子‿、令㆑祭吾‿者、則立平矣。亦有‿海外之国‿、自当帰伏。

## Article 3:『日本書紀』崇神七年八月己酉条
(Kiyū, August, the seventh year of Emperor Sujin, *Nihonshoki*)

倭迹速神浅茅原目妙姫・穂積臣遠祖大水口宿禰・伊勢麻績君、参人共同㆑夢、而奏言、昨夜夢之、有‿一貴人‿、誨曰、以‿大田々根子命‿、為㆘祭‿大物主大神‿之主㆖、亦以‿市磯長尾市‿、為㆘祭‿倭大国魂神‿主㆖、必天下太平矣。天皇得‿夢辞‿、益歓‿於心‿。布告‿天下‿、求‿大田々根子‿、即於‿茅渟県陶邑‿得‿大田々根子‿而貢之。天皇、即親臨‿于神浅茅原‿、会‿諸王卿及八十諸部‿、而問‿大田々根子‿曰、汝其誰子。対曰、父曰‿大物主大神‿。母曰‿活玉依媛‿。陶津耳之女。亦云、奇日方天日方武茅渟祇之女也。天皇曰、朕当栄楽。乃卜㆑使‿物部連祖伊香色雄‿、為㆗神班物者㆖、吉之。又卜㆓便祭‿他神‿、不㆑吉。

## Article 4:『日本書紀』崇神七年十一月己卯条
(Kibō, November, the seventh year of Emperor Sujin, *Nihonshoki*)

命‿伊香色雄‿、而以‿物部八十平瓮‿、作‿祭神之物‿。即以‿大田々根子‿、為㆘祭‿大物主大神‿之主㆖。又以‿長尾市‿、為㆘祭‿倭大国魂神‿之主㆖。然後、卜㆑祭‿他神‿、吉焉。便別祭‿八十万群神‿。仍定‿天社・国社、及神地・神戸‿。於是、疫病始息、国内漸謐。五穀既成、百姓饒之。

## Article 5:『日本書紀』崇神八年四月乙卯条
(Itsubō, April, the eighth year of Emperor Sujin, *Nihonshoki*)

以‿高橋邑人活日‿為‿大神之掌酒‿。〈掌酒、此云‿佐介弭苔‿。〉

## Article 6:『日本書紀』崇神八年十二月乙卯条
(Itsubō, December, the eighth year of Emperor Sujin, *Nihonshoki*)

天皇、以‿大田々根子‿、令㆑祭‿大神‿。是日活日自挙神酒、献天皇。(略)所謂大田々根子、今三輪君等之始祖也。

Ōtataneko also appears in these articles in *Nihonshoki*. This story's plot is very similar to that of *Kojiki*. In these articles, many people died of an epidemic in the era of Emperor Sujin. Princess Yamatototohimomoso-hime[4] (倭迹迹日百襲姫命) told the emperor that the epidemic was a curse from the god Ōmononushi. Later, the god appeared in the emperor's dream and told the emperor how to worship the god. So the emperor found Ōtataneko in Sue Village, Chinu Region (茅渟県陶邑), and commanded him to worship the god at Mt. Miwa. As a result, the epidemic came to an end. The next year, the emperor appointed Takahashimura-no-Ikuhi (高橋邑活日) to be the manager of the rice wine[5] (神酒). The emperor again commanded Ōtataneko to worship the god at Mt. Miwa and commanded Ikuhi to present the rice wine to the god. Ōtataneko was the ancestor of the Ōmiwa clan.

The principal objectives of this series of legends are as follows. First, Ōtataneko, who was a descendant of the Ōmiwa god, lifted the curse of the god who lived in Mt. Miwa. Second, Ōtataneko, who was the ancestor of the Ōmiwa clan, served the Yamato Kingdom (大和王権) by conducting religious services at Mt. Miwa. In short, these legends explain the legitimacy of the Ōmiwa clan. This is the opinion of most researchers.

However, there is one point on which researchers have differed. This relates to the place where the emperor found Ōtataneko. In *Kojiki*, he was found in Mino Village. In *Nihonshoki*, he was found in Sue Village. Although these two villages are referred to by different names, they indicate the same area; therefore, in what follows I refer to this place as Suemura Village. Suemura Village was in present-day Sakai, Osakasayama, Izumi, and Kishiwada Cities, in Ōsaka Prefecture (大阪府堺市, 大阪狭山市, 和泉市, 岸和田市), in western Japan. In this place, there are now ruins of Suemura kilns (陶邑窯跡群). From the fifth century to the tenth century, the Suemura kilns (陶邑窯) produced extravagant Sue ware[6] (須恵器). In the fifth century in particular, the Suemura kilns played a major role in the production of Sue ware in ancient Japan. In addition, a large amount of Sue ware produced in the Suemura kilns has been excavated or discovered around Mt. Miwa.

Many previous researchers have argued, first, about why Ōtataneko was found in Suemura Village, not around Mt. Miwa, despite the fact that he was an ancestor of the Ōmiwa clan, which was based at the foot of the mountain. Second, researchers have argued about the extent to which the Ōmiwa clan was involved with the production of Sue ware in the Suemura kilns. I analyze and explain these two points of contention in this chapter. In other words, this chapter contains the central arguments of this book.

## 7.2  The production of Sue ware and the Miwabe clan

In this section, I consider the latter point. The first researcher to consider this point was Mikio Sasaki (佐々木幹雄) (Sasaki 1975, Sasaki 1976, Sasaki 1979a, Sasaki 1979b, Sasaki 1984, Sasaki 1986).

Sasaki focused on Sue ware that was excavated or discovered at the foot of Mt. Miwa and now owned by the Ōmiwa-jinja Shrine. He then noted the following points. The quantity and the years of production of these pieces of Sue ware correspond with the prosperity and decline of the Suemura kilns. These pieces of Sue ware included some pieces that were produced before other kilns, apart from the Suemura kilns, were established. The Sue ware that was discovered at Mt. Miwa, and the Sue ware that was produced at the Suemura kilns, have a similar shape. Based on these points, Sasaki insists that the greater part of the Sue ware that was excavated or discovered at the foot of Mt. Miwa was produced at the Suemura kilns. He also speculates that this Sue ware was used for religious services, because the items show no signs of everyday use.

Furthermore, Sasaki speculates that a group of craftsmen immigrated to Suemura Village from the Korean Peninsula in ancient times. They produced Sue ware, supplying these items to a certain group living at the foot of Mt. Miwa for religious services. The group of craftsmen living in Suemura Village came to be known as the Miwa-no-Atai clan (神直氏) and as the local Tomo-no-Miyatsuko[7] (伴造). According to Sasaki's argument, some members of the Miwa-no-Atai clan who had lived in Suemura Village later immigrated to the foot of Mt. Miwa. They came to be called the Ōmiwa clan and inherited the right to conduct religious services at Mt. Miwa from the group that had previously lived there.[8]

In a series of pieces of research, Sasaki used archaeological materials to elucidate the mutual relationships between Mt. Miwa and Suemura Village. His research should be respected as pioneering. However, it was based on the change of dynasties theory[9] (王朝交替説), which has been criticized by Yasutami Suzuki (鈴木靖民), Teiji Kadowaki (門脇禎二), Ryoichi Maenosono (前之園亮一), Kimio Kumagai (熊谷公男), and others (Suzuki Y. 1980, Kadowaki 1984, Maenosono 1986, Kumagai 2001). In particular, Jūichirō Inobe (伊野部重一郎) and Takashi Tanaka (田中卓) have criticized Sasaki's work in detail (Inobe 1983, Tanaka 1987). For more detail on this, see their research.

In addition, according to recent research trends, the Miwa-no-Atai clan was a professional group whose members originally lived in various places. As the local ruling system of the Yamato Kingdom spread to various parts of ancient Japan, the Miwa-no-Atai clan was organized as the Tomo-no-Miyatsuko in the local district, while the Ōmiwa clan was organized as the Tomo-no-Miyatsuko in the central district. It is not possible that the Miwa-no-Atai clan was previously organized as the Tomo-no-Miyatsuko locally and that the Ōmiwa clan was later organized as the Tomo-no-Miyatsuko in the central district. Furthermore, it is not possible that some members of the Miwa-no-Atai clan moved to the foot of Mt. Miwa and came to be called the Ōmiwa clan. We have to separate the argument about the religious services at Mt. Miwa from the change of dynasties theory.

Next, I will focus on the research of Kazutoshi Sakamoto (坂本和俊), Tetsuo Hishida (菱田哲郎), and Yūki Mizoguchi (溝口優樹). Sakamoto, who analyzed the places that are recorded in *Wamyōruijūshō*[10] (和名類聚抄) and the shrines that are listed in *Engishiki-Jinmyōchō*[11] (延喜式神名帳), points out that the Sue ware kilns were distributed in various places; the Miwabe clan (神部氏), which was presided over and controlled by the Ōmiwa clan, was also distributed in various places, and these areas roughly overlapped. Sakamoto then speculates that the Miwabe clan played an important role in the production of Sue ware in local areas[12] (Sakamoto 1987).

Hishida develops the arguments from Sakamoto's research and makes the following points. Earthenware that was inscribed "Ōga-no-Kimi" (大神君) and "Ōgabe" (大神部) on the surface was excavated from the ruins of the Ushikubi kilns[13] (牛頸窯跡群) (Ōnojō City Board of Education 1989, Ōnojō City Board of Education 2008a, Ōnojō City Board of Education 2008b). According to the field-tax report of Hamana County, Tōtoumi Province,[14] (遠江国浜名郡輸租帳) the Miwa-no-Atai clan (神直氏), the Miwahito clan (神人氏), and the Miwahitobe clan (神人部氏) were distributed around the ruins of the Kosai kilns[15] (湖西窯跡群) (Gotō 1997). According to the family register of Naka Village, Kakamu County, Mino Province[16] (御野国各牟郡中里戸籍), the Miwa-no-Atai clan and the Miwahito clan were distributed around the ruins of the Minosue kilns[17] (美濃須衛窯跡群). Based on these points, Hishida claims that one of the occupations of the Miwabe clan[18] was the production of Sue ware. He then insists that, from the late sixth century to the early seventh century, the production system was reorganized, the Miwabe clan took primary charge of the production of Sue ware, and kilns in various places were able to begin the stable production of Sue ware. In addition, Hishida insists that the Miwabe clan in various places did not originally worship the Ōmiwa god but began to worship the god after they constructed vocational relationships with the Ōmiwa clan in the central district (Hishida 2005, Hishida 2007).

Mizoguchi studied this point, making reference to the research of Hishida, Takehiko Yoshimura (吉村武彦), and Nagato Satō (佐藤長門) (Yoshimura 1993, Satō 1994). According to Mizoguchi, initially the Miwahito clan, which was organized on the basis of the Hito system[19] (人制), gathered from various places to Suemura Village and engaged in the production of Sue ware. After the Bemin system[20] (部民制) was introduced, the Miwahitobe clan and the Miwabe clan were established in various places as economic bases for the Miwahito clan.[21] Furthermore, at first, the right of managing craftsmen, called Be (部), belonged only to the emperor, but the governing system of the Yamato Kingdom was enriched in the sixth century, and the right was entrusted to powerful clans. In the same way, the production of early Sue ware was managed directly by the emperor, but the right was later entrusted to the Ōmiwa clan, which presided over and controlled the Miwabe clan in the central district (Mizoguchi Y. 2009, Mizoguchi Y. 2012).

In recent years, as above, some researchers have insisted that the Miwabe clan played a central role in the production of Sue ware. It is certainly thought that the Miwabe clan was distributed in various places as the local ruling systems of the Yamato Kingdom spread to eastern and western Japan. In Chapter 4, I explained that the Miwahito clan, the Miwahitobe clan, and the Miwabe clan are related to the Hito system, the Bemin system, and the Kokuzō system[22] (国造制).

However, many other pieces of research also relate to who made Sue ware. Shō Ishimoda (石母田正) and Shōichi Narasaki (楢崎彰一) state that the craftsmen who made Sue ware were organized as Suebe (陶部) (Ishimoda 1955, Narasaki 1963, Narasaki 1965). According to Yoshimura, these craftsmen's title changed from Suehito (陶人) to Suebe (Yoshimura 1993, Yoshimura 2005, Yoshimura 2006). Toshiki Asaka (浅香年木) argues that the craftsmen of Sue ware were not organized as Suebe and were not included in the Bemin system (Asaka 1971). Up to this point, there has been no commonly accepted theory about this point of contention. In addition, Teruhiko Takahashi (高橋照彦) and Hiroyuki Sagimori (鷺森浩幸) have criticized other research in detail. They have cast doubt on the idea that the Miwabe clan and the production of Sue ware were directly connected (Takahasi 2007, Sagimori 2010). I also disagree with the research on this topic. In particular, the following points are questionable.

First, as I showed in Chapter 4, the names of places, shrines, and clans were distributed over a wide area of the Japanese islands, apart from a few provinces, as far north as Mutsu Province (陸奥国) and Dewa Province,[23] (出羽国) and as far south as Satsuma Province[24] (薩摩国). It is quite possible that the distribution areas of the ruined Sue ware kilns and the Miwabe clan could overlap, even if there was no connection between the two. In addition, according to Hishida's research, there is roughly one ruined kiln for every one or two counties, especially around the Kinai district[25] (畿内地方) and Setouchi district[26] (瀬戸内地方), at the time when the Sue ware kilns in local places were reorganized. Hishida describes this situation as a one-county one-kiln system (一郡一窯体制) (Hishida 2005, Hishida 2007). In these districts, it is even more likely that the distribution of the Sue ware kilns and the distribution of the Miwabe clan overlapped. Therefore, we cannot necessarily conclude that the Miwabe clan engaged in the production of Sue ware simply because this clan was distributed near the kilns.

Furthermore, Hishida points out that many clans could be engaged in the same handicraft. For example, the Karakanuchibe clan (韓鍛治部), the Kanatsukuribe clan (金作部), and the Oshinumibe clan (忍海部) were engaged in metal production, and the Yamabe clan (山部) and the Wanibe clan (丸部) were engaged in iron manufacturing. It is not clear, says Hishida, that only the Miwabe clan was engaged in the production of Sue ware; many clans, including the Miwa clan, were engaged in the production of Sue ware. The following evidence supports this idea.

- The characters "Kurahito" (内椋人) and "Oshisaka" (押坂) were inscribed on the surface of some of the Sue ware that was excavated from the ruins of the Ushikubi kilns (Ōnojō City Board of Education 2008a).
- The characters "Ujibe-no-Kimi" (宇治部君) were inscribed on the surface of some of the Sue ware that was excavated from the Site of Dazaifu Government Office[27] (大宰府政庁跡) (Kyūshū Historical Museum 1985).
- The characters "Awata" (阿〔波〕田) were inscribed on the surface of the Sue ware that was excavated from the ruins of the Natanikonpirayama kilns[28]

(那谷金比羅山窯跡) (Ishikawa Prefecture Center for Archaeological Operations 1985).
- The characters "Sakahitobe-no-Obito" (酒人首) were inscribed on the surface of the Sue ware that was excavated from the Sakurabasama-kofun Tumulus[29] (桜生古墳) (Shiga Prefectural Board of Education 1992)
- The characters "Ōshihitobe" (凡人部) were inscribed on the surface of the Sue ware that was excavated from the Kōzōji ruins of the second kiln[30] (高蔵寺二号窯跡) (Tatsumi 1999).
- The characters "Hatahitobe" (秦人部) were inscribed on the surface of the Sue ware that was excavated from the Ishigami ruins[31] (石神遺跡) (Nara National Research Institute of Cultural Properties 1993a, Nara National Research Institute of Cultural Properties 1993b).
- The characters "Hatahito" (秦人) were inscribed on the surface of the Sue ware that was excavated from the ruins of Kosugi distribution housing complex No. 16[32] (小杉流通団地No. 16遺跡) (Toyama Prefectural Board of Education 1980).

These inscriptions on the surface of the Sue ware indicate either the craftsmen who produced the items or the clans that managed their production. Therefore, rather than just the Miwabe clan, many other clans are thought to have been engaged in the production of Sue ware. If all the craftsmen were organized as part of the Miwabe clan, the clan should have been distributed intensively around Suemura Village, which took a principal position in the production of Sue ware at that time. However, in fact, various clans were distributed there, as I mention later.

In previous research, it was thought that the production of Sue ware was reorganized into a new system centering on the Miwabe clan, and that the right of managing the production of Sue ware was entrusted from the emperor to the Ōmiwa clan from the late sixth century to the early seventh century. However, we already know that the Ōmiwa clan's power was declining at that time.

As I mentioned in Chapter 2, Sakau (逆) was known as a favorite retainer of Emperor Bidatsu[33] (敏達天皇). He came from the Ōmiwa clan in the late sixth century, but he was murdered by Prince Anahobe (穴穂部皇子) and Mononobe-no-Moriya (物部守屋) because he disobeyed Anahobe's orders during Emperor Bidatsu's funeral.[34] At that time, Moriya killed not only Sakau, but also two of his children. After that, no members of the clan appeared in written history for half a century. Finally, Osazaki (小鷦鷯) appeared in the record of the early seventh century, but he was suspected of illicit intercourse with Uneme[35] (采女), so he committed suicide in 636 to assert his innocence.[36] Next, Fumiya (文屋) appeared in the era of Emperor Kōgyoku[37] (皇極天皇), but he committed suicide with Yamashiro-no-Oe-no-miko[38] (山背大兄王). The Ōmiwa clan rapidly declined in the late sixth century. Incidentally, the clan revived in the late seventh century when Koobito (子首) and Takechimaro (高市麻呂) played an active part in the Jinshin War (壬申の乱) in 672.

If the production of Sue ware was reorganized from the late sixth to the early seventh century, it is not clear why the Ōmiwa clan and the Miwabe clan were chosen, as there were many more powerful clans. It seems unlikely that the right of managing the production of Sue ware would be entrusted to the Ōmiwa clan, which was in a slump. Mizoguchi said that it was the Miwabe clan, whose members lived in various places, that was entrusted with the right to produce Sue ware, whereas the Ōmiwa clan was only entrusted with the right to manage it, so there would not be a problem even if the Ōmiwa clan declined further (Mizoguchi Y. 2012). However, in this model, if the Ōmiwa clan could not adequately manage the production of Sue ware, stable production could not be implemented in the kilns, which were located in various places.

From the above, it seems impossible that the production of Sue ware was reorganized into a new system centering on the Miwabe clan and that the Ōmiwa clan managed the system in the central district from the late sixth century to the early seventh century. We do know that the Yamato Kingdom sent troops to or advanced into western Japan, eastern Japan, and foreign countries, the Ōmiwa god was worshipped as a war god, and the Ōmiwa-jinja Shrine was established in various places, so the Miwabe clan was distributed across the Japanese islands. In times of peace or times of war, the Miwabe clan supplied commodities, a work force, and soldiers to the Ōmiwa clan, whose members lived in Yamato Province as the Tomo-no-Miyatsuko in the central district. In addition, the Miwabe clan worshipped the Ōmiwa god in various places. These were thought to be the primary occupations of the Miwabe clan. If the Ōmiwa clan and the Miwabe clan were engaged in the production of Sue ware, it is because they used Sue ware for religious services at Mt. Miwa and various other places.

## 7.3 Clans that lived in Suemura Village

Next, as stated earlier in this chapter, I explain how the Ōmiwa clan was involved in the production of Sue ware in Suemura kilns.

The ruins of the Suemura kilns can be found in six zones[39] (Tanabe 1981, Nakamura 2001): the Tōkiyama zone (MT, 陶器山), the Takakuraji zone (TK, 高蔵寺), the Toga zone (TG, 栂), the Kōmyōike zone (KM, 光明池), the Ōnoike zone (ON, 大野池), and the Taniyamaike zone (TN, 谷山池). These zones are separated by natural topography such as hills and valleys. According to *Wamyōruijushō*, the following villages were within these zones in ancient times (Nakamura 2001).

- Ōmura Village, Ōtori County (大鳥郡大村郷)
- Kamitsumiwa Village, Ōtori County (大鳥郡上神郷)
- Nigita Village, Ōtori County (大鳥郡和田郷)
- Shinoda Village, Izumi County (和泉郡信太郷)
- Ikeda Village, Izumi County (和泉郡池田郷)

Kamitsumiwa Village (上神郷) is identified as present-day Niwadani, Minami Ward, Sakai City, Ōsaka Prefecture (大阪府堺市南区上神谷). Nigita Village is identified as present-day Mikita, Minami Ward, Sakai City, Ōsaka Prefecture (大阪府堺市南区美木多). Shinoda Village is identified as Mt. Shinoda (信太山) in Izumi City, Ōsaka Prefecture (大阪府和泉市). Ikeda Village is identified as Ikedashimochō, Izumi City, Ōsaka Prefecture (大阪府和泉市池田下町).

According to *Gyōkinenpu*[40] (行基年譜), the Ōsue-in Temple (大修恵院) was in Takakura, Ōmura Village. In the present day, there is a place called Takakuraji (高蔵寺) in Naka Ward, Sakai City, Ōsaka Prefecture, and a place called Takakuradai (高倉台) in Minami Ward, Sakai City, Ōsaka Prefecture. It is also said that the Takakura-ji Temple (高倉寺) was known as the Ōsuesan-ji Temple (大修恵山寺) or the Sue-ji Temple (修恵寺) in ancient times. In the same way, the Ōniwa-in Temple (大庭院) was located in Kamitsumiwa Village, and the Hinooike-in Temple (檜尾池院) and the Hinooike-pond (檜尾池) were located in Nigita Village. In the present day, the place names Ōbadera (大庭寺) and Hinoo (檜尾) can be found in Minami Ward, Sakai City, Ōsaka Prefecture. According to *Oriin and history of Chōfuku-ji Temple*[41] (鉢峰山長福寺縁起), the Chōfuku-ji Temple (長福寺) was located in Kamitsumiwa Village. In the present day, the place name Hachigamineji can be found in Minami Ward, Sakai City, Ōsaka Prefecture.

From the above, many place names and temple names from ancient times still remain in modern place names. In terms of current administrative areas, Ōmura Village ranges from the southeastern part of Naka Ward, Sakai City, Ōsaka Prefecture, to the northeastern part of Minami Ward, Sakai City, Ōsaka Prefecture. Kamitsumiwa Village is the central part of the same ward. Nigita Village is in the northwestern part of the same ward. Shinoda Village is in the northern part of Izumi City, Ōsaka Prefecture. Ikeda Village is in the central part of the same city (Tanabe 1981, Nakamura 2001).

Among these villages, Kamitsumiwa Village, which included "Miwa" in its name, is thought to be related to the Ōmiwa clan. This place name was also written as "Miwa-no-Sato" (三輪里) in *Sumiyoshi-taisha Shrine Jindaiki*[42] (住吉大社神代記). The Sakurai-jinja Shrine (桜井神社), which is listed in *Engishiki-Jinmyōchō*, is identified as the Sakurai-jinja Shrine, in present-day Katakura, Minami Ward, Sakai City, Ōsaka Prefecture (大阪府堺市南区片蔵). This shrine was also called the Niwatani-hachimangū Shrine (上神谷八幡宮). The Kuni-jinja Shrine (国神社), which is listed in *Engishiki-Jinmyōchō*, was written as "the Miwakuni-jinja Shrine" (三輪国神社) in *Ōmiwabunshinruishashō*[43] (大神分身類社抄). This shrine was formerly located in Hachigamineji, Minami Ward, Sakai City, Ōsaka Prefecture (大阪府堺市南区鉢ケ峯寺), but it was later enshrined with the Sakurai-jinja Shrine (Shikinaisha Research Society 1976). Therefore, the Ōmiwa clan was closely linked to Kamitsumiwa Village, along with some other villages, which were included within Suemura Village.

Next, in *Shinsenshōjiroku*[44] (新撰姓氏録), the following clans, which were distributed across the area around the ruins of the Suemura kilns, are listed.[45]

### Article 7:『新撰姓氏録』和泉国皇別
(Kōbetsu,[46] Izumi Province, *Shinsenshōjiroku*)

池田首。景行天皇皇子大碓命之後也。日本紀漏。

### Article 8:『新撰姓氏録』和泉国神別
(Shinbetsu,[47] Izumi Province, *Shinsenshōjiroku*)

狭山連。同上(大中臣朝臣同祖。天児屋命之後也―筆者注)。
和太連。同上(大中臣朝臣同祖。天児屋命之後也―筆者注)。
民直。同上(大中臣朝臣同祖。天児屋命之後也―筆者注)。
韓国連。采女臣同祖。武烈天皇御世、被ν遣_韓国_。復命之日、賜_姓韓国連_。
和山守首。同上(神魂命五世孫天道根命之後也―筆者注)。
和田首。同上(神魂命五世孫天道根命之後也―筆者注)。
大庭造。神魂命八世孫天津麻良命之後也。
神直。同神(神魂命―筆者注)五世孫生玉兄日子命之後也。
大村直。紀直同祖。大名草彦命男机彌都彌命之後也。
荒田直。高魂命五世孫剣根命之後也。
民直。同神(天穂日命―筆者注)十七世孫若桑足尼之後也。
末使主。天津彦根命子彦稲勝命之後也。

### Article 9:『新撰姓氏録』和泉国諸蕃
(Shoban,[48] Izumi Province, *Shinsenshōjiroku*)

池辺直。坂上大宿禰同祖。阿智王之後也。
信太首。百済国人百千之後也。
取石造。百済国人阿麻意彌之後也。

Among these clans, the Ōmura clan (大村氏), the Arata clan (荒田氏), and the Sue clan (末氏) lived in Ōmura Village. The Ōniwa clan (大庭氏) and the Miwa clan (神氏) lived in Kamitsumiwa Village. The Nigita clan (和太氏), the Nigiyamamori clan (和山守氏), the Nigita clan (和田氏), the Mitami clan (民氏), and the Sayama clan (狭山氏) lived in Nigita Village. The Shinoda clan (信太氏) and the Toroshi clan (取石氏) lived in Shinoda Village. The Ikeda clan (池田氏), the Ikebe clan (池辺氏), and the Karakuni clan (韓国氏) lived in Ikeda Village (Yoshida 1970, Saeki 1982a, Saeki 1982b, Saeki 1982c, Saeki 1983a, Saeki 1983b).

It is thought that the Miwa clan, who included "Miwa" in the Uji[49] (氏), was related to the Ōmiwa clan. In addition, previous research has suggested that the Ōniwa clan was related to the Ōmiwa clan (Nakamura 2001). I will detail the Miwa clan later, and I explain the Ōniwa clan here.

In previous research, it was thought that this clan was originally named Ōmiwa and later changed its name to Ōniwa. I think that this assumption must be reexamined. The head of the lineage of the Ōmiwa clan was originally called the Miwa clan and came to be called the Ōmiwa clan after the era of Emperor

Tenmu[50] (天武天皇) [673–686]. It is not possible that the other clan was called the Ōmiwa clan, before the head of the lineage of the Ōmiwa clan was described in that way. If I base my argument on the above assumption, the Ōniwa clan was also previously called the Miwa clan, later changed its name to the Ōmiwa clan, and finally changed its name to the Ōniwa clan.

However, the earliest appearance of the Ōniwa clan in recorded history was in the wooden tablets (木簡) that were excavated from the site of Fujiwara-Kyō[51] (藤原京). Among the other wooden tablets that were excavated from the same area, there is one with the inscription "the year of Kōshi"[52] (庚子), which is 700, and another with the inscription "the first year of Taiho" (大宝), which is 701. Therefore, the above-mentioned wooden tablet was made around the year 700. This wooden tablet showed that the clan was called the Ōniwa clan around the year 700, because the clan name was written clearly on it.

Based on this example, it seems impossible that the clan name changed from Miwa to Ōmiwa and finally to Ōniwa during the course of only a few decades. In principle, an Uji name cannot be easily changed. Therefore, the clan must have been called Ōniwa initially. This clan was different from the Ōmiwa clan. Of course, these two clans interacted with each other through the Miwa clan whose members lived in Kamitsumiwa Village, but it is not appropriate to treat the Ōmiwa clan and the Ōniwa clan as if they are the same entity.

## 7.4 The Miwa clan of Suemura Village and the Ōmiwa clan

Now, I consider the Miwa clan. This clan was organized as the Tomo-no-Miyatsuko in its local area (地方伴造), in equivalence to the Ōmiwa clan, which was the Tomo-no-Miyatsuko in the central district (中央伴造). In the Bemin system, the Ōmiwa clan presided over and controlled the Miwa clan. However, the Miwa clan's genealogy was not connected to that of the Ōmiwa clan. This is noteworthy. In many cases, two specific clans with a political relationship also constructed a genealogical relationship with each other.

In Article 8, the Miwa clan is described as being descended from Kamimusuhi-no-Mikoto (神皇産霊命). This clan built a genealogical relationship with the Kii clan (紀氏) based in Nagusa County, Kii Province (紀伊国名草郡).[53] In addition, in Suemura Village, the Ōmura clan, the Nigiyamamori clan, the Nigita clan, and the Ōniwa clan constructed genealogical relationships with the Kii clan. How should the relationship between the Ōmiwa clan and the Kii clan be understood?

To the present day, many previous researchers have analyzed this controversial point. Kōyū Sonoda (薗田香融) and Akira Yoshida (吉田晶) point out that many clans that built genealogical relationships with the Kii clan were based in Ōtori County, Kawachi Province, so Sonoda and Yoshida assumed that the Kii clan engaged in the production of Sue ware at the Suemura kilns (Sonoda 1967, Yoshida 1970). Hiroyuki Sagimori supposes two possibilities. One is that the

Kii clan expanded in power to Izumi Province. Another is that the Kii clan constituted a group of immigrant craftsmen who had moved from the Korean Peninsula to Suemura Village. Sagimori insists that the Kii clan and the clans that lived in Suemura Village built their genealogical relationships with each other in this way (Sagimori 2010). Takayuki Nakabayashi (中林隆之) assumes that the Kazuraki clan (葛城氏) and the Kii clan originally managed the production of Sue ware at the Suemura kilns, but the Yamato Kingdom plundered the right to produce Sue ware from these two clans later (Nakabayashi 2006). Yūki Mizoguchi speculates that a certain group was previously controlled under the Kii clan, and that these two mutually built a genealogical relationship, but after the Ōmiwa clan came to manage the production of Sue ware at the Suemura kilns, the group came to be called the Miwa clan, because it was presided over and controlled by the Ōmiwa clan (Mizoguchi Y. 2012). In this way, some previous researchers have insisted that the relationships that were built between the Kii clan and the Miwa clan based in Suemura Village dated back to ancient times.

However, these relationships were not homogeneous. The Ōmura clan was descended from Kimitsumi-no-Mikoto (君積命, 枳弥都弥命). Kimitsumi was a child of Ōnagusahiko-no-Mikoto (大名草彦命). Ōnagusahiko was the fifth head of the Kii clan in *Kii-Kokuzō-Shidai*[54] (紀伊国造次第). The Ōmura clan was genealogically connected to the Kii clan through Ōnagusahiko. In the same way, the Nigita clan and the Nigiyamamori clan were the descendants of Amenomichine-no-Mikoto (天道根命). Amenomichine was a descendant of the fifth generation of Kamimusuhi, and Amenomichine was the first head of the Kii clan in *Kii-Kokuzō-Shidai* and *Kokuzōhongi*[55] (国造本紀). The Nigita clan and the Nigiyamamori clan were genealogically connected to the Kii clan through Amenomichine.

In contrast, the Miwa clan was descended from Ikutamaehiko-no-Mikoto (生玉兄日子命), who was a fifth-generation descendant of Kamimusuhi. The Ōniwa clan was descended from Amatsumara-no-Mikoto (天津麻良命), who was an eighth-generation descendant of Kamimusuhi. Ikutamaehiko does not appear in other historical documents. Amatsumara was described as having engaged in iron manufacturing.[56] In *Tenjinhongi*[57] (天神本紀), Amatsumara was the ancestor of the Mononobe-no-Miyatsuko clan (物部造氏), and the Ōmiwa clan was one of the clans that accompanied Tenson Kōrin[58] (天孫降臨). In any case, Ikutamaehiko and Amatsumara are thought to have originally been ancestors of the Miwa clan and the Ōniwa clan. These two clans were genealogically connected to the Kii clan through Kamimusuhi.

The clans that lived in Suemura Village differed in terms of how their genealogy was connected to the ancestors of the Kii clan. They can be divided into three groups, as follows.

Connected to the Kii clan through Ōnagusahiko

- The Ōmura clan

Connected to the Kii clan through Amenomichine

- The Nigita clan
- The Nigiyamamori clan

Connected to the Kii clan through Kamimusuhi

- The Miwa clan
- The Ōniwa clan

I have analyzed the genealogy of the Kii clan (Suzuki M. 2012). In my research, I have noted the following facts. Ōnagusahiko had a concrete name, including the place name "Nagusa," but Amenomichine and Kamimusuhi had abstract names, including "Ame"[59] and "Kami."[60] Ōnagusahiko appeared in a history book in the early eighth century, but Amenomichine and Kamimusuhi appeared in a history book in the early ninth century. A few clans connected their genealogy to the Kii clan through Ōnagusahiko, but many clans connected their genealogy to the Kii clan through Amenomichine, and many more connected their genealogy to the Kii clan through Kamimusuhi. Therefore, the Kii clan described Ōnagusahiko as its ancestor in the mid-sixth century when they expanded their power to the whole of Nagusa County. They described Amenomichine as their ancestor from the end of the seventh century to the early eighth century, when the Hinokuma-Kunikakasu-jingū Shrine[61] (日前・国懸神宮), which the Kii clan worshipped, came to receive special offerings from the imperial family. The clan described Kamimusuhi as their ancestor in the late eighth century to the early ninth century, when many clans connected their genealogies to the Zōkasanshin[62] (造化三神).

Furthermore, in *Shinsenshōjiroku*, the clans that were genealogically connected to the Kii clan through Ōnagusahiko were as follows:

- The Ōmura clan
- The Naosiirinoie clan (直尻家)
- The Takano clan (高野)

These clans lived in Izumi Province. They interacted with the Kii clan and so built their genealogical relationships when the Kii clan's power expanded to Izumi Province.

In contrast, twelve clans connected themselves genealogically to the Kii clan through Amenomichine.

- The Kii clan[63]
- The Nigita clan
- The Nigiyamamori clan
- The Ōmura clan
- The Shigeno clan (滋野氏)
- The Ōyake clan (大家氏)
- The Ōsaka clan (大坂氏)

*The legend of religious services* 125

- The Isoshi clan (伊蘇志氏)
- The Ōmura-no-Atai-ta clan (大村直田氏)
- The Mononobe clan (物部氏)
- The Takaya clan (高家氏)
- The Kawase clan (川瀬氏)

These clans lived in Izumi, Kawachi, Yamato, and Yamashiro Provinces, as well as Ukyō (右京) of the Heian-Kyō[64] (平安京).

In the same way, thirty-four clans connected themselves genealogically to the Kii clan through Kamimusuhi.

- The Kii clan[65]
- The Miwa clan
- The Ōniwa clan
- The Mononobe clan
- The Nigiyamamori clan
- The Nigita clan
- The Takaya clan
- The Kawase clan
- The Shigeno clan
- The Agatainukai clan (県犬養氏)
- The Ōkura-no-Okisome clan (大椋置始氏)
- The Takeda clan (竹田氏)
- The Hashihito clan (間人氏)
- The Hatakumi clan (爪工氏)
- The Tame clan[66] (多米氏)
- The Mishima clan (三島氏)
- The Amagatari clan (天語氏)
- The Kume clan (久米氏)
- The Ya clan (屋氏)
- The Tame clan (多米氏)
- The Hata-no-Kadobe clan (波多門部氏)
- The Wakayamatobe clan (若倭部氏)
- The Kamo clan (賀茂氏)
- The Kamo clan (鴨氏)
- The Shidori clan (委文氏)
- The Tanabe clan (田辺氏)
- The Tame clan (多米氏)
- The Tame clan (多米氏)
- The Inukai clan (犬養氏)
- The Mashikobenomatoki clan (目色部真時氏)
- The Tame clan (多米氏)
- The Kihara clan (城原氏)
- The Hatakumi clan (爪工氏)
- The Takumi clan (工氏)

These clans lived in Izumi, Kawachi, Yamato, Settsu, and Yamashiro Provinces, as well as Ukyo and Sakyō (左京) of the Heian-Kyō.

As above, several of these clans were distributed across a wide area, so it is not thought that these clans interacted with the Kii clan and built their genealogical relationships accordingly. If anything, a certain clan initially built a genealogical relationship with the Kii clan, and the relationship later expanded to the other nearby clans, or the relationship was shared with specific cognate clans.

If this situation applies to the clans living in Suemura Village, it is thought that the Ōmura clan built a genealogical relationship with the Kii clan. Sue ware, which was produced in Suemura kilns, was transported via the Ishizu-gawa River (石津川) (Nakamura 2001). The oldest of the Suemura kilns is in Ōmura Village, the site of the Ōmura clan's stronghold. These kilns in Ōmura Village took a principal position among Suemura kilns from the fifth century to the sixth century (Nishimura 1983, Higuchi Y. 1999, Nakamura 2001, Sugawara 2006, Sogō 2010).

In contrast, the Kii clan seized control of the port called "Kii-no-Minato[67]" (紀伊水門) in the fifth century. Ki-no-Oshikatsu (紀忍勝) was dispatched to Baekje (百済) to bring a diplomatic adviser in 583.[68] This was the first person to form the Kii clan (Shinokawa 1996, Suzuki M. 2012).

Therefore, the Ōmura clan transported Sue ware down the Ishizu-gawa River into Osaka Bay. On the other hand, the Kii clan engaged in diplomatic negotiations from the Kii Channel (紀伊水道) to the Seto Inland Sea (瀬戸内海). These two clans interacted with each other via sea traffic; together they built a relationship through Ōnagusahiko before the relationships between other clans developed.

In the case of the Nigita clan and the Nigiyamamori clan, they did not individually interact with the Kii clan. In Suemura Village, these clans had a territorial connection with the Ōmura clan, and the Nigita clan and the Nigiyamamori clan built their genealogical relationship with the Kii clan through the Ōmura clan. In the same way, the Miwa clan and the Ōniwa clan built a genealogical relationship with the Kii clan through the Ōmura clan, based on a territorial connection with the Ōmura clan in Suemura Village. Therefore, the Ōmura clan built a genealogical relationship with the Kii clan in the early days, but the Miwa clan built its genealogical relationship with the Kii clan later. The Miwa clan and the Kii clan did not have relations with each other in the fifth and sixth centuries.

As I mentioned in earlier chapters, many pieces of Sue ware have been excavated or discovered around Mt. Miwa. Most of these were produced in the Suemura kilns. Over seventy-four pieces of Sue ware are now owned by the Ōmiwa-jinja Shrine. According to Sasaki's report, 21 per cent of these items were made in the late fifth century, 35 per cent were made in the early sixth century, 24 per cent were made in the late sixth century, 3 per cent were made in the late seventh century, and we do not know when the other 17 per cent were made (Sasaki 1975, Sasaki 1976, Sasaki 1979a, Sasaki 1979b, Sasaki 1984,

Sasaki 1986). Sue ware, which was conveyed from Suemura kilns to Mt. Miwa, was used in large quantities in the fifth and sixth centuries but was not in use after the seventh century.

In addition, the Ōmiwa clan's power obviously declined from the late sixth century to the early seventh century because of Sakau's death. At that time, the Yamato Kingdom founded a new system of religious services. For example, the Ise-jingū Grand Shrine[69] (伊勢神宮) was worshipped, the Saikan system[70] (祭官制) was introduced, the Nakatomi clan (中臣氏) and the Inbe clan (忌部氏) became more significant, and the Hiokibe (日置部) and Himatsuribe[71] (日祀部) were established (Naoki 1951, Ueda 1964, Okada Seishi 1960, Okada Seishi 1962). Furthermore, the imperial palaces were relocated from near Mt. Miwa to the Asuka region[72] (飛鳥地方). As a result of these changing circumstances, Mt. Miwa's political and religious position in the Yamato Kingdom was altered dynamically, and the religious services at Mt. Miwa declined or changed gradually.

Therefore, it seems likely that the time during which the Ōmiwa clan interacted with the Miwa clan of Suemura Village to use Sue ware for religious services at Mt. Miwa was mostly from the late fifth century to the late sixth century, and the relationship became weaker year by year starting in the seventh century. At this point, the Miwa clan came to place more significance on the territorial connection with the Ōmura clan in Suemura Village, so the Miwa clan became incorporated into a genealogical relationship with the Kii clan through the Ōmura clan. This is why the Ōmiwa clan presided over and controlled the Miwa clan living in Suemura Village under the Bemin system, but they did not build a genealogical relationship with each other.

## 7.5 The nodal point of the genealogical relationships

It is necessary to understand the relationship between the Ōmiwa clan and Suemura Village specifically. The Ōmiwa clan interacted with the Miwa clan, whose members lived in Kamitsumiwa Village from the late fifth century to the late sixth century. The Ōmiwa clan did not always have constant, long-term interaction with all the other clans that lived in Suemura Village. The legend of Ōtataneko, which I mentioned in the introduction, explains the origin of the Ōmiwa clan, so it must be reexamined based on this historical background.

Regarding this legend, previous researchers have lumped many clans living in Suemura Village together as "the Suemura group" and have argued about whether Ōtataneko was the ancestor of the Ōmiwa clan or the ancestor of the entire Suemura group. For example, Atsumu Wada (和田萃) assumes that Ōtataneko was the ancestor of the Suemura group. He insists that the Suemura group produced and supplied Sue ware to the Ōmiwa clan. According to Wada, the Ōmiwa clan used these pieces of Sue ware for religious services at Mt. Miwa. This is how, he argues, the Ōmiwa clan and the Suemura group came to interact. The Ōmiwa clan came to preside over and control the Suemura group, and Ōtataneko, who was the ancestor of the Suemura group, was incorporated into the genealogy of the Ōmiwa clan (Wada 1985).

Hishida argues that the Miwa clan – whose members lived in Suemura Village and various other places – was engaged in the production of Sue ware, the Ōmiwa clan controlled the production, and this relationship was reflective of Ōtataneko's legend. He also insists that this legend explains the origin of the Suemura group's worship of the Ōmiwa god, in that this legend was handed down by the Suemura group (Hishida 2005).

Mizoguchi criticizes these pieces of research. He insists that if Ōtataneko was the ancestor of the Suemura group, the Ōmiwa clan would describe the neighboring clans' ancestors as their own ancestors, but it seems hard to accept this. If anything, the legend was handed down by the Ōmiwa clan. The legend explains that the Ōmiwa clan presided over and controlled the Suemura group, and it explains the Ōmiwa clan's legitimacy in leading the production of Sue ware (Mizoguchi Y. 2009).

However, as seen above, the Ōmiwa clan did not control the whole of the Suemura group. Nor did the Ōmiwa clan lead the production of Sue ware in the Suemura kilns and various other places. In Articles 1, 3, and 4, a person named Ikagashikoo (伊迦賀色許男命, 伊香色雄) made Hiraka (毘羅訶, 平瓮), or flat drinking vessels used for a religious service.[73] Some researchers have insisted that "Ikagashikoo" included the words "Ika" and "Ga." "Ika" means sacred and "Ga" means earthenware, so the name itself indicates the production of earthenware (Noda 1968). Furthermore, in Article 3, Ikagashikoo was the ancestor of the Mononobe clan (物部氏). In the context of these articles, the person who produced and supplied Sue ware to use for religious services at Mt. Miwa was not Ōtataneko, who was the ancestor of the Ōmiwa clan, but Ikagashikoo, who was the ancestor of the Mononobe clan (Shinokawa 2009). Unless this point can be explained logically, we cannot infer from the legend of Ōtataneko a direct relationship between the Ōmiwa clan and the production of Sue ware.

The alternative argument, regarding whether Ōtataneko was the ancestor of the Ōmiwa clan or of the Suemura group, is insignificant. Ōtataneko's place in the genealogy of the Ōmiwa clan seems a more important point. I focus on the following two facts.

First, although previous researchers have not paid sufficient attention to the fact, Ōtataneko was not the only ancestor of the Ōmiwa clan.

### Article 10: 『日本書紀』垂仁三年三月条
(March, the third year of Emperor Suinin, *Nihonshoki*)

時天皇遣下三輪君祖大友主、与二倭直祖長尾市一於播磨上、而問二天日槍一日(略)

### Article 11: 『日本書紀』仲哀九年二月丁未条
(Teibi, February, the ninth year of Emperor Chūai, *Nihonshoki*)

則皇后詔二大臣及中臣烏賊津連・大三輪大友主君・物部膽咋連・大伴武以連一曰(略)

### Article 12:『日本三代実録』貞観二年（八六〇）十二月甲戌条
(Kōjutsu, December, the second year of Jōgan [860], *Nihonsandaijitsuroku*[74])

従五位下行内薬正大神朝臣虎主卒。虎主者、右京人也。自言、大三輪<u>大田々根子</u>之後。虎主、姓<u>神直</u>、成名之後、賜_姓大神朝臣_。(略)

In these articles, Ōtomonushi is also described as the ancestor of the Ōmiwa clan. In particular, it is worth noting that he is described as being the ancestor of only the Ōmiwa clan. In contrast, in Article 6, Ōtataneko is described as the ancestor of both the Ōmiwa clan and other clans. According to Article 1 and *Nihonshoki*, the Kamo clan (賀茂氏) was included among these other clans.[75] In *Shinsenshōjiroku*, the ancestors of the Ōmiwa clan, the Kamo clan, the Miwahito clan, and the Mitoshi-no-Hahuri clan (三歳祝氏) are the same. In *Awagadaimyōjinganki*[76] (粟鹿大明神元記), Ōtataneko is described as the father of Ōtomonushi, Ōkamotsumi-no-Mikoto (大鴨積命), Ōtatahiko-no-Mikoto (太多彦命), and Ōmikemochi-no-Mikoto (意富弥希毛知命). Likewise, in this article, Ōmononushi is described as the ancestor of the Ōmiwa clan; Ōkamotsumi is described as the ancestor of the Kamo clan; Ōtatahiko is described as the ancestor of the Miwa clan, the Miwabe clan, and so on; and Ōmikemochi is described as the ancestor of the Miwahitobe clan. That is to say, Ōtataneko was the ancestor of all these clans. Among these clans, the Miwa clan was mentioned in Article 12. This article states that the Miwa clan comprised descendants of Ōtataneko.[77]

Based on the above articles, it is clear that Ōtomonushi was the ancestor of only the Ōmiwa clan and that Ōtataneko was a common ancestor of the Ōmiwa clan, the Kamo clan, the Miwa clan, the Miwahitobe clan, the Miwabe clan, and so on. In other words, Ōtataneko was placed at the nodal point of the different clans' genealogical relationships. This fact shows that Ōtataneko was created as an ancestor for the Ōmiwa clan and added to the genealogy that each clan handed down individually (Takemoto 2006, Suzuki M. 2012).

When were these relationships constructed? The first clue to answering this is that, in *Nihonshoki*, Ōmiwa-no-Takechimaro (大神高市麻呂) and Kamo-no-Emishi (鴨蝦夷) met and became retainers of General Ōtomo-no-Fukei (大伴吹負) in the Jinshin War.[78] The Jinshin War took place in 672 and included the largest battle in ancient times. Ancient clans generally confirmed, constructed, and reconstructed their genealogical relationships when they participated in military operations. In the Jinshin War, the Ōmiwa clan and the Kamo clan acted together. This shows that the genealogical relationship between two clans was constructed before the war.

In regard to the legend of Ōtataneko, as I mentioned in the introduction, the accounts in *Kojiki* and *Nihohshoki* were similar. Taro Sakamoto (坂本太郎) has said that this legend did not represent the first time the Ōmiwa clan's *Boki*[79] (墓記) was edited. This legend had already been written in *Kyūji* (旧辞), a now-defunct history book that was written in the sixth century and which was the source document of *Kojiki* (Sakamoto 1946). It is possible that the close relationship between the Ōmiwa clan and the Kamo clan dates back at least to the sixth century.

Furthermore, the Miwa clan was included in the genealogy of the Ōmiwa clan. This clan was established in various places according to the expansion of the local ruling systems in the Yamato Kingdom and was presided over and controlled by the Ōmiwa clan. In concrete terms, the Miwa clan, the Miwahitobe clan, and the Miwabe clan were organized from the mid-fifth century to the end of the fifth century, according to the introduction of the Bemin system. The Miwa-no-Atai clan and the Miwbe-no-Atai clan (神部直氏) were organized from the mid-sixth century to the end of the sixth century, according to the introduction of the Kokuzō system. After the organization of these clans, they began to interact with the Ōmiwa clan, and their interactions developed into genealogical relationships. Therefore, the Ōmiwa clan interacted with the Miwa clan and other clans from the sixth century at the earliest.

In this way, we can see that the genealogical relationships among the Ōmiwa clan, the Kamo clan, and the Miwa clan date back to approximately the sixth century. This time corresponds precisely with the time when the Ōmiwa clan was interacting with the Miwa clan living in Suemura Village. This fact should be noted.

Incidentally, it is also important to note secondarily that the ancient clans living in Yamato Province had other strongholds beyond Yamato Province. Major examples are as follows (Naoki 1964, Kamei 1976, Saeki 1981, Katō 1983, Shinokawa 2009).

The Ōtomo clan (大伴氏)

- The Suminoe territory[80] (住吉宅)

The Mononobe clan (物部氏)

- Eganonagano Village[81] (餌香長野邑)
- The Ato territory[82] (阿都家)
- The Shibukawa territory[83] (渋河家)
- The Naniwa territory[84] (難波宅)
- Arimaka Village[85] (有真香邑)

The Soga clan (蘇我氏)

- The Ishikawa territory[86] (石川宅)
- The Ishikawa secondary residence[87] (石川別業)

The Suminoe territory was in Suminoe County, Settsu Province[88] (摂津国住吉郡). Eganonagano Village was in Shiki County, Kawachi Province[89] (河内国志紀郡). The Ato territory and the Shibukawa territory were in Atobe Village, Shibukawa County, Kawachi Province[90] (河内国渋川郡跡部郷). The Naniwa territory was in Higashinari and Nishinari County, Settsu Province[91] (摂津国東

生郡, 西生郡). Arimaka Village was in Izumi County, Izumi Province[92] (和泉国和泉郡). The Ishikawa territory and the Ishikawa secondary residence were both in Ishikawa County, Kawachi Province[93] (河内国石川郡). These locations were key junctions of Settsu, Kawachi, and Izumi Provinces.

In regard to the Haji clan (土師氏), members of the clan lived in each of these places[94] (Naoki 1960).

- Haji Village, Tajihi County, Kawachi Province[95] (河内国丹比郡土師里)
- Haji Village, Shiki County, Kawachi Province[96] (河内国志紀郡土師郷)
- Haji Village, Ōtori County, Izumi Province[97] (和泉国大鳥郡土師郷)

In regard to the Nakatomi clan, the cognate clans were distributed in Ōtori County, Izumi Province, and Tajihi County, Kawachi Province. The clan had a base of operations there, and it engaged in the production and management of Sue ware, which was used for religious services (Sagimori 2006).

From these examples, it seems likely that the Ōmiwa clan had two strongholds. One of these was at the foot of Mt. Miwa in Yamato Province. The Ōmiwa-jinja Shrine was established there. Another was Suemura Village, particularly Kamitsumiwa Village, Ōtori County, Izumi Province. That location was also referred to as Mino Village or Sue Village in Articles 1 and 3. The Miwa clan, which was presided over and controlled by the Ōmiwa clan, lived there and supplied Sue ware to the Ōmiwa clan to use for religious services at Mt. Miwa.

Previous researchers have insisted that the Ōmiwa clan's stronghold was at the foot of Mt. Miwa and that there were other political groups in Suemura Village, and they have argued about the relationship between these two places. However, both of these places were equally important strongholds for the Ōmiwa clan. The previous arguments seem less relevant when we underline this.

Furthermore, the Kamo-jinja Shrine (鴨神社) was listed in *Engishiki-Jinmyōchō*, alongside the Sakurai-jinja Shrine and the Kuni-jinja Shrine. In modern times, this Kamo-jinja Shrine is described as the Kamota-jinja Shrine (鴨田神社) and enshrined with the Tajihayahime-jinja Shrine[98] (多治速比売神社), but the Kamo-jinja Shrine was said to have been originally located in Taiheiji, Kitaniwa Village (北上神村大平寺).[99] This location was at the site of the ancient Kamitsumiwa Village. In *Jingihōten*[100] (神祇宝典) and *Tokusen-Jinmyōchō*[101] (特選神名牒), the enshrined deity of the Kamo-jinja Shrine was Kotoshironushi-no-Kami (事代主神), and it was written that this was the same as the deity of the Kamotsuba-jinja Shrine[102] (鴨都波神社) in Yamato Province. According to *Engishiki-Jinmyōchō* and *Shinsenshōjiroku*, this Kamotsuba-jinja Shrine was worshipped by the Kamo clan. Therefore, the Kamo-jinja Shrine, which was located in Suemura Village, was also worshipped by the Kamo clan.

I cannot find a place name or clan that is related to the Kamo clan in Suemura Village in existing historical documents. However, as above, the Kamo-jinja Shrine in Kamitsumiwa Village was one of the Ōmiwa clan's strongholds in ancient times. This fact indicates that a certain clan,[103] which was presided over and

132  *The legend of religious services*

controlled by the Kamo clan, lived in or around Kamitsumiwa Village, and this place was similarly a stronghold for the Kamo clan, which engaged in the production and management of Sue ware for religious services at the Kamotsuba-jinja Shrine.

That is to say, the Suemura area, especially the area around Kamitsumiwa Village, was an important stronghold not only for the Ōmiwa clan but also for the Kamo clan, and these two clans interacted with each other through the production of Sue ware. In this way, these two clans built a close genealogical relationship.

This historical situation could also be applied to the Miwa clan. In ancient times, the Miwa clan lived in Kamitsumiwa Village and provided Sue ware, which was produced in the Suemura kilns, to the Ōmiwa clan. At that time, the members of the Miwa clan frequently visited the foot of Mt. Miwa to present Sue ware. Likewise, members of the Ōmiwa clan frequently visited Kamitsumiwa Village for instruction and to manage the production of Sue ware.

At first, these clans built a political and vocational relationship, but this developed into a genealogical relationship, and the Ōmiwa clan created Ōtataneko as their common ancestor and as the nodal point of their genealogies. Likewise, they created the legend of Ōtataneko to explain the origin of the religious services at Mt. Miwa. At that time, they chose Suemura Village as the stage of the legend of Ōtataneko, because they were actually interacting with each other in Suemura Village through the production of Sue ware. This is why, in *Kojiki* and *Nihonshoki*, Ōtataneko was described as being found in Suemura Village.

## 7.6 Conclusion

In this chapter, as the core of this book, I took up the most important argument in order to understand the religion and clans of ancient Japan. This is the legend of Ōtataneko. I have explained why Ōtataneko was found in Suemura Village, not around Mt. Miwa, despite the fact that he was the ancestor of Ōmiwa clan, which was based at the foot of the mountain. Furthermore, I have explained how the Ōmiwa clan was connected to the production of Sue ware in Suemura kilns. I noted the following points.

- There was no production system centering on the Miwabe clan. The original occupations of the Miwabe clan were worshipping the Ōmiwa god and conducting religious services in various local places, so they engaged in the production of Sue ware for its use in religious services.
- The Ōmiwa clan had a very limited connection to Suemura Village and its kilns. The Ōmiwa clan interacted with the Miwa clan, whose members lived in Kamitsumiwa Village, from the late fifth century to the late sixth century. The Ōmiwa clan did not interact in a constant or long-term way with all the clans that lived in Suemura Village.
- The Ōmiwa clan had more than one ancestor. Ōtomonushi was only the ancestor of the Ōmiwa clan. In contrast, Ōtataneko was the common ancestor

of the Ōmiwa clan, the Kamo clan, the Miwa clan, and others. Ōtataneko was created as a nodal point of their genealogies.

- Suemura Village, in particular the area of Kamitsumiwa Village, was a stronghold of the Ōmiwa clan, just like the foot of Mt. Miwa. Suemura Village was the place where the Ōmiwa clan, the Kamo clan, and the Miwa clan actually interacted with each other. Therefore, it was chosen as the stage of the legend of Ōtataneko, and he was described as being found there in the legend.

Until now, previous researchers have presented the Ōmiwa clan and the Suemura group as in binary opposition and argued about the relationship that Ōtataneko had with them both. However, Ōtataneko was the common ancestor for many clans, and Suemura Village was the stage where these clans interacted with each other. This helps us understand the legend of Ōtataneko more deeply and develop a more accurate understanding of the real images of religion and clans in ancient Japan.

## Notes

1 *Kojiki* (古事記) is a record of ancient matters in Japan. It was edited in 712.
2 *Nihonshoki* (日本書紀) is a chronicle of ancient Japan. It was edited in 720.
3 Sujin (崇神天皇) was the tenth emperor.
4 Princess Yamatototohimomoso-hime (倭迹迹日百襲姫命) was a daughter of Emperor Kōrei (孝霊天皇), the seventh emperor. She was later the grand-aunt of Emperor Sujin.
5 Today, the Ōmiwa-jinja Shrine is worshipped as the god of rice wine production.
6 Sue ware (須恵器) is a type of unglazed earthenware produced from the latter half of the Kofun period (古墳時代) to the Heian period (平安時代). The Kofun period was from the fourth century to the seventh century. The Heian period was from the end of the eighth century to the beginning of the twelfth century.
7 Tomo-no-Miyatsuko (伴造) referred to groups that served the Yamato Kingdom through specific occupations. Most of these groups were small or middle-sized clans.
8 Sasaki insists that the Ōmiwa clan comprised people from overseas (Sasaki 1975, Sasaki 1976, Sasaki 1979a, Sasaki 1979b, Sasaki 1984, Sasaki 1986). Takeshi Matsumae (松前健) and Masaaki Ueda (上田正昭), for example, agree with this (Matsumae 1975, Ueda 1976). However, I state in what follows that present research trends have shown that Sasaki's hypothesis cannot be supported as it stands. I cannot agree with it. In regard to this point, Machio Terakawa (寺川眞知夫) also criticizes Sasaki's hypothesis from the viewpoint of the indigenous people of the Ōmiwa clan (Terakawa 1992).
9 The change of dynasties theory (王朝交替説) was proposed by Yū Mizuno (水野祐). According to this theory, the imperial family in ancient Japan changed several times (Mizuno 1952).
10 *Wamyōruijushō* (和名類聚抄) was an encyclopedia edited in the era of Jōhei (931–938).
11 *Engishiki Jinmyōchō* (延喜式神名帳) is a record of Shintō shrines in ancient Japan. It was edited in 927.

12 Sakamoto insists that the Miwabe clan, too, played an important role in iron manufacturing (Sakamoto 1987).
13 The ruins of the Ushikubi kilns (牛頸窯跡群) are in present-day Ōnojō City, Fukuoka Prefecture (福岡県大野城市). Takuma Yogo (余語琢磨) insists that the production system in which the "Ōga-no-Kimi" (大神君) presided over "Ōgabe" (大神部) could also be found in this area (Yogo 1990).
14 The field-tax report of Hamana County, Tōtoumi Province (遠江国浜名郡輸租帳), was written in 740. It was included in *Dainihon-Komonjyo* (大日本古文書), 2–258.
15 The ruins of the Kosai kilns (湖西窯跡群) are in present-day Kosai City, Shizuoka Prefecture (静岡県湖西市).
16 The family register of Mino Province (御野国戸籍) was edited in 702. It was included in *Dainihon-Komonjyo* 1–114.
17 The ruins of the Minosue kilns (美濃須衛窯跡群) are in present-day Kakamigahara City, Gihu Prefecture (岐阜県各務原市).
18 Hishida uses the term "the Miwabe clan" as the general term for the Miwa-no-Atai clan, the Miwa clan, the Miwahito clan, the Miwahitobe clan, and the Miwabe clan.
19 In the Hito system (人制), the government moved people to the capital from various districts to serve the emperor as government officials according to their business and gave them the title of Hito (人). Hito means "person."
20 In the Bemin system (部民制), the government moved people to the capital from various districts to serve the emperor as government officials according to their business and gave them the title of Be (部). Be means "group." Furthermore, the government gave the title of Be (部) to people who stayed in their hometowns and supported the people who came to the capital to serve the emperor. Bemin was strictly called Be-no-Tami in Japanese. However, in recent works, it is common to refer to it using the sound of the Chinese character, "Bemin."
21 Mizoguchi has argued that the Miwahitobe clan was established as an economic base for the Miwahito clan, based on both the Hito system and the Bemin system (Mizoguchi Y. 2012). However, if the Miwahitobe clan was established after the introduction of the Bemin system, it should be referred to not as "Miwahitobe" but as "Miwabe." Therefore, the Miwahito clan was actually established already and was then reorganized after introduction of the Bemin system and was renamed the Miwahitobe clan as a result (Suzuki M. 2014).
22 In the Kokuzō system (国造制), the government appointed a powerful local clan as the chief officer of a region or the Kokuzō (国造) and granted it local rule. In return, the Kokuzō was required to supply goods, workers, and military power to the government. For example, in Kii Province, the Kii-uji clan was appointed as Kii-Kokuzō (紀伊国造) by the Yamato Kingdom. The Kokuzō was strictly called Kuni-no-Miyatsuko in Japanese. However, in recent research, it is common to refer to it using the sound of the Chinese character, "Kokuzō."
23 Mutsu Province (陸奥国) and Dewa province (出羽国) were in present-day Tohoku District (東北地方) in eastern Japan.
24 Satsuma Province (薩摩国) was in the western part of present-day Kagoshima Prefecture (鹿児島県).
25 Kinai District (畿内地方) indicates Yamato Province (大和国), Yamashiro Province (山城国), Kawachi Province (河内国), Settsu Province (摂津国), and Izumi Province (和泉国). In the present day, these provinces are Nara Prefecture (奈良県), Kyōto Prefecture (京都府), and Ōsaka Prefecture (大阪府).
26 Setouchi District (瀬戸内地方) is near the Seto Inland Sea (瀬戸内海). In the present day, this district indicates Hyōgo Prefecture (兵庫県), Okayama

Prefecture (岡山県), Hiroshima Prefecture (広島県), Yamaguchi Prefecture (山口県), Kagawa Prefecture (香川県), and Ehime Prefecture (愛媛県).
27 The Site of Dazaifu Government Office (大宰府政庁跡) is in present-day Dazaifu City, Fukuoka Prefecture (福岡県太宰府市).
28 The ruins of the Natanikonpirayama kilns (那谷金比羅山窯跡) are in present-day Komatsu City, Ishikawa Prefecture (石川県小松市).
29 The Sakurabasama-Kofun Tumulus (桜生古墳) is in present-day Yasu City, Shiga Prefecture (滋賀県野洲市).
30 The ruins of the second kiln at Kōzōji (高蔵寺二号窯跡) are in present-day Kasugai City, Aichi Prefecture (愛知県春日井市).
31 The Ishigami ruins (石神遺跡) are in present-day Asuka Village, Takaichi County, Nara Prefecture (奈良県高市郡明日香村).
32 The ruins of Kosugi distribution housing complex No. 16 (小杉流通団地 No. 16遺跡) are in present-day Imizu City, Toyama Prefecture (富山県射水市).
33 Bidatsu (敏達天皇) was the thirtieth emperor.
34 May, the first year of Emperor Yōmei (用明天皇) [586], *Nihonshoki*. Yōmei was the thirty-first emperor.
35 Uneme (采女) were beautiful maids of honor who served the emperor and prepared meals for him. They were presented to the emperor by local ruling clans of various provinces.
36 March, in the eighth year of Emperor Jomei (舒明天皇) [636], *Nihonshoki*. Jomei was the thirty-fourth emperor.
37 Kōgyoku (皇極天皇) was the thirty-fifth emperor.
38 Heishi, November, in the second year of Emperor Kōgyoku [643], *Nihonshoki*.
39 In addition to these six zones, some researchers include the Sayamaike zone (SY, 狭山池) or the Tomikura zone (TM, 富蔵) in the ruins of the Suemura kilns.
40 Tokio Shinkawa (新川登亀男) studied *Gyōkinenpu* (行基年譜) in detail (Shinkawa 1999).
41 *Origin and history of Chōfuku-ji Temple* (鉢峰山長福寺縁起) was edited in 930. This is included in the documents of Hōdō-ji temple (法道寺) No. 1 (Sakai City 1973).
42 *Sumiyoshi-taisha Shrine Jindaiki* (住吉大社神代記) was an ancient history book introducing the origin of the Sumiyoshi-taisha Shrine (Okimori et al. 2012). This shrine is in present-day Sumiyoshi Ward, Ōsaka City, Ōsaka Prefecture.
43 *Ōmiwabunshinruishashō* (大神分身類社抄) contains the records of the Sessha (摂社, auxiliary shrine) and Massha (末社, affiliated sub-shrines) of the Ōmiwa-jinja Shrine. It was edited in 1265. This is included in *Ōmiwajinja-shiryō* Vol. 1.
44 *Shinsenshōjiroku* (新撰姓氏録) was a newly compiled register of clan names and noble titles. It was edited in 815.
45 In addition to those clans, the Miwahito clan is listed in *Shinsenshōjiroku*, but this clan comprised foreign settlers from Goguryeo (高句麗). The relationship between these clans and the Ōmiwa clan is not clear. If this clan engaged in the production of Sue ware under the management of the Miwa clan, it is possible that some foreign settlers who brought techniques of manufacturing and producing Sue ware also were organized as part of the Miwahitobe clan.
46 Kōbetsu (皇別) refers to the social status of a clan whose members were descended from the imperial family. Ko means "the imperial family." Betsu means "branching."
47 Shinbetsu (神別) refers to the social status of a clan whose members were descended from a god. Shin means "god."

48 Shoban (諸蕃) refers to the social status of a clan whose members came from overseas.
49 Uji (氏) was an ancient family name showing the clan's stronghold or occupation.
50 Tenmu (天武天皇) was the fortieth emperor.
51 The wooden tablets are included in *Asuka-Fujiwara-Kyō-Mokkan* (飛鳥藤原京木簡) 2–1488. Fujiwara-Kyō (藤原京), in present-day Kashihara City, Nara Prefecture (奈良県橿原市), was the capital city of the ancient Japanese nation from 694 to 710.
52 The year of Kōshi (庚子) was the fourth year of Emperor Monmu (文武天皇) [700]. Monmu was the forty-second emperor.
53 In present-day Wakayama City and Kainan City, Wakayama Prefecture (和歌山県和歌山市, 海南市).
54 *Kii-Kokuzō-Shidai* (紀伊国造次第) is the genealogy of the Kii-uji clan (Teranishi 2003, Suzuki M. 2012).
55 *Kokuzōhongi* (国造本紀) is the record of Kokuzō, which was established in various local regions. This history book is included in *Sendaikujihongi* (先代旧事本紀) Vol. 10.
56 The record before the enthronement of Emperor Suizei (綏靖天皇), *Nihonshoki*. Suizei was the second emperor.
57 *Tenjinhongi* (天神本紀) is a record of ancient Japanese myths. This history book is included in *Sendaikujihongi* Vol. 3.
58 Tenson Kōrin (天孫降臨) is one of the most famous myths in ancient Japan. It describes how Ninigi-no-Mikoto (瓊瓊杵尊), who was the ancestor of the imperial family, descended from heaven to earth.
59 Ame (天) means "heaven."
60 Kami (神) means "god."
61 The Hinokuma-Kunikakasu-jingū Shrine (日前国懸神宮) is in present-day Wakayama City, Wakayama Prefecture (和歌山県和歌山市).
62 The Zokasanshin (造化三神) are the three gods of creation in the myths of ancient Japan. Their names were Amenominakanushi-no-Kami (天御中主神), Takamimusuhi-no-Kami (高皇産霊神), and Kamimusuhi-no-Kami (神皇産霊神).
63 This Kii-uji clan lived in Kawachi Province. This clan was the cognate clan of the head of the lineage of the Kii-uji clan based in Kii Province.
64 Heian-Kyō (平安京), in present-day Kyōto City, Kyōto Prefecture (京都府京都市), was the capital city of Japan from 794 to 1869. This is divided between the eastern side, or Sakyō (左京), and the western side, or Ukyō (右京).
65 This Kii-uji clan lived in Izumi Province. This clan was the cognate clan of the head linage of the Kii-uji clan based in Kii Province.
66 Some of these clans have the same name, such as the Tame clan, but they were different clans living in different places.
67 The record before the enthronement of Empress Jingū (神功皇后), *Nihonshoki*. April, the ninth year of Emperor Ōjin (応神天皇), *Nihonshoki*. Jingū was the wife of Chūai (仲哀天皇), the fourteenth emperor. Ōjin was the fifteenth emperor.
68 Teiyū, July, the twelfth year of Emperor Bidatsu, *Nihonshoki*. October, the twelfth year of Emperor Bidatsu, *Nihonshoki*.
69 The Ise-jingu Grand Shrine (伊勢神宮) is in present-day Ise City, Mie Prefecture (三重県伊勢市).
70 A Saikan (祭官) was an official priest who conducted Shintō rituals.
71 Hiokibe (日置部) and Himatsuribe (日祀部) conducted the imperial family's religious services, especially services related to the emperor. Other opinions about this also exist.

72 Near present-day Asuka Village, Takaichi County, Nara Prefecture (奈良県高市郡明日香村).
73 The first part of *Kojiki*. The record before the enthronement of Emperor Jinmu (神武天皇), *Nihonshoki*. Jinmu was the first emperor.
74 *Nihonsandaijitsuroku* (日本三代実録) is a history book that recorded the era of Emperors Seiwa (清和天皇), Yōzei (陽成天皇), and Kōkō (光孝天皇). It was edited in 901. Seiwa was the fifty-sixth emperor, Yōzei was the fifty-seventh emperor, and Kōkō was the fifty-eighth emperor.
75 The first book of the eighth part of Jindaiki, *Nihonshoki*. Jindaiki (神代紀) is part of the myth in *Nihonshoki*.
76 *Awagadaimyōjinganki* (粟鹿大明神元記) was the genealogy of the Miwabe clan based in Awaga Village, Asako County, Tajima Province (但馬国朝来郡粟鹿郷), in present-day Asako County, Hyōgo Prefecture (兵庫県朝来市).
77 Mizoguchi suggests that the members of the Miwa clan were not actually descendants of Ōtataneko; they used the name of Ōtataneko to try to connect themselves genealogically to the Ōmiwa clan because the Ōmiwa clan was powerful and the two clans had the same occupation (Mizoguchi Y. 2012). However, at that time, the Ōmiwa clan was only comprised of Shintō priests of the Ōmiwa-jinja Shrine, so it was not particularly powerful. If the Miwa clan members were not actually descendants of Ōtataneko, there would have been no reason for the clan to connect itself genealogically to the Ōmiwa clan. In *Awagadaimyōjinganki*, the other Miwa clan members were described as descendants of Ōtataneko. Therefore, the genealogy in this article was not created later by the Miwa clan. In fact, they had insisted on this genealogy, and their connection with the Ōmiwa clan, for a long time.
78 Kichū, June, the first year of Emperor Tenmu [672], *Nihonshoki*.
79 *Boki* (墓記) was a clan's genealogy. The specific order for editing and presenting a *Boki* was encoded in 691. Shingai, October, the fifth year of Emperor Jitō [691], *Nihonshoki*. Jitō was the forty-first emperor.
80 Teibō, September, the first year of Emperor Kinmei (欽明天皇) [538], *Nihonshoki*. Kinmei was the twenty-ninth emperor.
81 March, the thirteenth year of Emperor Yūryaku (雄略天皇), *Nihonshoki*. Yūryaku was the twenty-first emperor.
82 Heigo, April, the second year of Emperor Yōmei [587], *Nihonshoki*.
83 The record before the enthronement of Emperor Sushun (崇峻天皇), *Nihonshoki*. Sushun was the thirty-second emperor.
84 The record before the enthronement of Emperor Sushun, *Nihonshoki*.
85 The record before the enthronement of Emperor Sushun, *Nihonshoki*.
86 September, the thirteenth year of Emperor Bidatsu [584], *Nihonshoki*.
87 Kishi, December, the first year of Jōgan [877], *Nihondsandaijitsuroku*.
88 In present-day Sumiyoshi Ward, Ōsaka City, Ōsaka Prefecture (大阪府大阪市住吉区).
89 In present-day Fujiidera City, Ōsaka Prefecture (大阪府藤井寺市).
90 In present-day Yao City, Ōsaka Prefecture (大阪府八尾市).
91 In present-day Ōsaka City, Ōsaka Prefecture (大阪府大阪市).
92 In the southern part of present-day Ōsaka Prefecture.
93 In the southeastern part of present-day Ōsaka Prefecture.
94 *Dainihon-Komonjyo* (大日本古文書) 4–227. *Wamyōruijūshō*.
95 In present-day Matsubara City, Ōsaka Prefecture (大阪府松原市).
96 In present-day Fujiidera City, Ōsaka Prefecture.
97 In present-day Sakai City, Ōsaka Prefecture (大阪府堺市).
98 The Tajihayahime-jinja Shrine (多治速比売神社) is in present-day Miyayamadai, Minami Ward, Sakai City, Ōsaka Prefecture (大阪府堺市南区宮山台).

99 In present-day Taiheiji, Minami Ward, Sakai City, Ōsaka Prefecture, and Taiheiji Nishi Ward, Sakai City, Ōsaka Prefecture (大阪府堺市南区太平寺・堺市西区太平寺).
100 *Jingihōten* (神祇宝典) is a list of Shintō shrines. It was edited in 1646, and it included *Jingi Zensho* (神祇全書) Volume 2 (Saeki 1907).
101 *Tokusen-Jinmyōchō* (特選神名牒) is a list of shrines. It was edited in 1876 and published in 1925 (Kyōbusho 1925).
102 The Kamotsuba-jinja Shrine (鴨都波神社) is in present-day Gose City, Nara Prefecture (奈良県御所市).
103 The Kamobe-uji clan (鴨部氏) was the cognate clan of the Kamo clan in various places in ancient Japan. These clans were presided over and controlled by the central Kamo-uji clan. It is possible that there were also Kamobe-uji clans living in or around Kamitsumiwa Village.

# 8 Conclusion and future prospects

## 8.1 Introduction

In this book, I have discussed the religion and clans of ancient Japan. Specifically, I have investigated the Ōmiwa clan in Chapters 2–4 and the religious services conducted at Mt. Miwa in Chapters 5–7. The Ōmiwa clan's stronghold was at the foot of Mt. Miwa. It played an active part in constructing the ancient Japanese nation. I have tried to examine this clan by paying attention to the process of growth and distribution, the legends about it, its political position, and its genealogical relationships with other clans. In this chapter, I present the conclusions of each chapter and discuss the future prospects.

## 8.2 Summary and conclusion of each chapter

In Chapter 1, "History of study and points of controversy," I confirmed the changing process of the Uji (氏) and Kabane (姓) of the Ōmiwa clan as a basis for the discussion in the following chapters. I then reviewed previous research on the Ōmiwa-jinja Shrine and the history of studies on the Ōmiwa clan.

In Chapters 2, 3, and 4, I principally focused on the Ōmiwa clan.

In Chapter 2, "The rise and decline of the Ōmiwa clan," I investigated the fictional members of this clan and members of the clan in the fifth and sixth centuries, the early to mid-seventh century, and the late seventh century to early eighth century. I then analyzed their achievements one by one in detail and examined the general trends of the Ōmiwa clan. I can divide the trends into four phases: the rising period, the prosperous period, the decline period, and the revival period. The rising period was during the era of Emperor Yūryaku[1] (雄略天皇), in the late fifth century. The prosperous period was during the era of Emperor Kinmei[2] (欽明天皇) and Emperor Bidatsu[3] (敏達天皇), in the sixth century. The decline period was from the era of Emperor Yōmei[4] (用明天皇) to that of Emperor Kōgyoku[5] (皇極天皇), from the early to mid-seventh century. The revival period was from the era of Emperor Kōtoku[6] (孝徳天皇) to the era of Emperor Tenmu[7] (天武天皇) and Emperor Jitō[8] (持統天皇), in the late seventh century.

In Chapter 3, "The constitution of the Ōmiwa clan," I analyzed the relationship of the head linage of the Ōmiwa clan with the cognate clans and looked at the achievements and distribution of the cognate clans. The head linage of the Ōmiwa clan, its cognate clans, and other clans were reorganized according to politics and genealogy from the early eighth century to the early ninth century. The cognate clans were distributed across the territories adjacent to the capital and western Japan. Some clans were connected with each other through a territorial relationship. The distribution of the cognate clans was related to sea traffic. Some of the cognate clans' strongholds were of strategic importance to the Ōmiwa clan. The Ōmiwa clan built political and genealogical relationships with the cognate clans in these places.

In Chapter 4, "The dispersal process of the Ōmiwa clan," I extracted the place names, Shintō shrine names, and clan names related to the "Miwa" (神, 三輪) or "Ōmiwa" (大神, 大三輪) from ancient historical documents. I found that they were distributed throughout almost all the Japanese islands, and some of the clans overlapped geographically. If a related place name or a Shintō shrine name is found somewhere now, it is likely that the Miwa clan, who were presided over and controlled by the Ōmiwa clan, lived there in ancient times. When the Yamato Kingdom sent troops to or advanced into western and eastern Japan, or foreign countries, ancient people came to view the Ōmiwa god as a war god. They then established the shrines to worship the Ōmiwa god, and the Miwa clan (神氏), the Miwahito clan (神人氏), the Miwahitobe clan (神人部氏), and the Miwabe clan (神部氏) were established in various places to worship the god, according to the local ruling systems of the Yamato Kingdom, including the Hito system[9] (人制), Bemin system[10] (部民制), and Kokuzō system[11] (国造制).

In Chapters 5, 6, and 7, I focused on the religious services rendered at Mt. Miwa.

In Chapter 5, "Characterizations of the Ōmiwa god," I reexamined the basis of much of the previous research on this topic, which has assumed that the religious services rendered at Mt. Miwa could be split into two periods. This previous research claims that the imperial family worshipped the sun god and conducted the Kunimi ceremony[12] (国見儀礼) at Mt. Miwa from the fourth century to the mid-fifth century, when the religious services were discontinued. The Ōmiwa clan resumed religious services, worshipping the Ōmiwa god as the god of curses, in the mid-sixth century. However, there is no evidence that the Kunimi ceremony and the services for the sun god took place at Mt. Miwa. If anything, on the basis of ruins and relics that have been discovered around Mt. Miwa, we can see that the religious services were continuously conducted from the late fifth to the late sixth century. Furthermore, the Ōmiwa god had many characterizations, and they were indivisible by nature. Ancient people consistently worshipped the Ōmiwa god as a multilayered god.

In Chapter 6, "The transition of religious services at Mt. Miwa," I analyzed the relationship between the Ōmiwa clan and the religious services conducted at Mt. Miwa. The relics that were excavated and discovered around Mt. Miwa continued to be manufactured from the late fifth century to the sixth century, and no changes in their quality or quantity have been recognized, so it seems very unlikely that there was any interruption in the rendering of religious services during that period. In *Kojiki*[13] (古事記) and *Nihonshoki*[14] (日本書紀), the notation "Mt. Mimoro" (御諸山, 三諸山) was used when the religious services were actually being conducted at Mt. Miwa, in contrast to the notation "Mt. Miwa" (三輪山, 美和山), which was used when people's consciousness that the mountain had been a site for conducting religious services was fading. *Miwa-Takamiya-Kakeizu*[15] (三輪髙宮家系図) states that the April Ōmiwa-sai Festival[16] (大神祭) was begun by Kotohi (特牛) in the era of Emperor Kinmei, but this is not an original description, so we cannot trust this article unquestioningly. In fact, the fortunes of the Ōmiwa clan correspond to the quantity of relics that have been excavated or discovered around Mt. Miwa, so we can argue that the Ōmiwa clan continuously took charge of the religious services performed at Mt. Miwa from the fifth century to the mid-sixth century.

In Chapter 7, "The legend of religious services at Mt. Miwa," I explained why Ōtataneko (大田田根子) was found in Suemura Village (陶邑) in the legend about him and described how the Ōmiwa clan was involved with the production of Sue ware (須恵器) in the Suemura kilns (陶邑窯跡群). It is quite possible that the areas of distribution of Sue ware and the Miwa clan could overlap, even if there was no connection between the two. Not only the Miwa clan, but also many other clans, were engaged in the production of Sue ware. Researchers have stated that the emperor entrusted the right of managing the production of Sue ware to the Ōmiwa clan from the late sixth century to the early seventh century, but the Ōmiwa clan's power obviously declined over that time. Therefore, I cannot agree to the statement that the production system of Sue ware centered on the Miwa clan. Furthermore, the Ōmiwa clan interacted with the Miwa clan in Kamitsumiwa Village (上神郷) from the late fifth century to the late sixth century, but they did not have a constant, long-term interaction with all the clans living in Suemura Village. Ōtataneko was seen as the common ancestor of the Ōmiwa clan, the Kamo clan (賀茂氏), the Miwa clan, and other local clans. Both the foot of Mt. Miwa and Suemura Village were Ōmiwa clan strongholds. Suemura Village was the place where the Ōmiwa clan, the Kamo clan, and the Miwa clan actually interacted. Therefore, this place was chosen as the stage of the legend of Ōtataneko. This is why Ōtataneko was found in Suemura Village in the legend.

## 8.3 Future prospects

In the previous chapters, I focused on the Ōmiwa clan before the early eighth century. There are themes that I did not focus on, such as comparison with the religious services in other areas. I will analyze and explain these themes in the next book or on another occasion. I will now give an overview of the members of the Ōmiwa clan after the eighth century.

After the death of Takechimaro (高市麻呂), his younger brothers Yasumaro (安麻呂) and Komamaro (狛麻呂) led the Ōmiwa clan. In 698, Yasumaro was appointed as the Judge (判事); his official rank was Mudaishi (務大肆) at that time.[17]

### Article 1:『続日本紀』慶雲四年（七〇七）九月丁未条
### (Teibi, September, the fourth year of Keiun, *Shokunihongi*[18])

正五位下大神朝臣安麻呂、為﹍氏長﹍。

In this article, Yasumaro was appointed head of the Ōmiwa clan (氏長), and his official rank was Shōgoige[19] (正五位下). In 708, he was appointed Master of Settsu Province (摂津大夫).[20] When he died in 714, he was the Minister for Military Affairs (兵部卿) and his official rank was Jushiijō[21] (従四位上).

Regarding Komamaro, he was promoted from Shōrokuijō[22] (正六位上) to Jugoige[23] (従五位下) in 704.[24] He was appointed Master of Tanba Province[25] (丹波守) in 708, when his official rank was Jugoijō[26] (従五位上).[27] He was promoted from Jugoijō to Shōgoige in 711.[28] He was promoted from Shōgoige to Shōgoijō[29] (正五位上) in 715[30] and was appointed Master of Musashi Province[31] (武蔵守) in the same year.[32] During his continuance in office, he helped establish Koma County, Musashi Province (武蔵国高麗郡) (Suzuki M. 2015). It is unclear when he died, but approximately 170 years later, *Nihonsandaijitsuroku*[33] (日本三代実録) described his official rank as having been Shōgoijō, so this is thought to have been his rank when he died.

After Yasumaro and Komamaro, Oshihito (忍人) inherited the head linage of the Ōmiwa clan, followed by Ikaho (伊可保), Saigusa (三支), Nonushi (野主), and Chinari (千成) in succession. According to *Ōmiwa-no-Ason-Honkeichōryaku* (大神朝臣本系牒略) and *Takamiya-Kakeizu*, Takechimaro's son was Oshihito, Oshihito's son was Ikaho, Ikaho's son was Saigusa, Saigusa's son was Nonushi, and Nonushi's son was Chinari.

Oshihito was promoted from Shōrokuijō to Jugoige in 712.[34]

### Article 2:『続日本紀』霊亀元年（七一五）二月丙寅条
### (Heiin, February, the first year of Reiki, *Shokunihongi*)

従五位下大神朝臣忍人、為﹍氏上﹍。

In this article, Oshihito was appointed the head of the Ōmiwa clan in 715. Yasumaro had died the previous year, so Oshihito is thought to have been his successor. Ikaho was "the Ōmiwa-no-Kannushi" (大神神主) in 747, and he was promoted from Jurokuijō[35] (従六位上) to Jugoige the same year.[36] In addition, the rank of Jugoige was conferred upon Saigusa in 779,[37] Nonushi in 837,[38] and Chinari in 854.[39]

As above, Yasumaro's highest official rank was Jushiijō, and Komamaro's was Shōgoijō, but Oshihito's was only Jugoige. After him, Ikaho, Saigusa, Nonushi, and Chinari's highest official rank was Jugoijō.

Allow me to discuss Ikaho's description as "the Ōmiwa-no-Kannushi." After Ikaho was appointed as Ōmiwa-no-Kannushi, the title "the Ōkannushi" (大神主)

appeared in *Honkeichōryaku* and *Takamiya-Kakeizu*. "The Ōmiwa-no-Kannushi" denotes a priest of the Ōmiwa-jinja Shrine, and "the Ōkannushi" was used as its abbreviation. In *Honkeichōryaku*, Oshihito, Ikaho, and Saigusa are referred to as "the Ōkannushi." In contrast, in *Takamiya-Kakeizu*, all the leaders from Oshihito to Chinari were called "the Ōkannushi," and the title was inherited by the following generation after the medieval period.

These facts show that the members of the Ōmiwa clan were lower-class aristocrats after the eighth century (Abe 1975, Watanabe 1988), the head of the clan was given the title "The Ōmiwa-no-Kannushi" or "the Ōkannushi," they stayed away from the central political world, and they devoted themselves to performing priestly duties at the Ōmiwa-jinja Shrine.

After the eighth century, under the Ritsuryō system (律令制), various festivals, such as the Chinka-sai Festival (鎮花祭) and the Ōmiwa-sai Festival (大神祭), were held at the Ōmiwa-jinja Shrine (Nishiyama 1975). In the Chinka-sai Festival, the government did not worship the god directly by dispatching a messenger but did so indirectly through a local powerful clan. This was known as the "entrusted-type religious service" (委託型祭祀). Kaoru Fujimori (藤森馨) notes that this type of religious service had something in common with what was described in the legend of Ōtataneko (Fujimori 2008a, Fujimori 2008b). The Ōmiwa-sai Festival was conducted by the Ōmiwa clan in ancient times, and its origins have been explained in the legend of Ōtataneko.

Based on these facts, the Ōmiwa clan paradoxically tried to adapt to a new era by going back to its roots. The roots were precisely the religious services performed at Mt. Miwa, which their ancestor Ōtataneko had begun, and of which the clan had taken charge generation after generation. The members of the Ōmiwa clan absorbed the history of their ancestors, and they inherited and reinterpreted their own history for future generations. In this way, the Ōmiwa clan handed down its genealogy, legend, and religion to posterity.

Therefore, the Ōmiwa-jinja Shrine is of the greatest historical significance among the numerous Shintō shrines in Japan, and this shrine is indispensable in studying ancient Japanese history.

## Notes

1. Yūryaku (雄略天皇) was the twenty-first emperor.
2. Kinmei (欽明天皇) was the twenty-ninth emperor.
3. Bidatsu (敏達天皇) was the thirtieth emperor.
4. Yōmei (用明天皇) was the thirty-first emperor.
5. Kōgyoku (皇極天皇) was the thirty-fifth emperor.
6. Kōtoku (孝徳天皇) was the thirty-sixth emperor.
7. Tenmu (天武天皇) was the fortieth emperor.
8. Jitō (持統天皇) was the forty-first emperor.
9. In the Hito system (人制), the government moved people to the capital from various districts to serve the emperor as government officials according to their business and gave them the title of Hito (人). Hito means "person."
10. In the Bemin system (部民制), the government moved people to the capital from various districts to serve the emperor as government officials according to their

business and gave them the title of Be (部). Be means "group." Furthermore, the government also gave the title of Be (部) to people who stayed in their hometowns and supported the people who came to the capital to serve the emperor. Bemin was strictly called Be-no-Tami in Japanese. However, in recent works, it is common to call it by the sound of the Chinese character, "Bemin."

11 In the Kokuzō system (国造制), the government appointed a powerful local clan as the chief officer of a region or the Kokuzō (国造) and granted them local rule. In return, the Kokuzō was required to supply goods, workers, and military power to the government. For example, in Kii Province, the Kii-uji clan was appointed Kii-Kokuzō (紀伊国造) by the Yamato Kingdom. The Kokuzō was strictly called Kuni-no-Miyatsuko in Japanese. However, in recent research, it is common to call it by the sound of the Chinese character, "Kokuzō."

12 Kunimi (国見) was the ceremony in which the emperor supervised the territories under his control from a high place and ensured that the people lived peacefully.

13 *Kojiki* (古事記) is a record of ancient matters in Japan. It was edited in 712.

14 *Nihonshoki* (日本書紀) is a chronicle of ancient Japan. It was edited in 720.

15 *Miwa-Takamiya-Kakeizu* (三輪髙宮家系図) records the family tree of the Ōmiwa clan and their descendants, the Takamiya family (髙宮家).

16 The Ōmiwa-sai (大神祭) was the main festival held at the Ōmiwa-jinja Shrine.

17 Kiyū, February, the third year of Emperor Jitō [689], *Nihonshoki*.

18 *Shokunihongi* (続日本紀) was the history book that recorded the period after *Nihonshoki*. It was edited in 797.

19 Shōgoige (正五位下) was Senior Fifth Rank, Lower Grade.

20 Jinjyutsu, September, the first year of Wado [708], *Shokunihongi* (続日本紀). Settsu Province (摂津国) was in the western part of present-day Ōsaka Prefecture (大阪府).

21 Heijyutsu, January, the seventh year of Wado [714], *Shokunihongi*. Jushiijō (従四位上) was Junior Fourth Rank, Upper Grade.

22 Shōrokuijō (正六位上) was Senior Sixth Rank, Upper Grade.

23 Jugoige (従五位下) was Junior Fifth Rank, Lower Grade.

24 Kishi, January, the first year of Keiun [704], *Shokunihongi*.

25 In the center part of present-day Kyōto Prefecture (京都府).

26 Jugoijō (従五位上) was Junior Fifth Rank, Upper Grade.

27 Heishi, March, the first year of Wado, *Shokunihongi*.

28 Jingo, April, the fourth year of Wado [711], *Shokunihongi*.

29 Shōgoijō (正五位上) was Senior Fifth Rank, Upper Grade.

30 Heishi, April, the first year of Reiki [715], *Shokunihongi*.

31 In present-day Tōkyō Prefecture (東京都), Saitama Prefecture (埼玉県), and the northeastern part of Kanagawa Prefecture (神奈川県).

32 Jinin, May, the first year of Reiki, *Shokunihongi*.

33 Itsugai, March, the third year of Ninna [887], *Nihonsandaijitsuroku* (日本三代実録). *Nihonsandaijitsuroku* is the history book that recorded the era of Emperors Seiwa (清和天皇), Yōzei (陽成天皇), and Kōkō (光孝天皇). It was edited in 901. Seiwa was the fifty-sixth emperor. Yōzei was the fifty-seventh emperor. Kōkō was the fifty-eighth emperor.

34 Boshi, January, the fifth year of Wado [712], *Shokunihongi*.

35 Jurokuijō (従六位上) was Junior Sixth Rank, Upper Grade.

36 Teibo, April, the nineteenth year of Tenpyō [747], *Shokunihongi*.

37 Kasshi, January, the tenth year of Hōki, *Shokunihongi*.

38 Itsubō, April, the sixth year of Jōwa, *Shokunihonkōki* (続日本後紀). *Shokunihonkōki* was the history book that recorded the period after *Nihonkōki*. It was edited in 869.

39 Jinshin, January, the first year of Saikō [854], *Nihonmontokutennōjitsuroku* (日本文徳天皇実録). *Nihonmontokutennōjitsuroku* was the history book that recorded the period after *Shokunihonkōki*. It was edited in 879.

# Bibliography

Abe 1950: Takehiko Abe, "Clan Name and Genealogy of Kokuzō (Kokuzō no Sei to Keifu)," *Journal of the Historical Science Society (Shigaku Zasshi) 59–11*, 1950. Reprinted in: *Clan and Religious Services in Ancient Japan (Nihon Kodai no Shizoku to Saishi)*, Yoshikawa-Kōbunkan, Tōkyō, Japan, 1984.

Abe 1975: Takehiko Abe, "Ōmiwa Clan and Ōmiwa God (Ōmiwa-uji to Ōmiwa no Kami)," Publication Committee on Editing the Sourcebook of the Ōmiwa-jinja Shrine (Ōmiwa-jinja-shiryō), ed., *History of the Ōmiwa-jinja Shrine (Ōmiwa-jinja Shi)*, Yoshikawa-Kōbunkan, Tōkyō, Japan, 1975. Reprinted in: *Clan and Religious Services in Ancient Japan (Nihon Kodai no Shizoku to Saishi)*, Yoshikawa-Kōbunkan, Tōkyō, Japan, 1984.

Aboshi et al. 2003: Yoshinori Aboshi, Hironobu Ishino, Kunihiko Kawakami, Fuminori Sugaya, Yoshinobu Tsukaguchi, and Kōichi Mori, eds., *Archaeology of Mt. Miwa (Miwayama no Kōkogaku)*, Gakuseisha, Tōkyō, Japan, 2003.

Archaeological Institute of Kashihara 1984: Archaeological Institute of Kashihara (Kashihara Kōkogaku Kenkyūjo), ed., *Excavation Report of the Ōmiwa-jinja Shrine Precincts (Ōmiwa-jinja Keidaichi Hakkutsuchōsa Hōkokusho)*, Ōmiwa-jinja Shrine, Nara, Japan, 1984.

Archaeological Institute of Kashihara 2012: Archaeological Institute of Kashihara (Kashihara Kōkogaku Kenkyūjo), ed., *Summary Report of Ruins of Nara Prefecture (Naraken Iseki Chōsa Gaihō) 2011–2*, Archaeological Institute of Kashihara, Nara, Japan, 2012.

Asaka 1971: Toshiki Asaka, *Study of Handicrafts in Ancient Japan (Nihon Kodai Shukogyō no Kenkyū)*, Hosei University Press, Tōkyō, Japan, 1971.

Fujimori 2008a: Kaoru Fujimori, "Religious Services of Jingi-Ryō and Ōmiwa (Jingi-Ryō Saishi to Ōmiwa Saishi)," *Journal of Shintō Studies (Shintō Shūkyō) 210*, 2008.

Fujimori 2008b: Kaoru Fujimori, "Structure of Religious Services of Chinka-sai Festival and Saigusa-sai Festival (Chinka-sai to Saigusa-sai no Saishi Kōzō)," *Journal of Shintō Studies (Shintō Shūkyō) 211*, 2008.

Furuya 2010: Takeshi Furuya, "Religious Archaeological Study of Yamanokami Ruins Located in Baba, Miwa, Nara Prefecture (Naraken Miwa Baba Yamanokami Iseki no Saishi Kokōgakuteki Kentō)," Celebration of Shigetsugu Sugiyama's Seventieth Birthday Commemorative Editing Committee, ed., *Collection of Treatises of Japanese Basic Culture (Nihon Kiso Bunka Ronshū)*, Yūzankaku, Tōkyō, Japan, 2010.

Gotō 1997: Kenichi Gotō, "Kosai Kilns and the Kantō Districts (Kosaigama kara Mita Kantō)," Secretariat of Production History Society, ed., *Sue Ware of Eastern Japan (Tōgoku no Sueki)*, Production History Society, Tochigi, Japan, 1997.

Hashimoto 2002: Teruhiko Hashimoto, "Remains of Bead Production at the Foot of Mt. Miwa (Miwasanroku no Tamatsukuri Iseki)," *Ancient Culture of East Asia (Higashi Ajia no Kodai Bunka) 113*, 2002.
Higuchi K. 1927: Kiyoyuki Higuchi, "Huge Stones at the Top of Mt. Miwa (Miwasanchō niokeru Kyosekigun)," *Archaeological Study (Kōkogaku Kenkyū) 1*, 1927.
Higuchi K. 1928: Kiyoyuki Higuchi, "Study of Yamanokami Ruins Located in Miwa-chō, Nara Prefecture (Naraken Miwa-chō Yamanokami Iseki Kenkyū)," *Japanese Journal of Archaeology (Kōkogaku Zasshi) 18–10, 18–12*, 1928.
Higuchi K. 1959: Kiyoyuki Higuchi, "Establishment of Ōmiwa Ancient Culture (Ōmiwa Kodai Bunka no Kenkyū)," History of Ōmiwa-chō Town Editing Committee, ed., *History of Ōmiwa-chō Town (Ōmiwa-chō Shi)*, Ōmiwa-chō, Nara, Japan, 1959.
Higuchi K. 1971: Kiyoyuki Higuchi, "Miwa and the Ōmiwa Clan (Miwa to Ōmiwa-uji)," Publication Committee on Editing the Sourcebook of the Ōmiwa-jinja Shrine, ed., *Sourcebook of the Ōmiwa-jinja Shrine (Ōmiwa-jinja-shiryō) 3*, Yoshikawa-Kōbunkan, Tōkyō, Japan, 1971.
Higuchi K. 1972: Kiyoyuki Higuchi, "Mt. Miwa (Miwayama)," Iwao Ōba, ed., *Lectures on Shintō Archaeology (Shintō Kōkogaku Kōza) 5*, Yūzankaku, Tōkyō, Japan, 1972.
Higuchi K. 1975: Kiyoyuki Higuchi, "Archaeological Background of Sacred Mountain (Shintaisan no Kōkogakutekihaikei)," Publication Committee on Editing the Sourcebook of the Ōmiwa-jinja Shrine (Ōmiwa-jinja-shiryō), ed., *History of Ōmiwa-jinja Shrine (Ōmiwa-jinja Shi*, Yoshikawa-Kōbunkan, Tōkyō, Japan, 1975.
Higuchi K. 1977: Kiyoyuki Higuchi, "Japanese Mythology and the Ōmiwa Clan (Nihon Shinwa to Miwa-uji)," *Lectures on Japanese Mythology (Kōza Nihon no Shinwa) 8*, Yūseidō Shuppan, Tōkyō, Japan, 1977.
Higuchi K. 1990: Kiyoyuki Higuchi, "Mt. Miwa as Sacred Mountain and Iwakura (Shintaisan Miwayama to Iwakura)," Religious Association of Tōkyō Miwa Ikazuchi, ed., *Mt. Miwa as Village of God (Shinkyō Miwayama)*, Dōyūkan, Tōkyō, Japan, 1990.
Higuchi, Y. 1999: Yoshifumi Higuchi, "Recent Results of the Archaeological Study of Sue Village, Chinu Region (Chinu no Agata no Suemura no Saishin no Kōkogakutekiseika kaea)," *Sakai City Museum Research Bulletin (Sakaishi Hakubutukan Hō) 18*, 1999.
Hishida 2005: Tetsuo Hishida, "Producer of Sue Ware (Sueki no Seisansha)," Mahito Uehara, Taichirō Shiraishi, Shinji Yoshikawa, and Takehiko Yoshimura, eds., *Ancient History of the Japanese Islands (Rettō no Kodaishi) 4*, Iwanamishoten, Tōkyō, Japan, 2005.
Hishida 2007: Tetsuo Hishida, *Archaeology of Formation of the Ancient Japanese Nation (Kodai Nihon Kokka Keisei no Kōkogaku)*, Kyōto University Press, Kyōto, Japan, 2007.
Hōjō 2005: Katsutaka Hōjō, "Curse, Disease, Buddha and Gods (Tatari Byōki Busshin)," New Ancient History Society, ed., *Ancient History of Kingship and Faith (Ōken to Shinkō no Kodishi)*, Yoshikawa-Kōbunkan, Tōkyō, Japan, 2005.
Hozumi 2013: Hiromasa Hozumi, "Archaeological Interpretation of Religious Services at Mt. Miwa (Miwayama Saishi no Kōkogakuteki Kaishaku)," *Ōmiwa 125*, Shrine Office of the Ōmiwa-jinja Shrine, Nara, Japan, 2013.
Ikebe 1972: Wataru Ikebe, "Local Ōmiwa-jinja Shrines in Ancient Japan (Kodai niokeru Chihō no Ōmiwa-jinja)," *Ōmiwa 42*, Shrine Office of the Ōmiwa-jinja

Shrine, Nara, Japan, 1972. Reprinted in: *Study of Ancient Shrines (Kodai Jinjashi Ronkō)*, Yoshikawa-Kōbunkan, Tōkyō, Japan, 1989.

Ikeda 1971: Genta Ikeda, "Characteristics of the Ōmiwa God and the Guardian Spirit (Miwa no Kami no Shokeitai to Hogo Seirei)," *Ancient Culture (Kodai Bunka) 23*, 1971. Reprinted in: *Study of Folklore and Culture in Ancient Japan (Kodai Nihon Minzoku Bunka Ronkō)*, Gakuseisha, Tōkyō, Japan, 1979.

Ikeda 1975: Genta Ikeda, "Enshrinement of the Ōmiwa-jinja Shrine *(Ōmiwa-jinja no Chinza),"* Publication Committee on Editing the Sourcebook of the Ōmiwa-jinja Shrine (Ōmiwa-jinja-shiryō), ed., *History of Ōmiwa-jinja Shrine (Ōmiwa-jinja Shi)*, Yoshikawa-Kōbunkan, Tōkyō, Japan, 1975.

Ikeda 1990: Genta Ikeda, "Mt. Miwa in Ancient History (Kodaishi no Naka no Miwayama)," Religious Association of Tōkyō Miwa Ikazuchi, ed., *Mt. Miwa as Village of God (Shinkyō Miwayama)*, Dōyūkan, Tōkyō, Japan, 1990.

Inobe 1983: Jūichirō Inobe, "Ōtataneko and the Ōmiwa Clan (Ōtataneko to Miwa-no-Kimi)," *Japanese History (Nihon Rekishi) 418*, 1983. Reprinted in: *Kojiki Nihonshoki and Ancient Legend (Kiki to Kodai Denshō)*, Yoshikawa-Kōbunkan, Tōkyō, Japan, 1986.

Inoue 1951: Mitsusada Inoue, "The Establishment of the Kokuzō System (Kokuzōsei no Seiritsu)," *Journal of the Historical Science Society (Shigaku Zasshi) 60-11*, 1951. Reprinted in: *Selections from Mitsusada Inoue's Works (Inoue Mitsusada Chosakushū) 4*, Iwanamishoten, Tōkyō, Japan, 1985.

Inoue 1971: Mitsusada Inoue, "The Ancient Japanese Nation and Buddhism (Nihon Kodai no Kokka to Bukkyō)," Iwanamishoten, Tōkyō, Japan, 1971. Reprinted in: *Selections from Mitsusada Inoue's Works (Inoue Mitsusada Chosakushū) 8*, Iwanamishoten, Tōkyō, Japan, 1986.

Ishikawa Prefecture Center for Archaeological Operations 1985: Ishikawa Prefecture Center for Archaeological Operations, ed., *Archaeological Survey Summary Report (Maizō Bunkazai Chōsa Gaihō) FY1984*, Ishikawa Prefecture Center for Archaeological Operations, Ishikawa, Japan, 1985.

Ishimoda 1955: Shō Ishimoda, "Ancient Society and Culture Based on Material Things (Kodai Shakai to Busshitsu Bunka)," Shuichi Gotō and Shō Ishimoda, eds., *Lectures on Japanese Archaeology (Nihon Kōkogaku Kōza) 7*, Kawadeshobō, Tōkyō, Japan, 1955. Reprinted in: *Selections from Shō Ishimoda's Works (Shō Ishimoda Chosakushū) 2*, Iwanamishoten, Tōkyō, Japan, 1988.

Ishino 1977: Hronobu Ishino, "Ritual Form from the Fourth to Fifth Century and Development of the Yamato Kingdom (Shi Go Seiki no Saishi Keitai to Ōken no Shinchō)," *Historia 75*, 1977.

Ishino et al. 2008: Hironobu Ishino, Makoto Ueno, Kenichi Okamoto, Masano Sugano, Kazuhiro Tatsumi, Yoshinobu Tsukaguchi, and Kōichi Mori, eds., *Mt. Miwa and Ancient Japanese History (Miwayama to Nihon Kodaisi)*, Gakuseisha, Tōkyō, Japan, 2008.

Kadowaki 1984: Teiji Kadowaki, *Kazuraki and the Ancient Nation (Kazuraki to Kodai Kokka)*, Kyōikusha, Tōkyō, Japan, 1984.

Kageyama 1971: Haruki Kageyama, "Study of the Old Illustration of the Ōmiwa-jinja Shrine (Ōmiwa-jinja Koezu nitsuite)," Publication Committee on Editing the Sourcebook of the Ōmiwa-jinja Shrine, ed., *Sourcebook of the Ōmiwa-jinja Shrine (Ōmiwa-jinja-shiryō) 3*, Yoshikawa-Kōbunkan, Tōkyō, Japan, 1971.

Kamei 1976: Kiichirō Kamei, "Yamato River and Mononobe Clan (Yamatogawa to Mononobe-uji)," *Study of Nihonshoki (Nihonshoki Kenkyū) 9*, 1976.

## 148 Bibliography

Kanō 1993: Hisashi Kanō, "The Bemin System and the Kokuzō System (Beminsei to Kokuzōsei)," Naohiro Asao, Yoshihiko Amino, Susumu Ishii, Masanao Kano, Shōhachi Hayakawa, and Yoshio Yasumaru, eds., *Iwanami Lectures on Japanese History (Iwanami Kōza Nihon Tsūshi) 2*, Iwanamishoten, Tōkyō, Japan, 1993.

Kasai et al. 2008: Toshimitsu Kasai, Hiroshi Kanaseki, Minoru Senda, Yoshinobu Tsukaguchi, Haruto Maeda, and Atsumu Wada, eds., *Mt. Miwa and Himiko and Emperor Jinmu (Miwayama to Himiko Jinmu Tennō)*, Gakuseisha, Tōkyō, Japan, 2008.

Katō 1973: Kenkichi Katō, "Study of Establishment of Plural Names (Fukusei Seiritsu nikansuru Ichikōsatsu)," *Journal of Shokunihongi (Shokunihongi Kenkyū) 168*, 1973. Reprinted in: *Yamato Kingdom and Ancient Clan (Yamato Seiken to Kodai Shizoku)*, Yoshikawa-Kōbunkan, Tōkyō, Japan, 1991.

Katō 1983: Kenkichi Katō, *Soga Clan and Yamato Kingdom (Soga-uji to Yamato Ōken)*, Yoshikawa-Kōbunkan, Tōkyō, Japan, 1983.

Katō 1986: Kenkichi Katō, "Taifu System and Clans Appointed Taifu (Taifusei to Taifu Sennin Shizoku)," Second Kyōritsu Girls Junior and Senior High School Research Bulletin (Kyōritsu Daini Chūgaku Kōtōgakkō Kenkyū Ronshū) 9, 1986. Reprinted in: *Yamato Kingdom and Ancient Clan (Yamato Ōken to Kodai Shizoku)*, Yoshikawa-Kōbunkan, Tōkyō, Japan, 1991.

Katō 2004: Kenkichi Katō, "Nihonshoki and Its Original Historical Materials (Nihonshoki to sono Genshiryō)," *Journal of Japanese History (Nihonshi Kenkyū) 498*, 2004.

Kishi 1957: Toshio Kishi, "Historic Significance of Empress Kōmyō (Kōmyō Ritsugō no Shiteki Igi)," *Historia 20*, 1957. Reprinted in: *Study of Ancient Japanese Political History (Nihon Kodai Seijishi no Kenkyū)*, Hanawashobō, Tōkyō, Japan, 1966.

Kobayashi 1994: Toshio Kobayashi, "Tennōrei and Enthronement Ceremonies (Tennōrei to Sokuigirei)," A *Basic Study of the Ancient Emperor System (Kodai Tennōsei no Kisotekikenkyū)*, Azekurashobō, Tōkyō, Japan, 1994.

Koike 1997: Kazue Koike, "Ritual Sites around Mt. Miwa (Miwayama Shūhen no Saishi Iseki)," Society for the Study of Mt. Miwa and Culture, ed., *Kannabi, Ōmiwa and Miwamyōjin*, Tōhōshuppan, Ōsaka, Japan, 1997.

Kumagai 1985: Kimio Kumagai, "Oath of Emishi (Emishi no Seiyaku)," *Collection of Treatises of Ancient Nara (Nara Kodaishi Ronshū) 1*, Shinyōsha, Kyōto, Japan, 1985.

Kumagai 1991: Kimio Kumagai, "Emishi, Royal Palace and Kingdom (Emishi to Ōkyu to Ōken to)," *Collection of Treatises of Ancient Nara (Nara Kodaishi Ronshū) 2*, Shinyōsha, Kyōto, Japan, 1991.

Kumagai 1979: Kimio Kumagai, "Establishment of Jibushō (Jibushō no Seiritsu)," *Journal of the Historical Science Society (Shigaku Zasshi) 88–4*, 1979.

Kumagai 2001: Kimio Kumagai, *Japanese History (Nihon no Rekishi) 3*, Kōdansha, Tōkyō, Japan, 2001.

Kuramoto 1991: Kazuhiro Kuramoto, "Establishment of Clan Consultation System (Shizoku Gōgisei no Seiritsu)," *Historia 131*, 1991. Reprinted in: *Structure of the Government at the Time When the Ancient Japanese Nation Was Formed (Nihon Kodai Kokka Seiritsuki no Seikenkōzō)*, Yoshikawa-Kōbunkan, Tōkyō, Japan, 1997.

Kyōbusho 1925: Kyōbusho, ed., *Tokusen-Jinmyōchō*, Isobekōyōdō, Tōkyō, Japan, 1925. Reprinted in: Kyōbusho, ed., *Tokusen-Jinmyōchō*, Shibunkaku, Kyōto, Japan, 1972.

Kyūshū Historical Museum 1985: Kyūshū Historical Museum, ed., *Archaeological Survey Summary Report of Site of Dazaifu Government Office (Dazaifu Hakkutsu Chōsa Gaihō) FY1984*, Kyūshū Historical Museum, Dazaifu, Japan, 1985.

Maeda 2006: Haruto Maeda, *Mt. Miwa (Miwayama)*, Gakuseisha, Tōkyō, Japan, 2006.
Maekawa 1986: Akihisa Maekawa, "The Eastern Management of the Yamato Kingdom and the Ise-jingū Grand Shrine (Yamato Seiken no Tōgoku Keiei to Ise Jingū)," *Study of Clan and Kingdom in Ancient Japan (Nihon Kodai Shizoku to Ōken no Kenkyū)*, Hōsei Daigaku Shuppankyoku, Tōkyō, Japan, 1986.
Maenosono 1986: Ryoichi Maenosono, *Criticism of the Change-of-Dynasties Theory (Kodai Ōchokōtaisetsu Hihan)*, Yoshikawa-Kōbunkan, Tōkyō, Japan, 1986.
Matsukura 1985: Fumihiko Matsukura, "Mt. Mimoro and Mt. Miwa (Mimoroyama to Miwayama)," *Study of Nihonshoki (Nihonshoki Kenkyū) 13*, 1985.
Matsukura 1991: Fumihiko Matsukura, "Mt. Mimoro in Miwa (Miwa no Mimoroyama)," *Ōmiwa 81*, Shrine Office of the Ōmiwa-jinja Shrine, Nara, Japan, 1991.
Matsumae 1975: Ken Matsumae, "Legend of Mt. Miwa and the Ōmiwa Clan (Miwayama Densetsu to Ōmiwa Uji)," *Yamanobe 19*, 1975. Reprinted in: *Myth and Legend of the Yamato Kingdom (Yamato Kokka to Shinwa Denshō)*, Yūzankaku, Tōkyō, Japan, 1986.
Masuda 1976: Katsumi Masuda, "Invasion of Mono God (Monogami Shūrai)," *Island of Secret Ceremony (Higi no Shima)*, Chikumashobō, Tōkyō, Japan, 1976.
Mizoguchi, M. 1982: Mutsuko Mizoguchi, *Establishment of Genealogy of Ancient Japanese Clans (Nihon Kodai Shizoku Keifu no Seiritsu)*, Gakusyūin, Tōkyō, Japan, 1982.
Mizoguchi, Y. 2009: Yūki Mizoguchi, "Miwa Clan and Ruins of Suemura Kilns (Miwa Kei Shizoku to Suemurakoyōsekigun)," *Journal of Kokugakuin University (Kokugakuin Zasshi) 110–7*, 2009. Reprinted in: *Regional and Social Integration of Ancient Japan (Nihon Kodai no Chiiki to Shakai Tōgō)*, Yoshikawa-Kōbunkan, Tōkyō, Japan, 2015.
Mizoguchi, Y. 2012: Yūki Mizoguchi, "Miwa Clan and Reorganization of Sue Ware Production (Miwa-no-Kimi to Sueki Seisan no Saihen)," *Journal of Japanese History (Kokushigaku) 206, 207*, 2010. Reprinted in: *Regional and Social Integration of Ancient Japan (Nihon Kodai no Chiiki to Shakai Tōgō)*, Yoshikawa-Kōbunkan, Tōkyō, Japan, 2015.
Mizuno 1952: Yū Mizuno, *Introduction to the Theory on the History of Ancient Dynasties in Japan (Nihon Kodai Ōchō Shiron Josetsu)*, Tachikawa, Tōkyō, Japan, 1952. Reprinted in: *Selections from Yū Mizuno's Works (Mizuno Yū Chosakushū) 1*, Waseda University Press, Tōkyō, Japan, 1992.
Mori 1999: Hiromichi Mori, *Solving the Enigma of Nihonshoki (Nihonshoki no Nazo wo Toku)*, Chūōkōronshinsha, Tōkyō, Japan, 1999.
Moriya 1968: Toshihiko Moriya, "Study of Episode 25 in Volume 1 (Jōkan Dai25en Kō)," *Shintō Studies (Shintō Gaku) 59*, 1968. Reprinted in: *Study of Nihonryōiki (Nihonryōiki no Kenkyū)*, Miyaishoten, Tōkyō, Japan, 1974.
Naitō 1958: Kankichi Naitō, "Hōkan and Rikan of Ōmiryō (Ōmiryō no Hōkan Rikan nitsuite)," *Journal of Law and Politics (Hōgaku Zasshi) 4–1*, 1958.
Nakabayashi 2006: Takayuki Nakabayashi, "Kamitsukenu Clan and Izumi Province in Ancient Times (Kodai Izumi Chiiki to Kamitsukenu Kei Shizoku)," *Izumi City Historical Review (Izumishi Shi Kiyō) 11*, 2006.
Nakamura 1994: Ikuo Nakamura, *God and Kingship in Japan (Nihon no Kami to Ōken)*, Hōzōkan, Tōkyō Japan, 1994.
Nakamura 2001: Hiroshi Nakamura, *Historical Study of Ruins of Suemura Kilns in Izumi Province (Izumi Suemurayō no Rekishiteki Kenkyū)*, Fuyōshobōshuppan, Tōkyō, Japan, 2001.

## Bibliography

Nakamura 2009: Tomokazu Nakamura, *Clan System in Ancient Japan (Nihon Kodai no Shizokusei)*, Yagishoten, Tōkyō, Japan, 2009.

Nakayama 2002: Kaoru Nakayama, "Study of Miwa-no-Kimi-no-Sakau (Miwa-no-Kimi-no-Sakau nitsuiteno Ichikōsatsu)," *Study of Nihonshoki (Nihonshoki Kenkyū)* 24, 2002.

Nakayama 1971: Wakei Nakayama, *The Ōmiwa-jinja Shrine (Ōmiwa-jinja)*, Gakuseisha, Tōkyō, Japan, 1971.

Naoki 1951: Kōjirō Naoki, "Amaterasu-Ōmikami and Origin of Ise-jingū Grand Shrine (Amaterasu-Ōmikami to Ise-jingū no Kigen)," Naomoto Fuji, ed., *Society and Religion in Ancient Times (Kodai Shakai to Shūkyō)*, Wakatakeshobō, Ōsaka, Japan, 1951. Reprinted in: *Clan and Emperor in Ancient Japan (Nihon Kodai no Shizoku to Tennō)*, Hanawashobō, Tōkyō, Japan, 1964.

Naoki 1958: Kōjirō Naoki, "Study of the Hito System (Hitosei no Kenkyū)," *Structure of the Ancient Japanese Nation (Nihon Kodai Kokka no Kōzō)*, Aokishoten, Tōkyō, Japan, 1958.

Naoki 1960: Kōjirō Naoki, "Study of Haji Clan (Haji-uji no Kenkyū)," *Studies in the Humanities (Jinbun Kenkyū) 11–9*, 1960. Reprinted in: *Clan and Emperor in Ancient Japan (Nihon Kodai no Shizoku to Tennō)*, Hanawashobō, Tōkyō, Japan, 1964.

Naoki 1964: Kōjirō Naoki, "Introduction to the Ōjin Dynasty Theory (Ōjinōchōron Josetsu)," Ōsaka City University Association in Honor of the Remnants of Naniwakyūshi, ed., *Study of the Remnants of Naniwa no Miya Palace (Naniwakyūshi no Kenkyū) 5*, Association in Honor of the Remnants of Naniwakyūshi, Ōsaka, Japan, 1964. Reprinted in: *Clan and Emperor in Ancient Japan (Nihon Kodai no Shizoku to Tennō)*, Hanawashobō, Tōkyō, Japan, 1964. Reprinted in: *Study of the Kawachi Kingdom in Ancient Japan (Kodai Kawachi Seiken no Kenkyū)*, Hanawashobō, Tōkyō, Japan, 2005.

Naoki 1977: Kōjirō Naoki, "Mt. Amano Kaguyama and Mt. Miwa (Amanokaguyama to Miwayama)," *Window on Ancient History (Kodaishi no Mado)*, Gakuseisha, Tōkyō, Japan, 1977. Reprinted in: *Study of Kawachi Kingdom in Ancient Japan (Kodai Kawachi Seiken no Kenkyū)*, Hanawashobō, Tōkyō, Japan, 2005.

Nara National Research Institute of Cultural Properties 1993a: Nara National Research Institute of Cultural Properties, ed., *Archaeological Survey Summary Report of Asuka Fujiwara-Kyū (Asuka Fujiwara-Kyū Hakkutsu Chōsa Gaihō) 23*, 1993.

Nara National Research Institute of Cultural Properties 1993b: Nara National Research Institute of Cultural Properties, ed., *Annual Bulletin of Nara National Cultural Properties Research Institute (Nara Kokuritsu Bunkazai Kenkyūjo Nenpō) FY1993*, 1993.

Nara Prefecture 1914–1915: Nara Prefecture, ed., *Sourcebook of Yamato (Yamatoshiryō)*, Kōdōkan, Tōkyō, Japan, 1914–1915. Reprinted in: Nara Prefectural Board of Education, ed., *Sourcebook of Yamato (Yamatoshiryō)*, Rinsenshoten, Tōkyō, Japan, 1987.

Narasaki 1963: Shōichi Narasaki, "Sue Ware (Sueki)," Shō Ishimoda, ed., *Lectures on Ancient History (Kodaishi Kōza) 9*, Gakuseisha, Tōkyō, Japan, 1963.

Narasaki 1965: Shōichi Narasaki, "Ceramic Industry at the End of Ancient Times (Kodai Makki no Yōgyō Seisan)," *Journal of Japanese History (Nihonshi Kenkyū) 79*, 1965.

Niino 1974: Naoyoshi Niino, *A Historical Study of Kokuzō (Kenkyūshi Kokuzō)*, Yoshikawa-Kōbunkan, Tōkyō, Japan, 1974.

Nishiyama 1975: Isao Nishiyama, "Ritsuryō System and the Ōmiwa-jinja Shrine (Ritsuryō-sei to Ōmiwa-jinja)," Publication Committee on Editing the Sourcebook of the Ōmiwa-jinja Shrine (Ōmiwa-jinja-shiryō), ed., *History of the Ōmiwa-jinja Shrine (Ōmiwa-jinja Shi)*, Yoshikawa-Kōbunkan, Tōkyō, Japan, 1975. Reprinted in: *History of Shintō in Ancient Times (Jōdai Shintōshi no Kenkyū)*, Kokushokankōkai, Tōkyō, Japan, 1983.

Nishimiya 1990: Kazutami Nishimiya, "Kamunabi Mimuro Mimoro," *Religious Services and Language in Ancient Times (Jōdai Saishi to Gengo)*, Ōfūsha, Tōkyō, Japan, 1990.

Nishimiya 1999: Kazutami Nishimiya, "Mt. Miwa Is Like God (Miwayama wa Kami)," *Ōmiwa 97*, Shrine Office of the Ōmiwa-jinja Shrine, Nara, Japan, 1999.

Nishimura 1983, Yasushi Nishimura, "Suemura Sanage Ushikubi," Publication Committee on the Collection of Treatises of the 30th Anniversary of Nara National Research Institute of Cultural Properties, ed., *Collection of Treatises of Cultural Property (Bunkazai Ronshū) Volume 1*, Dōhōshashuppan, Kyōto, Japan, 1983.

Nitō 2011: Atsushi Nitō, "Establishment of Teiki, Kyūji and the Genealogy of the Imperial Family (Teiki Kyūji to Ōtōfu no Seiritsu)," Tokio Shinkawa and Mannen Hayakawa, eds., *Nihonshoki as Historical Materials (Shiryō toshiteno Nihonshoyoki)*, Benseishuppan, Tōkyō, Japan, 2011.

Noda 1968: Reishi Noda, "Basic Study of the Mononobe Clan (Mononobe-uji ni Kansuru Kisotekikenkyū)," *The Shirin or the Journal of History (Shirin) 51-2*, 1968.

Noguchi 1992: Takeshi Noguchi, "Boki and Nihonshoki (Boki to Nihonshoki)," Hirotoshi Nakamura, ed., *Collection of Treatises of Kojiki and Nihonshoki (Kiki Ronshū)*, Zokugunshoruijūkanseikai, Tōkyō, Japan, 1992.

Ōba 1951: Iwao Ōba, "Study of Ceremonial Implement Discovered around Mt. Miwa (Miwasanroku Hakken Kodai Saiki no Ichikōsatsu)," *Ancient Times (Kodai) 3*, 1951.

Ōe 2007: Atsushi Ōe, *God and Spirit in Ancient Japan (Nihon Kodai no Kami to Rei)*, Rinsen Shoten, Kyōto, Japan, 2007.

Ogasawara et al. 2008: Yoshihiko Ogasawara, Kunihiko Kawakami, Fuminori Sugaya, Chiyono Suzuka, Akihito Hirabayashi, Kazuo Hirose, and Atsumu Wada, eds., *Mt. Miwa and Ancient Religious Services (Miwayama to Kodai no Kami Matsuri)*, Gakuseisha, Tōkyō, Japan, 2008.

Ōhira 2007: Shigeru Ōhira, "Historical Background of Comma-Shaped Beads with Decorations Excavated around Mt. Miwa," Shigetsugu Sugiyama and Ryōji Yamagishi ed., *Religious Services of Japan in Primitive and Ancient Times (Genshi Kodai Nihon no Saishi)*, Dōseisha, Tōkyō, Japan, 2007.

Okada, Seishi 1960: Seishi Okada, "Origin of the Ise-jingū Grand Shrine (Ise-jingū no Kigen)," *Journal of Japanese History (Nihonshi Kenkyū) 49*, 1960. Reprinted in: *Religious Services and Myth of the Ancient Kingdom (Kodai Ōken no Saishi to Shinwa)*, Hanawashobō, Tōkyō, Japan, 1970.

Okada, Seishi 1962: Seishi Okada, "Himatsuribe and Predecessor of Jingikan (Himatsuribe to Jingikan Senkō Kanshi)," *Journal of Historical Studies (Rekishigakukenkyū) 278*, 1963. Reprinted in: *Religious Services and Myth of the Ancient Kingdom (Kodai Ōken no Saishi to Shinwa)*, Hanawashobō, Tōkyō, Japan, 1970.

Okada, Seishi 1966: Seishi Okada, "The Establishment of the Kawachi Imperial Family (Kawachi Daiōke no Seiritsu)," *Study of Nihonshoki (Nihonshoki Kenkyū) 2*, 1966. Reprinted in: *Religious Services and Myth of the Ancient Kingdom (Kodai Ōken no Saishi to Shinwa)*, Hanawashobō, Tōkyō, Japan, 1970.

## 152  Bibliography

Okada, Seishi 1968: Seishi Okada, "Establishment of the Imperial Family in Kawachi Province (Kawachi Daiōke no Seiritsu)," *Study of Nihonshoki (Nihonshoki Kenkyū)* 3, 1968. Reprinted in: *Religious Services and Myth of the Ancient Kingdom (Kodai Ōken no Saishi to Shinwa)*, Hanawashobō, Tōkyō, Japan, 1970.

Okada, Shōji 2005: Shōji Okada, "Circulate Religious Services of the Emperor and Gods (Tennō to Kamigami no Junkangata Saishi Keitai)," *Journal of Shintō Studies (Shintō Shūkyō) 199–200*, 2005.

Okimori et al. 2012: Takuya Okimori, Makoto Satō, and Izumi Yajima, eds., *Collection of Records of Ancient Clans (Kodai Ujibumi Shū)*, Yamakawashuppansha, Tōkyō, Japan, 2012.

Ōmiwa-jinja Shrine 2013: Ōmiwa-jinja Shrine, ed., *God of Mt. Miwa and Ancient Yamato (Kodai Yamato to Miwayama no Kami)*, Gakuseisha, Tōkyō, Japan, 2013.

Ōnojō City Board of Education 1989: Ōnojō City Board of Education, ed., *Ōnojō City Survey Report of Cultural Property (Ōnojōshi Bunkazai Chōsa Hōkokusho) 30*, Ōnojō, Japan, 1989.

Ōnojō City Board of Education 2008a: Ōnojō City Board of Education, ed., *Ōnojō City Survey Report of Cultural Property (Ōnojōshi Bunkazai Chōsa Hōkokusho) 77*, Ōnojō, Japan, 2008.

Ōnojō City Board of Education 2008b: Ōnojō City Board of Education, ed., *Ōnojō City Survey Report of Cultural Property (Ōnojōshi Bunkazai Chōsa Hōkokusho) 81*, Ōnojō, Japan, 2008.

Ōyama 1975: Seiichi Ōyama, "The Historical Development of Hamana County and Tōtoumi Province before the Taika Reforms (Taika Zendai Tōtoumi no Kuni Hamana Gun no Shiteki Tenkai)," *Japanese History (Nihon Rekishi) 321*, 1975. Reprinted in: *Diplomacy and Local Administration in Ancient Japan (Nihon Kodai no Gaikō to Chihō Gyōsei)*, Yoshikawa-Kōbunkan, Tōkyō, Japan, 1999.

Publication Committee on Editing the Sourcebook of the Ōmiwa-jinja Shrine 1968–1991: Publication Committee on Editing the Sourcebook of the Ōmiwa-jinja Shrine, ed., *Sourcebook of the Ōmiwa-jinja Shrine (Ōmiwa-jinja-shiryō)*, Yoshikawa-Kōbunkan, Tōkyō, Japan, 1968–1991.

Publication Committee on Editing the Sourcebook of the Ōmiwa-jinja Shrine 1975: Publication Committee on Editing the Sourcebook of the Ōmiwa-jinja Shrine (Ōmiwa-jinja-shiryō), ed., *History of the Ōmiwa-jinja Shrine (Ōmiwa-jinja Shi)*, Yoshikawa-Kōbunkan, Tōkyō, Japan, 1975.

Saeki 1907: Ariyoshi Saeki, ed., *Complete Collection of Jingi (Jingi Zensho) Volume 2*, Kōtenkōkyūjo, Tōkyō, Japan, 1907. Reprinted in: *Complete Collection of Jingi (Jingi Zensho) Volume 2*, Shibunkaku, Kyōto, Japan, 1971.

Saeki 1975: Arikiyo Saeki, "Formation of the Culture of Nobles (Kizoku Bunka no Hassei)," *Iwanami Lectures on Japanese History (Iwanami Kōza Nihon Rekishi) 2*, Iwanamishoten, Tōkyō, Japan, 1975.

Saeki 1981: Arikiyo Saeki, *Study of Shinsenshōjiroku (Shinsenshōjiroku no Kenkyū) Parts of Investigation (Kōshō Hen) Volume 1*, Yoshikawa-Kōbunkan, Tōkyō, Japan, 1981.

Saeki 1982a: Arikiyo Saeki, *Study of Shinsenshōjiroku (Shinsenshōjiroku no Kenkyū) Parts of Investigation (Kōshō Hen) Volume 2*, Yoshikawa-Kōbunkan, Tōkyō, Japan, 1982.

Saeki 1982b: Arikiyo Saeki, *Study of Shinsenshōjiroku (Shinsenshōjiroku no Kenkyū) Parts of Investigation (Kōshō Hen) Volume 3*, Yoshikawa-Kōbunkan, Tōkyō, Japan, 1982.

Saeki 1982c: Arikiyo Saeki, *Study of Shinsenshōjiroku (Shinsenshōjiroku no Kenkyū) Parts of Investigation (Kōshō Hen) Volume 4*, Yoshikawa-Kōbunkan, Tōkyō, Japan, 1982.
Saeki 1983a: Arikiyo Saeki, *Study of Shinsenshōjiroku (Shinsenshōjiroku no Kenkyū) Parts of Investigation (Kōshō Hen) Volume 5*, Yoshikawa-Kōbunkan, Tōkyō, Japan, 1983.
Saeki 1983b: Arikiyo Saeki, *Study of Shinsenshōjiroku (Shinsenshōjiroku no Kenkyū) Parts of Investigation (Kōshō Hen) Volume 6*, Yoshikawa-Kōbunkan, Tōkyō, Japan, 1983.
Sagimori 2006: Hiroyuki Sagimori, "Ruins of Suemura Kilns and Nakatomi Clan (Suemura Koyōsekigun to Nakatomi Kei Shizoku)," *Izumi City Historical Review (Izumishi Shi Kiyō) 11*, 2006.
Sagimori 2010: Hiroyuki Sagimori, "Suemura and Suebe," Towao Sakaebara, ed., *Kingdom and Society in Ancient Japan (Nihon Kodai no Ōken to Shakai)*, Hanawashobō, Tōkyō, Japan, 2010.
Sakai City 1973: Sakai City, ed., *Sequel to History of Sakai City (Sakaishi Shi Zokuhen) Volume 4*, Sakai City, Sakai, Japan, 1973.
Sakamoto 1946: Tarō Sakamoto, "Sanki and Nihonshoki (Sanki to Nihonshoki)," *Journal of the Historical Science Society (Shigaku Zasshi) 56–7*, 1946. Reprinted in: *Basic Study of Ancient Japanese History (Nihon Kodaishi no Kisoteki Kenkyū) Volume 1*, Tōkyōdaigaku Shuppankai, Tōkyō, Japan, 1964. Reprinted in: *Selections from Tarō Sakamoto's Works (Sakamoto Tarō Chosakushū) Volume 2*, Yoshikawa-Kōbunkan, Tōkyō, Japan, 1988.
Sakamoto 1970: Tarō Sakamoto, "The Ōmiwa Clan and Manyoshū (Ōmiwa-uji to Manyoshū)," *Ōmiwa 38*, Shrine Office of the Ōmiwa-jinja Shrine, Nara, Japan, 1970. Reprinted in: *Selections from Tarō Sakamoto's Works (Sakamoto Tarō Chosakushū) 4*, Yoshikawa-Kōbunkan, Tōkyō, Japan, 1988.
Sakamoto 1987: Kazutoshi Sakamoto, "Research Task of Old Sue Ware in Eastern Japan (Tōgoku niokeru Koshiki Sueki Kenkyū no Kadai)," Research Institute for Chikuma-gawa River System and Ancient Culture, ed., *Problems of Old Sue Ware in Eastern Japan (Tōgoku niokeru Koshiki Sueki womeguru Shomondai)*, Nagano, Japan, 1987.
Sakurai City Center for Archaeological Operations 2000: Sakurai City Center for Archaeological Operations (Sakuraishiritsu Maizōbukaza Center), ed., *Archaeology around Mt. Miwa (Miwayama Shūhen no Kōkogaku)*, Sakurai City Center for Archaeological Operations, Nara, Japan, 2000.
Sakurai City Institute for Cultural Properties 1998: Sakurai City Institute for Cultural Properties (Sakuraishi Bunkazai Kyōkai), *Excavation Report of Sakurai City (Sakuraishinai Maizōbunkazai Hakkutsuchōsa Hōkokusho) Volume 2*, Sakurai City Institute for Cultural Properties, Nara, Japan, 1998.
Sasaki 1975: Mikio Sasaki, "Miwa and Sue Village (Miwa to Suemura)," Publication Committee on Editing the Sourcebook of the Ōmiwa-jinja Shrine (Ōmiwa-jinja-shiryō), ed., *History of the Ōmiwa-jinja Shrine (Ōmiwa-jinja Shi)*, Yoshikawa-Kōbunkan, Tōkyō, Japan, 1975.
Sasaki 1976: Mikio Sasaki, "Miwa and Sue Village, Continued (Zoku Miwa to Suemura)," *Study of Popular History (Minshūshi Kenkyū) 14*, 1976.
Sasaki 1979a: Mikio Sasaki, "Historical Background of Religious Services at Mt. Miwa (Miwayama Saishi no Rekishitekihaikei)," Celebration of Hiroshi Takiguchi's Seventieth Birthday Commemorative Editing Committee, ed., *Collection of Treatises of Ancient History (Kodai Tansō) 1*, Waseda University Press, Tōkyō, Japan, 1980.

## 154  Bibliography

Sasaki 1979b: Mikio Sasaki, "Sue Ware Discovered around Mt. Miwa (Miwayama Shitsudo no Sueki)," *Ancient Times (Kodai) 66*, 1979.

Sasaki 1981: Mikio Sasaki, "Comma-Shaped Beads with Decorations Excavated around Mt. Miwa (Miwayama oyobi sono Shūhen Shutsudo no Komochi Magatama)," *Journal of Ancient Times (Kodai) 71*, 1981.

Sasaki 1984: Mikio Sasaki, "The Ōmiwa Clan and Religious Services at Mt. Miwa (Miwa-no-Kimi-uji to Miwayama Saishi)," *Japanese History (Nihon Rekishi) 429*, 1984.

Sasaki 1985: Mikio Sasaki, "Study of Comma-Shaped Beads with Decorations (Komochi Magatama Shikō)," Hiroshi Takiguchi, ed., *Collection of Treatises of Ancient Times (Kodai Tansō) 2*, Waseda University Press, Tōkyō, Japan, 1985.

Sasaki 1986: Mikio Sasaki, "New Version of Sue Ware Discovered around Mt. Miwa (Shin Miwayama Shitsudo no Sueki)," *Ancient Times (Kodai) 88*, 1986.

Satō 1976: Makoto Satō: "Kōfu of the Jinshin War and Establishment of Taihō-Kōfu System (Jinshin no Kōfu to Taihō Kōfusei no Seiritsu)," *Review of Historical Studies (Shigaku Ronsō) 6*, 1976. Reprinted in: *Capital and Wooden Tablets in Ancient Japan (Nihon Kodai no Kyūto to Mokkan)*, Yoshikawa-Kōbunkan, Tōkyō, Japan, 1979.

Satō 1994: Nagato Satō, "Function and Structure of the Council System of Wa Kingdom (Wa Ōken niokeru Gōgisei no Kinō to Kōzō)," *Journal of Historical Studies (Rekishigakukenkyū) 661*, 1994. Reprinted in: *Structure and Development of the Kingdom in Ancient Japan (Nihon Kodai Ōken no Kōzō to Tenkai)*, Yoshikawa-Kōbunkan, Tōkyō, Japan, 2009.

Shida 1971: "Junichi Shida, the Ōmiwa clan," *Feature and Legend of Ancient Clans (Kodai Shizoku no Seikaku to Denshō)*, Yūzankaku, Tōkyō, Japan, 1971.

Shiga Prefectural Board of Education 1992: Shiga Prefectural Board of Education, ed., *Archaeological Survey Report of Sakurabasama-Kofun Tumulus Cluster (Sakurabasama Kofungun Hakkutsu Chōsa Hōkokusho)*, Shiga Prefectural Board of Education, Shiga, Japan, 1992.

Shikinaisha Research Society 1976: Shikinaisha Research Society, ed., *Survey Report of Shikinaisha (Shikinaisha Chōsa Hōkoku) Volume 5*, Kōgakukan University Press, Mie, Japan, 1976.

Shimizu 1998: Shinichi Shimizu, "Religious Services at Mt. Miwa and Archaeology (Miwayama Saishi to Kōkogaku)," Kōichi Mori, ed., *Research of Ancient Times (Kodai Tankyū)*, Chūōkōronsha, Tōkyō, Japan, 1998.

Shinkawa 1994: Tokio Shinkawa, *Conception of Cultural History in Ancient Japan (Nihon Kodai Bunkashi no Kōsō)*, Meichokankōkai, Tōkyō, Japan, 1994.

Shinkawa 1999: Tokio Shinkawa, *Basic Study of Gyōki Group as Sociality (Shakaiteki Ketsugō toshiteno Gyōki Shūdan nikansuru Kisoteki Kenkyū)*, Waseda University, Tōkyō, Japan, 1999.

Shinokawa 1996: Ken Shinokawa, *Study of the Kokuzō System in Ancient Japan (Nihon Kodai Kokuzōsei no Kenkyū)*, Yoshikawa-Kōbunkan, Tōkyō, Japan, 1996.

Shinokawa 2009: Ken Shinokawa, *Study of Mononobe Clan (Mononobe-uji no Kenkyū)*, Yūzankaku, Tōkyō, Japan, 2009.

Shirai 1984: Isamu Shirai, "Study of the Remaining Site of the Main Shrine Building of the Ōmiwa-jinja Shrine (Ōmiwa-jinja Goshuden-Ato Kō)," Archaeological Institute of Kashihara (Kashihara Kōkogaku Kenkyūjo), ed., *Excavation Report of the Ōmiwa-jinja Shrine Precincts (Ōmiwa-jinja Keidaichi Hakkutsuchōsa Hōkokusho)*, Ōmiwa-jinja Shrine, Nara, Japan, 1984.

Shrine Office of the Ōmiwa-jinja Shrine 1928: Shrine Office of the Ōmiwa-jinja Shrine, ed., *Sourcebook of Miwa (Miwasōsho)*, Shrine Office of the Ōmiwa-jinja Shrine, Nara, Japan, 1928. Reprinted in: Shrine Office of the Ōmiwa-jinja Shrine, ed., *Sourcebook of Miwa (Miwasōsho)*, Shrine Office of the Ōmiwa-jinja Shrine, Nara, Japan, 1986.

Sogō 2010: Yoshikazu Sogō, "The Western Part and the Eastern Part of Ruins of Suemura Kilns in the Fifth Century (Go Seikidai niokeru Suemurayōsekigun no Tōbu to Seibu)," *Historia* 223, 2010.

Sonoda 1967: Kōyū Sonoda, "Iwase Senzuka-Kofun Tumulus Cluster and Kii-Kokuzō (Iwase Senzuka to Kii-Kokuzō)," Archaeological Research Laboratory of Kansai University, ed., *Iwase Senzuka-Kofun Tumulus Cluster (Iwase Senzuka)*, Archaeological Research Laboratory of Kansai University, Ōsaka, Japan, 1967. Reprinted in: *Aristocrats and Local Clans in Ancient Japan (Nihon Kodai no Kizoku to Chihō Gōzoku)*, Hanawashobō, Tōkyō, Japan, 1992.

Sugano 2008: Masao Sugano, "The Ōmiwa Clan in the Era of Emperor Tenmu and Jitō (Tenmu Jitō Chō no Ōmiwa-uji)," Hironobu Ishino, Makoto Ueno, Kenichi Okamoto, Masano Sugano, Kazuhiro Tatsumi, Yoshinobu Tsukaguchi, and Kōichi Mori, eds., *Mt. Miwa and Ancient Japanese History (Miwayama to Nihon Kodaisi)*, Gakuseisha, Tōkyō, Japan, 2008.

Sugawara 2006: Yūichi Sugawara, "Locality of Ruins of Suemura Kilns and the Spread of Techniques (Suemura Yōsekigun no Chiikisei to Gijutsu Kakusan)," *Archaeological Study (Kōkogaku Kenkyū)* 53-1, 2006.

Suzuki, M. 2012: Masanobu Suzuki, *Basic Study of Genealogy of Ancient Japanese Clans (Nihon Kodai Shizoku Keifu no Kisoteki Kenkyū)*, Tōkyōdō-shuppan, Tōkyō, Japan, 2012.

Suzuki, M. 2014: Masanobu Suzuki, *Study of Ōmiwa Clan (Ōmiwa-uji no Kenkyū)*, Yūzankaku, Tōkyō, Japan, 2014.

Suzuki, M. 2015: Masanobu Suzuki, "Establishment of Koma County and Ōmiwa-no-Ason-Komamaro (Komagun no Kengun to Ōmiwa-no-Ason-Komamaro)," Ō Yū and Kimiko Kōno, eds., *Collision and Fusion of Culture (Bunka no Shōtotsu to Yūgō)*, Benseishuppan, Tōkyō, Japan, 2015.

Suzuki, Y. 1980: Yasutami Suzuki, *History of Study of Ancient Nation (Kodai Kokkashi Kenkyū no Ayumi)*, Shinjinbutsuōraisha, Tōkyō, Japan, 1980.

Takahashi 1920: Kenji Takahashi, "Tatsunosuke Nishizaki, "Yamanokami Kofun Tumulus Located in Baba, Miwa-chō (Miwa-chō Baba Yamanokami Kofun)," *Report of Historic Site Designated by Nara Prefecture (Naraken Shiseki Shōchi Chōsakai Hōkokusho)* 7, 1920.

Takahashi 2007: Teruhiko Takahashi, *Study of Change in Processes of Sue Ware Production from Ancient Times to the Middle Ages in Japan (Sueki Seisan niokeru Kodai kara Chūsei heno Henshitu Katei no Kenkyū)*, Ōsaka University, Ōsaka, Japan, 2007.

Takemitsu 1981: Makoto Takemitsu, *A Historical Study of the Bemin System (Kenkyūshi Beminsei)*, Yoshikawa-Kōbunkan, Tōkyō, Japan, 1981.

Takemoto 2006: Akira Takemoto, "Earliest Ancestor and Clan in Nihonshoki (Nihonshoki niokeru Shiso to Uji)," *Cultura Antiqua (Kodai Bunka)* 58, 2006.

Tamura 1996: Enchō Tamura, *Establishment of the Ise-jingū Grand Shrine (Ise-jingū no Seiritsu)*, Yoshikawa-Kōbunkan, Tōkyō, Japan, 1996.

Tanabe 1981: Shōzō Tanabe, *Encyclopedia of Sue Ware (Sueki Taisei)*, Kadokawashoten, Tōkyō, Japan, 1981.

Tanaka 1987: Takashi Tanaka, "Establishment of the Ōmiwa-jinja Shrine (Ōmiwa-jinja no Sōshi)," *Shinto History Review (Shintōshi Kenkyū) 35–1*, 1987. Reprinted in: *Selections from Takashi Tanaka's Works (Tanaka Takashi Chosakushū) 1*, Kokusho-Kankōkai, Tōkyō, Japan, 1986.

Tanaka 1990: Hisao Tanaka, *Ujigami Worship and Religious Services for Ancestors (Ujigami Shinkō to Sosen Saishi)*, Meicho shuppan, Tōkyō, Japan, 1990.

Tatsumi 1999: Junichirō Tatsumi, "Study of Presentation of Earthenware in Ancient Times (Kodai no Yakimono Chōnōsei ni Kansuru Kenkyū)," Celebration of Ikuo Mori's Sixtieth Birthday Commemorative Editing Committee, ed., *Tiles and Clothes 1,000 Years Ago (Gai Sennen)*, Celebration of Ikuo Mori's Sixtieth Birthday Commemorative Editing Committee, Kyōto, Japan, 1999.

Terakawa 1992: Machio Terakawa, "Legend regarding Control of the Right of Religious Services of Ōmononushi-no-Kami (Ōmononushi-no-Kami no Saishiken Keishō Denshō)," *Ōmiwa 83*, Shrine Office of the Ōmiwa-jinja Shrine, Nara, Japan, 1992.

Teranishi 2003: Sadahiro Teranishi, "Study of Kii-Kokuzō-Shidai," *Wakayama City Musium Research Bulletin 17*, 2003. Reprinted in: *Study of the Kii Clan (Kii-uji no Kenkyū)*, Yūzankaku, Tōkyō, Japan, 2013.

Terasawa 1984: Kaoru Terasawa, "Comma-Shaped Beads with Decorations Excavated around Mt. Miwa (Miwasannroku Shutsudo no Komochi Magatama wo Megutte)," Archaeological Institute of Kashihara, ed., *Excavation Report of the Ōmiwa-jinja Shrine Precincts (Ōmiwa-jinja Keidaichi Hakkutsuchōsa Hōkokusho)*, Ōmiwa-jinja Shrine, Nara, Japan, 1984.

Terasawa 1988: Kaoru Terasawa, "Ritual Sites and Religious Services at Mt. Miwa (Miwayama no Saishiiseki to sono Matsuri)," Atsumu Wada, ed., *Ōmiwa and Isonokami (Ōmiwa to Isonokami)*, Chikumashobō, Tōkyō, Japan, 1988.

Tosa 1999: Hidesato Tosa, "Restoration of Ōmiwa-no-Takechimaro (Ōmiwa-no-Takechimaro no Fukken)," *Journal for the Study of Japanese Literature (Kokubungaku Kenkyū) 128*, 1999.

Toyama Prefectural Board of Education 1980: Toyama Prefectural Board of Education, ed., *The Second Urgent Archaeological Survey Summary Report of Ruins Kosugi Distribution Business Parks in Kosugi-machi and Ōkado-machi, Toyama Prefecture (Toyamaken Kosugi-machi Ōkado-Machi Kosugi Ryutsū Gyōmu Danchinai Isekigun Dainiji Kinkyū Hakkutsu Chōsa Gaiyō)*, Toyama Prefectural Board of Education, Toyama, Japan, 1968.

Tsuda 1946: Sōkichi Tsuda, *Study of Japanese Classical Literature (Nihon Koten no Kenkyū) Volume 1*, Iwanamishoten, Tōkyō, Japan, 1948. Reprinted in: *Selections from Sōkichi Tsuda's Works (Tsuda Sōkichi Zenshū) Volume 1*, Iwanamishoten, Tōkyō, Japan, 1963.

Tsuda 1950: Sōkichi Tsuda, *Study of Japanese Classical Literature (Nihon Koten no Kenkyū) Volume 2*, Iwanamishoten, Tōkyō, Japan, 1950. Reprinted in: *Selections from Sōkichi Tsuda's Works (Tsuda Sōkichi Zenshū) Volume 2*, Iwanamishoten, Tōkyō, Japan, 1963.

Tsukaguchi 2003: Yoshinobu Tsukaguchi, "Emperor Bidatsu and Mt. Miwa Worship (Bidatsu Tennō to Miwayama Shinkō)," Masaaki Ueda, Teiji Kadowaki, Haruo Kadowaki, Yoshinobu Tsukaguchi, and Atsumu Wada, eds., *Gods of Mt. Miwa (Miwayama no Kamigami)*, Gakuseisha, Tōkyō, Japan, 2003.

Ueda 1964: Masaaki Ueda, "Establishment of Priest (Saikan no Seiritsu)," Shōei Mishina, ed., *Study of Nihonshoki (Nihonshoki Kenkyū) 1*, 1964. Reprinted in:

*Study of the Ancient Japanese Nation (Nihon Kodai Kokka Ronkyū)*, Hanawashobō, Tōkyō, Japan, 1968.

Ueda 1967: Masaaki Ueda, *Yamato Imperial Court (Yamato Chōtei)*, Kōdansha, Tōkyō, Japan, 1967.

Ueda 1976: Masaaki Ueda, "Development of Myth Dealing with Marriages between Gods (Shinkon Denshō no Tenkai)," Celebration of Minoru Shibata's Seventieth Birthday Commemorative Editing Committee, ed., *Collection of Treatises of Japanese Cultural History (Nihon Bunka Shi Ronsō)*, Celebration of Minoru Shibata's Seventieth Birthday Commemorative Editing Committee, Suita, Japan, 1976.

Ueda et al. 2003: Masaaki Ueda, Teiji Kadowaki, Haruo Kadowaki, Yoshinobu Tsukaguchi, and Atsumu Wada, eds., *Gods of Mt. Miwa (Miwayama no Kamigami)*, Gakuseisha, Tōkyō, Japan, 2003.

Ueno 2001: Makoto Ueno, "Mori and Mimoro in Manyōshū (Manyō no Mori to Mimoro)," *Journal of Religious Services (Saishi Kenkyū) 1*, 2001.

Ueno et al. 2003: Makoto Ueno, Teiji Kadowaki, Minoru Senda, Yoshinobu Tsukaguchi, and Atsumu Wada, eds., *Ancient History of Mt. Miwa (Miwayama no Kodaishi)*, Gakuseisha, Tōkyō, Japan, 2003.

Umeda 1982: Yoshihiko Umeda, Miwanimasu-Himuka-jinja Shrine (Miwanimasu-Himuka-jinja), Society for Shikinaisha, ed., *Shikinaisha Survey Report (Shikinaisha Chosa Hokoku-sho) 3*, Kōgakkandaigaku-Shuppanbu, Ise, Japan, 1982.

Wada 1973: Atsumu Wada, "Historic Study of the Iware District (Iware Chihō no Rekishitek Kenkyū)," Archaeological Institute of Kashihara (Kashihara Kōkogaku Kenkyūjo), ed., *Iware and Ikenouchi-kofun Tumuli Cluster (Iware Ikenouchi Kofun-gun)*, Nara Prefectural Board of Education, Nara, Japan, 1973.

Wada 1979: Atsumu Wada, "Yamato Province and Sakurai City (Yamato to Sakurai)," Publication Committee on Editing History of Sakurai City, ed., *History of Sakurai City (Sakuraishi Shi) Volume 1*, Sakurai City, Nara, Japan, 1979.

Wada 1985: Atsumu Wada, "Reexamination of Religious Services at Mt. Miwa (Miwayama Saishi no Saikentō)," *Bulletin of the National Museum of Japanese History (Kokuritsu Rekishi Minzoku Hakubutsukan Kenkyū Hōkoku) 7*, 1985. Reprinted in: *Courtesy, Religious Services, and Faith in Ancient Japan (Nihon Kodai no Girei to Saishi Shinkō) Volume 2*, Hanawashobō, Tōkyō, Japan, 1995.

Wada 1989: Atsumu Wada, "Fortune-Teller of Isagawa-jinja Shrine (Isagawa-jinja no Sōhakkeyomi)," Celebration of Kōjirō Naoki's Seventieth Birthday Commemorative Meeting, ed., *Collection of Treatises of Ancient History (Kodaishi Ronshū) Volume 3*, Hanawashobō, Tōkyō, Japan, 1989. Reprinted in: *Courtesy, Religious Services, and Faith in Ancient Japan (Nihon Kodai no Girei to Saishi Shinkō) Volume 2*, Hanawashobō, Tōkyō, Japan, 1995.

Wada 2003: Atsumu Wada, "God of Mt. Miwa (Miwayama no Kami)," Masaaki Ueda, Teiji Kadowaki, Haruo Kadowaki, Yoshinobu Tsukaguchi, and Atsumu Wada, eds., *Gods of Mt. Miwa (Miwayama no Kamigami)*, Gakuseisha, Tōkyō, Japan, 2003.

Watanabe 1988: Kan Watanabe, "Ōmiwa-no-Ason-Takechimaro and His Surroundings (Ōmiwa-no-Ason-Takechimaro tosono Shūhen)," *Ōmiwa 75*, Shrine Office of the Ōmiwa-jinja Shrine, Nara, Japan, 1988.

Yogo 1990: Takuma Yogo, "Sue Ware Craftsmen at the Beginning of the Eighth Century (Hasseiki Shotō no Sueki Kōjin)," *Bulletin of the Graduate Division of Literature of Waseda University (Waseda daigaku Daigakuin Bungaku Kenkyūka Kiyō) Separate Volume 17*, Tōkyō, Japan, 1990.

Yoshida 1970: Akira Yoshida, "Preliminary Study of Distribution of Clan in Izumi Province (Izumi Chihō no Shizoku Bunpu ni Kansuru Yobiteki Kōsatsu)," Kobata Atsushi Retirement Commemorative Committee, ed., *Collection of Treatises of Japanese History (Kokushi Ronshū)*, Kobata Atsushi Retirement Commemorative Committee, Kyōto, Japan, 1970.

Yoshii 1974: Iwao Yoshii, "Change of the Ancestral Legend of the Imperial Court of the Emperor Sujin (Sujin Ōcho no Shiso Denshō to sono Hensen)," *Manyo 86*, 1974. Reprinted in: *The Genealogy and Myth of the Emperor (Tennō no Keifu to Shinwa)*, Hanawashobō, Tōkyō, Japan, 1976.

Yoshimura 1993: Takehiko Yoshimura, "Nation of the Wa and the Yamato Kingdom (Wakoku to Yamato Ōken)," Naohiro Asao, Yoshihiko Amino, Susumu Ishii, Masanao Kano, Shōhachi Hayakawa, and Yoshio Yasumaru, eds., *Iwanami Lectures on Japanese History (Iwanami Kōza Nihon Tsūshi) Volume 2*, Iwanamishoten, Tōkyō, Japan, 1993.

Yoshimura 2005: Takehiko Yoshimura, "King, Hito System and Province in the Fifth Century (Goseiki no Ō Hitosei Kuni)," *New Development of Ancient History (Kodaishi no Shin Tenkai)*, Shinjinbutsuōraisha, Tōkyō, Japan, 2005.

Yoshimura 2006: Takehiko Yoshimura, "Formation of the Yamato Kingdom and Japanese Nation Managed under the Ritsuryō System (Yamato Ōken to Ritsuryōsei Kokka no Keisei)," Mahito Uehara, Taichirō Shiraishi, Shinji Yoshikawa, and Takehiko Yoshimura, eds., *Ancient History of the Japanese Islands (Rettō no Kodaishi) Volume 8*, Iwanamishoten, Tōkyō, Japan, 2006.

# Index

Abe, Takehiko 6–7, 14, 22, 53
Ahe-no-Kunimi 102
Amaterasu-Ōmikami 31, 73
Ame-no-Hiboko 13
archaeological ruins and relics 89–96
Asaka, Toshiki 117
Asuka-dera Temple 37
Awaga-jinja Shrine 56

Baba ruins 90
Bemin system 59–61, 116–17
Bidatsu, Emperor 20–2, 58–9, 100
*Boki* 28
Buddhism 21, 25
Bushi system 59
Buzen province 41–3

change of dynasties theory 7–9, 59, 62, 66, 84, 86–9, 108, 115, 133, 149
Chihara-Gensui-Hotta site 90
Chihara-Maruta site 91
Chiisakobe-no-Ikazuchi 17
Chiisakobe-no-Sugaru 17, 81–2, 87, 100
Chinka-sai Festival 31, 143
cognate clans 40–3

Emishi 57–8
Emperor Chūai 13
Emperor Jinmu 68, 77–8
Emperor Jitō 29, 30
Emperor Jomei 23
Emperor Keikō 57
Emperor Kōgyoku 23, 118
Emperor Sujin 7, 12, 17, 40, 56–7, 67, 69–70, 78, 80, 86–8, 98–9, 103, 112, 114
Emperor Tenmu 5, 7, 37–8
Emperor Yōmei 20, 32

Emperor Yūryaku 15–19, 82
Empress Jingūō 53–4, 81

Fujimori, Kaoru 143
Fujiwara-no-Maro 29
Fumiya 23–4, 32
Fushimiinari-jinja Shrine 1

genealogical relationships 43–4, 122–4, 126–7, 129–30, 132, 139–40
Genpindani ruins 89
Gobu system 59
god of curses 7, 17, 54, 58, 66, 75, 79–83, 86–9, 95, 106, 140

Hashihaka legend 81, 87, 99
Hatsuse-gawa River 92
head lineage 36–8, 42, 44
Hegurinimasu-Iwatoko-jinja Shrine 14
Heguri-no-Matori 16
Higuchi, Kiyoyuki 6, 74, 89, 92
Hikitabe-no-Akaiko 18–19
Hikita-jinja Shrine 36–7
Himuka-jinja Shrine 71–2
Hishida, Tetsuo 7–8, 115–17, 128
Hito system 59–61, 116
Hōzu 25

Ikeda, Genta 75
Ikutamayori-bime 79–80
Inobe, Jūichiro 88, 115
Isagawa-jinja Shrine 22, 102
Ise-jingu Grand Shrine 1, 30, 100
Ishimoda, Shō 117
Isonokami-jingō Shrine 102
Iwakura-jinja Shrine 90
Iwatoko 14–15
*Izumo-Kokusō-Kamuyogoto* ritual 77
Izumo-taisha Shrine 1

160  *Index*

Jibushō 27
Jikidaini 30
Jindaiki 76–7, 99
Jinshin War 28, 38, 118, 129

Kabane 4–5
Kadowaki, Teiji 115
Kagami-ike pond of Sai-jinja Shrine 90
Kageyama, Haruki 72
Kamitsumiwa Village 120, 132–3
Kamo clan 27, 131–2
Kamo-jinja Shrine 131
Kanatsukuribe clan 117
Karakanuchibe clan 117
Katayashiki site 89
Kawachi dynasty 7, 87–8
Kii clan 122–4
Kii-no-Masume 102
Kobayashi, Toshio 58
Koike, Kazue 89
*Kojiki* 10, 12, 15–16, 98
Kokugakuin University Museum 93
Kokuzō system 116
Koobito 38–9
Kotohi 19
Kumagai, Kimio 27
Kumano-taisha Shrine 1
Kunichi-jinja Shrine 91
Kunimi ceremony 66–71, 75, 82–3, 88, 140
Kunitsu-jinja Shrine 91
Kusakabe-no-Shikobu 25

local ruling systems 59–60, 62–3, 115–16, 130, 140

Maeda, Haruto 62
Masuda, Katsumi 88
Matsukura, Fumihiko 88, 96–8, 103–4
Matsumae, Takeshi 88
Matsunomoto ruins 92
Meotoiwa site 90
Mimoro-jinja Shrine 97
Minokurayama ruins 90
Mitsutorii Shrine 91
Miwabe clan 60, 114–19
Miwa clan 121, 122–7
Miwa Elementary School 91
Miwahitobe clan 60
Miwa-no-Kurukuma clan 36, 40–1
Miwa-no-Miyabe clan 40–1
Mizoguchi, Yūki 115–16, 119, 123, 128
Mononobe clan 21, 130
Moriya, Toshihiko 22, 30
Moro-jinja Shrine 97
Mt. Miwa 1, 4–8, 10, 12, 14–20, 22, 26, 30–2, 41, 57–8, 66–7, 69–77, 79–83, 86–9, 92–8, 101–7, 112, 114–5, 119, 126–8, 131–3, 139–41, 143

Nakabayashi Takayuki 123
Nakatomi clan 21, 131
Nakayama, Kaoru 22
Nakayama, Wakei 6
Naoki, Kōjiro 7, 86–8
Narasaki Shōichi 117
Nemaro 26
Nigita clan 122
Nigiyamamori clan 122
*Nihonshoki* 10, 12, 14–16, 18
Ninotorii 90
Nishiyama, Isao 6, 30

Ōba, Iwao 74, 89
Oda Elementary School 91
Odamaki legend 98–9
Okada, Seishi 58, 88
Ōkamidani Iwakura unit 89
Ōkamotsumi-no-Mikoto 129
Ōkuchi 25
Okugaito ruins 90, 94
Ōkuninushi-no- Kami 76, 77, 87, 112
Ōmiwa god 4, 7–8, 17–19, 30, 52–4, 56–9, 62–3, 66, 75–83, 86–9, 95, 97–9, 101, 106, 112, 114, 116, 119, 128, 132, 140
Ōmiwa-no-Kannushi 142–3
Ōmiwa-no-Hikita clan 43–4
Ōmiwa-no-Makamuta clan 37, 44
Ōmiwa-no-Ōyosami clan 40–1
Ōmiwa-no-Shimotota clan 42–3
Ōmiwa-sai Festival 19–20, 104, 143
Ōmura clan 121–2
Ōnamuchi-jinja Shrine 54
Ōniwa clan 121–2
Ōsaka Prefecture 120
Osazaki 23, 32
Oshinumibe clan 117
Ōtomo clan 130
Ōtomo-no-Kanamura 16
Ōtomonushi 129

Prince Anahobe 21–2, 100

red arrow legend 77–8
Ritsuryō system 143

Sagimori, Hiroyuki 117, 122–3
Sai-jinja Shrine 90, 93, 94
Saitō, Misumi 5
Sakamoto, Kazutoshi 115–16
Sakamoto, Tarō 16, 29, 129
Sasaki, Mikio 6, 74, 88, 94, 114–19
Satō, Nagato 116
Shiba ruins 91, 95
Shida, Junichi 6
Shikinomiagatanimasu-jinja Shrine 91
Shinokawa, Ken 60–2
Shintō 1, *2–3*
Shirai, Isamu 93
Soga clan 21, 130
Sogo-no-Iruka 23
Sonoda, Kōyō 122
Sotōri-no- Iratsume 60
Suemura Village 119–22
Sue ware 7–8, 74, 89–94, 114–19, 122–3, 126–8, 131–2, 141
Suminoe-jinja Shrine 55
sun god worship 7, 41, 66, 71, 73–5, 82–3, 88, 140
Susanoo-jinja Shrine 91
Suzuki, Yasutami 115

tabooed land 31, 73, 90–3, 95
Tajihayahime-jinja Shrine 131
Takahashi, Teruhiko 117
Takechimaro 26–9, 32
Takehani-no-Yasuhiko 69–71
Takuhata-no-Himemiko 102
Tamoni-no-Sukune 54

Tamura, Enchō 31
Tanaka, Takashi 58, 88, 115
Tennōrei 58
Tenrikyō Shikishima Church 91
Terasawa, Kaoru 69, 74, 89
Togane 24
Tokio Shinkawa 135
Tomo-no-Miyatsuko 115, 122
Tosa, Hidesato 29
Tsumori clan 54

Ueda, Masaaki 88
Uji 4–5

Wada, Atsumu 7–8, 19–20, 53, 66–7, 69, 71, 73–5, 82, 88, 95, 104, 108, 127
Wakamiya-jinja Shrine 90, 94

Yamabe clan 117
Yamanokami ruins 90, 93–4
Yamashirono-Ōe-no-miko 23–4, 32, 34
Yamato Kingdom/dynasty 4, 6–7, 12–13, 16, 28, 31–2, 53, 56, 58–60, 62–3, 69, 86, 98, 100, 105–7, 114–16, 119, 123, 127, 130, 140
Yamato-no-Ōkunitama-no-Kami 73
Yamatototohimomoso-hime, Princess 87
Yoshida, Akira 122
Yoshii, Iwao 88
Yoshimura, Takehiko 60, 116–17
Yoshiomi 39